THE 1966

WORLD
BOOK

REVIEWING EVENTS OF 1965

YEAR
BOOK

An Annual Supplement to
THE WORLD BOOK ENCYCLOPEDIA

FIELD ENTERPRISES EDUCATIONAL CORPORATION, PUBLISHERS
Merchandise Mart Plaza, Chicago, Illinois 60654
CHICAGO · LONDON · ROME · STOCKHOLM · SYDNEY · TORONTO

Photographs identified as *PICTURES OF THE YEAR* were entries in the national photography competition sponsored jointly by the National Press Photographers Association, the University of Missouri School of Journalism, and THE WORLD BOOK ENCYCLOPEDIA SCIENCE SERVICE.

PREFACE

"In Europe, many people think that America is a country resisting change. But this, obviously, is not so. You speak of your 'continuing revolution' in social welfare, in education, in economics. If only the rest of the world could understand the revolutionary nature of America, then the estrangement between your country and people of the developing nations would not continue."

Paul-Henri Spaak, foreign minister of Belgium, was summing up his reactions to the annual meeting of THE YEAR BOOK Board of Editors held last fall in Bermuda. James Reston, Lawrence Cremin, Sylvia Porter, and the other Board Members had just reviewed the many changes that were taking place on the American scene. They were, figuratively speaking, standing apart from current events and looking back on the year. From the perspective of 12 months, a master plan of change began to emerge from the apparent formlessness of the year's events. Only then could the true dimensions of the "continuing American revolution" be seen. And from this master plan, THE YEAR BOOK Editors could lay down the guidelines for this 1966 edition.

The ability to stand off from the events of the day and to see them with the perspective of a year is one of the special values of THE YEAR BOOK. Certainly the *Focus* articles have become valuable commentaries on current affairs because of this perspective. The *Special Reports*, which may reach back six or a dozen years—or more—to draw their conclusions, extend this matter of perspective even further. A prime example in this edition is *Paths to Dialogue* in which theologian Jaroslav Pelikan goes back to before World War I to pick up the beginning of the ecumenical movement, and traces its development through 1965's historic session of Vatican Council II. Occasionally, it may even be necessary to look into the future to get a realistic perspective on where we stand today. In *How Far Will We Go in Space*, Dr. Isaac Asimov looks beyond the heady successes of the year's Gemini flights and evaluates man's limitations—as well as his possibilities—in space.

With this edition, Dr. Asimov assumes a new role in THE YEAR BOOK. He becomes a Contributing Editor and in this capacity will write *Special Reports* on the dynamic world of science. Taking Dr. Asimov's place on the Board of Editors is Harrison S. Brown. Dr. Brown is professor of geochemistry at California Institute of Technology and foreign secretary of the National Academy of Science. As witnessed by his *Focus* article in this volume, Dr. Brown has a firm grasp on the problems—as well as the progress—of science.

The relentless pattern of change, of which Paul-Henri Spaak spoke, has not left THE YEAR BOOK untouched. In the past five years, THE YEAR BOOK has evolved into a new kind of publication; one that goes beyond the recording of facts and attempts to capture the excitement of the year's events and put them in their proper perspective in the current of time. As Executive Editor, Roy M. Fisher has been the guiding hand behind this transformation. On Jan. 1, 1966, he became the Editor of the *Chicago Daily News*, a newspaper published by our parent company, Field Enterprises, Inc. We wish him well on his new assignment, and pledge ourselves to implementing the objectives which have guided THE YEAR BOOK thus far.   A.R.H.

TABLE OF CONTENTS

A Chronology of the Most Important Events of 1965 Will Be Found on Pages 10 to 14. A Preview of 1966 Will Be Found on Pages 625 and 626.

THE YEAR IN FOCUS .... page 15

The members of THE YEAR BOOK Board of Editors focus their attention on significant developments of the year.

YEAR BOOK SPECIAL REPORTS .. page 63

Eight special articles and the exclusive YEAR BOOK Trans-Vision® bring special treatment to subjects chosen for their current importance and lasting interest.

EDITORIAL STAFF

THE GOLDEN ANNIVERSARY
of THE WORLD BOOK ENCYCLOPEDIA

In terms of a human life, 50 years represent a considerable span of time. This is true even in the life of a publishing company, such as ours. And yet, as we now find ourselves in our 50th year, we do not *feel* old; in fact, we feel quite young and hearty. Nonetheless, this is an appropriate time to look back on the record of the past and to assess the challenges and responsibilities of the future.

The first edition of THE WORLD BOOK ENCYCLOPEDIA was published on January 24, 1917. Countless changes have taken place in the world since that distant time, and these startling, often even fantastic changes, have been mirrored in the development of THE WORLD BOOK itself. The Encyclopedia has, for example, grown from eight volumes to 20. Now, in our 50th year, it is still undergoing constant revision, still molding its character to meet the expanding demands of the "knowledge explosion."

No one man can be given credit for conceiving the Encyclopedia or bringing it to life, but of the many who worked on the first edition, the name of Editor in Chief Michael Vincent O'Shea stands out. O'Shea dreamed of THE WORLD BOOK as a unique reference work and, until his death in 1932, directed a program of continuing revision and expansion, highlighted by a "new" edition of 13 volumes in 1929.

Four years later, in 1933, THE WORLD BOOK ENCYCLOPEDIA appeared in 19 volumes. It was arranged in the unit-letter system, one of the many ease-of-use features that firmly established the Encyclopedia as the leader in its field. The 1930s also saw the formation of an Editorial Advisory Board, composed of distinguished educators, including Dr. Hollis L. Caswell, now General Chairman of all our Editorial Advisory Boards.

In 1945, THE WORLD BOOK ENCYCLOPEDIA became the property of Field Enterprises, Inc. Two years later, a major revision of the Encyclopedia was published under the guidance of Editor in Chief J. Morris Jones. Throughout the 1940s and 1950s, Mr. Jones pushed the dynamic current revision program, culminating in the 1960 edition of 20 volumes.

Each year, at a cost of more than a million dollars, between 4,000 and 5,000 pages of the Encyclopedia undergo some type of revision to keep the set up-to-date, authoritative, and easy to use. The funds needed for these revisions have been available, not only because of the wide acceptance of our publications, but because of the deep dedication to education of our late publisher, Marshall Field. Mr. Field passed away in 1965, and our sense of personal loss can never be erased. But we pledge ourselves to continue the commitment to education which was so much a part of him.

That commitment is reflected, not only in our program of continually updating the Encyclopedia, but in the existence of our other publications: CHILDCRAFT, The *How and Why*® Library, THE WORLD BOOK ENCYCLOPEDIA DICTIONARY, the *Cyclo-teacher*® Learning Aid, THE WORLD BOOK ATLAS, THE WORLD BOOK YEAR BOOK, and THE CHILDCRAFT ANNUAL. It is reflected, too, in our newest publication, SCIENCE YEAR, and in the World Book Encyclopedia Science Service, Inc.

Our attitude toward all our publications is one of "eternal discontent." We constantly try to make them more useful, more vital, more interesting, and more colorful. The challenge we face is clear: as people engaged in the great adventure of education, we must keep abreast of mankind's ever-increasing search for knowledge, and we must present that knowledge to you in a manner that is meaningful and easy to grasp. We assure you that we will always continue this quest.

CHAIRMAN OF THE BOARD
AND CHIEF EXECUTIVE OFFICER
FIELD ENTERPRISES EDUCATIONAL CORP.

CONTRIBUTORS

Anderson, Joseph P., M.S.S.A., Ph.B.; Exec. Director, National Association of Social Workers. Social Organizations

Asimov, Isaac, Ph.D.; Associate. Professor of Biochemistry, Boston University School of Medicine. Special Report

Atkinson, Brooks, A.B.; Journalist; Drama Critic; Pulitzer Prize for Journalism, 1947. Special Report

Bedingfield, Robert E.; Assistant to the Financial-Business Editor, *The New York Times.* Industry Articles

Bhote, Keki R., B.E., M.Sc.; Author; Lecturer. India; Pakistan Special Report

Bradley, Van Allen, B.J.; Literary Editor, *Chicago Daily News.* Literature

Bregman, Jacob I., B.S., M.S., Ph.D.; Director, Chemical Sciences, Illinois Institute of Technology Research Institute. Special Report

Brown, Kenneth; Journalist. Europe Articles

Bryan, Leslie A., Ph.D., LL.B.; Dir., Institute of Aviation, University of Illinois. Aviation

Burnet, Alastair, B.A.; Editor, *The Economist.* British Commonwealth Articles

Cain, Charles C., III, A.B.; Automotive Editor, Associated Press. Automobile; Rubber

Carner, Charles; Public Relations Officer, American Library Association. American Library Association

Carruth, Hayden, A.B., M.A.; Poet. Literature (Poetry)

Churchill, Rhona; Feature Writer, *Daily Mail,* London. Great Britain (Close-Up)

Colegrove, Kenneth, Ph.D., Litt. D.; Professor Emeritus, Northwestern University. Civil Rights

Commager, Henry Steele, Ph.B., A.M., Ph.D.; Sperenza Lecturer, Columbia University; Author, *The Blue and the Gray.* Deaths (Close-Up)

Conley, Clare, B.A.; Managing Editor, *Field & Stream.* Hunting and Fishing

Cook, Robert C.; President, Population Reference Bureau. Population

Covell, Florence Byerly, B.S.; Home Fashion Coordinator, Famous-Barr Co. Interior Decoration

Csida, June Bundy; Former Radio-TV Editor, *Music Business Magazine.* Radio; Television

Dammann, Harle; Foreign Correspondent. Eastern Europe Articles

Dammann, Tom, B.A.; Foreign Correspondent. Eastern Europe Articles

Darby, Edwin W., B.S.J.; Financial Editor, *Chicago Sun-Times.* Business Articles

Dewald, William G., Ph.D.; Associate Professor of Economics, Ohio State University. Finance Articles

Dumouchel, J. Robert; Director of Community Relations, Land Clearance for Redevelopment Authority of Kansas City, Mo. City Planning; Housing

Dunaway, James O., B.S.; Eastern Editor, *Track and Field News.* Sports Articles

Eckler, A. Ross, A.B., A.M., Ph.D.; Director, U.S. Bureau of the Census. Census

Farr, David M. L., M.A., D.Phil.; Dean of Arts, Carleton University, Ottawa. Canada

Feather, Leonard G.; Author, *Encyclopedia of Jazz.* Music Articles

Feinberg, Harold, B.A., M.A., Ph.D.; Assoc. Prof., University of Ill. School of Medicine. Biochemistry; Biology

Fenner, Frank E., B.S., FPSA, ARPS; World Book Encyclopedia Photographs Editor. Photography

Freeman, Leslie G., Jr., Ph.D.; Assistant Professor, Department of Anthropology, University of Chicago. Anthropology; Archaeology

French, Charles E., B.S., A.M., Ph.D.; Professor, Department of Agricultural Economics, Purdue University. Agriculture

Freudenheim, Milt, A.B.; United Nations Correspondent, *Chicago Daily News.* United Nations

Friesen, Ernest C., A.B., LL.B.; Assistant Deputy Attorney General, Department of Justice. Law Articles

Gassner, John, M.A.; Sterling Professor of Playwriting and Dramatic Literature, Yale University. Theater

Gayn, Mark, B.A.; Communist Affairs Analyst, *Toronto Star.* Special Report

Goy, Robert W., B.S., Ph.D.; Senior Scientist, Oregon Regional Primate Research Center. Psychology

Grevatt, Ren, B.A., M.B.A.; Public Relations Specialist. Recordings for Children

Griffin, Alice, M.A., Ph.D.; Associate Professor of English, Hunter College. Theater, Amateur

Haefele, Edwin T.; Senior Staff, Economics Division, The Brookings Institution. Transportation Articles

Harper, Frank B., A.B., B.J.; Agricultural writer. Agricultural Articles

Havighurst, Robert J., Ph.D.; Prof. of Education, University of Chicago; Author, *Older People.* Old Age

Hechinger, Fred M., B.A., LL.D.; Education Editor, *The New York Times.* Education

Holmes, Jay E., B.A.; Deputy Director, Special Operations, Manned Space Flight Center, NASA. Space Travel

Husén, Torsten, M.A., Ph.D.; Prof. of Education, University of Stockholm. Education (Close-Up)

Hussey, Hugh H., M.D.; Director of Scientific Activities, American Medical Association. Medical Articles

Isaacs, Stanley, B.A.; Sports Columnist, *Newsday.* Sports Articles

Jessup, M.E., A.B.; News Editor, *Civil Engineering.* Engineering Articles

Johnson, Robert I., A.B.; Director, Adler Planetarium. Astronomy

Jones, Virgil Carrington, B.A. (J); Author. Civil War Centennial

Joseph, Lou, B.A.; Asst. Director, Bureau of Public Information, American Dental Association. Dentistry

Kennedy, Rose F. (Mrs. Joseph P.), Hyannis Port, Mass. Special Report

Kertzer, Morris N., M.A., D.H.L.; Rabbi, Larchmont Temple, New York. Jews and Judaism

Knight, Arthur, B.A.; Professor, University of So. California Department of Cinema. Motion Pictures

Knight, George A. F., M.A., D.B.; Professor of Old Testament, McCormick Theological Seminary. Trans-Vision®

Koczy, F. F., Ph.D.; Chairman, Division of Physical Sciences, University of Miami. OCEAN

Koenig, Louis W., M.A., Ph.D.; Professor of Government, New York University. PRESIDENT (Close-Up)

Lach, Alma, Diplome de Cordon Bleu. FOOD

Lenormand, Sergei; Manager, Public Information, Illinois Institute of Technology Research Institute. Science Articles; Special Report

Lewis, Ralph H., A.B., M.A.; Chief, Museum Branch, National Park Service. MUSEUMS

Lief, Donald W., A.B.; Managing Editor, *Nation's Cities.* City Articles

Lisagor, Peter, A.B.; Chief, Washington Bureau, *Chicago Daily News.* Political Party Articles

Logan, Rayford W., A.B., A.M., Ph.D.; Professor of History, Howard University. NEGRO

Lohman, Joseph D., B.A., M.A.; Dean, School of Criminology, University of California. CRIME; PRISON

MacFarland, Douglas C., Ph.D.; Chief, Division of Services to the Blind, Dept. of Health, Education, and Welfare. BLINDNESS

Maki, John M., B.A., M.A., Ph.D.; Professor of Japanese Politics, University of Washington. JAPAN; KOREA

Malia, Thomas M., Ph.B.; Executive Editor, *Telecommunications Reports.* COMMUNICATIONS

Manchester, P. W.; Managing Editor, *Dance News;* New York Dance Critic, *Christian Science Monitor.* DANCING

Marsh, Robert C., A.M., Ed.D.; Music Critic, *Chicago Sun-Times.* MUSIC

Marty, Martin E., B.D., S.T.M., Ph.D.; Associate Editor, *The Christian Century.* PROTESTANT

Mattick, Hans W., B.A., M.A.; Director, Chicago Youth Development Project. JUVENILE DELINQUENCY

Mauldin, William H.; Editorial Cartoonist, *Chicago Sun-Times;* Pulitzer Prize, 1944 and 1958. Cartoons

Maxon, John, M.A., Ph.D.; Director of Fine Arts, The Art Institute of Chicago. PAINTING AND SCULPTURE

McCaul, Eugene B.; Director, Statistical Department, American Transit Association. TRANSIT

McGaffin, William, A.B., B.Sc.; Washington Correspondent, *Chicago Daily News.* U.S. Government Articles

Mencher, Melvin, B.A.; Assoc. Professor, Graduate School of Journalism, Columbia University. PUBLISHING

Miller, Richard, A.B., B.Arch.; Partner, Helge Westermann, Richard Miller, Associates. ARCHITECTURE

Milne, Lorus J., Ph.D.; Professor of Zoology, University of New Hampshire. Special Report

Milne, Margery, Ph.D.; Honorary Fellow in Zoology, University of New Hampshire. Special Report

Morse, Walter F., B.A.; Assistant City Editor, *Chicago Sun-Times.* Biographies

Morton, Elizabeth H., B.A.; Executive Director, Canadian Library Association. CANADIAN LITERATURE

Mullen, Frances A., Ph.D.; Assistant Superintendent, Chicago Public Schools. CHILD WELFARE

Muller, Herbert J., A.B., A.M., Ph.D.; Distinguished Service Professor, University of Indiana. DEMOCRACY

Newman, Andrew L., A.B., M.A.; Deputy Director of Information, U.S. Department of the Interior. Conservation Articles

O'Brien, Lawrence Francis, LL.B.; Postmaster General. POST OFFICE

O'Leary, Theodore M., A.B.; Special Correspondent, *Sports Illustrated* Magazine. PET, Hobby Articles

Patterson, William D., A.B.; Vice President and Associate Publisher, *The Saturday Review.* HOTEL; TRAVEL

Pelikan, Jaroslav, B.D., Ph.D.; Titus Street Professor of Ecclesiastical History, Yale University. Special Report

Perkins, R. Marlin; Director, St. Louis Zoo. ZOOS AND AQUARIUMS

Prastein, S. Matthew, A.B., M.S., Ph.D.; Assistant Professor of Physics, Illinois Institute of Technology. PHYSICS

Pyle, Howard; President, National Safety Council. SAFETY

Ravenholt, Albert; Special Foreign Correspondent, *Chicago Daily News.* Asia Articles

Rogers, Warren; Chief Washington Correspondent, Hearst Newspapers. Military Articles

Rue, Eloise, M.A., B.A. in L.S.; Associate Professor of Library Science, University of Wisconsin, Milwaukee. LITERATURE FOR CHILDREN

Russell, I. Willis, A.B., M.A., Ph.D.; Professor of English, University of Alabama. WORDS AND PHRASES

Schmemann, The Rev. Alexander, S.T.D.; Dean, St. Vladimir's Seminary. EASTERN ORTHODOX

Shearer, Warren W., Ph.D.; Chairman, Department of Economics, Wabash College. Business Articles

Sheen, Fulton J., Ph.D., D.D., LL.D.; National Director, Society for the Propagation of the Faith, New York City. ROMAN CATHOLIC

Skilling, H. Gordon, B.A., M.A., Ph.D.; Professor of Political Science, Univ. of Toronto. COMMUNISM; RUSSIA

Smothers, Frank; Director of Publications, The Council of State Governments. STATE GOVERNMENT

Spencer, William, A.B., A.M., Ph.D.; Director, Institute of Non-Western Studies, The American University. Africa and Middle East Articles

Stalker, John N., B.A., M.A., Ph.D.; Professor of History, University of Hawaii. Asia Articles

Stern, James L., B.S., Ph.D.; Professor of Economics, University of Wisconsin. AUTOMATION; LABOR

Thomas, Benjamin E., M.A., Ph.D.; Professor of Geography, University of California. Africa Articles

Thompson, Carol L., A.B., M.A.; Editor, *Current History* Magazine. U.S. Government Articles

Uphaus, Robert A., B.S., M.S., Ph.D.; Chemist, Argonne National Laboratory. CHEMISTRY

Wallbank, T. Walter, A.B., A.M., Ph.D.; Professor of History, Univ. of So. California. WORLD, HISTORY OF

Webster, Mary C., B.A.; Editor, *Noticias* Magazine. Latin America Articles

White, Ruth M., B.S. in Ed., B.S. in L.S., A.M.; Headquarters Librarian, American Library Assoc. LIBRARY

Zwecker, Peg, B.S.; Fashion and Beauty Editor, *Chicago Daily News.* FASHION

1965 · CHRONOLOGY · 1965

JANUARY

1—First World Weather Center Opens at Suitland, Md., World Meteorological Organization unit.

4—89th Congress of U.S. Opens its first session in Washington, D.C. President Johnson delivers State of Union Message, outlining his "Great Society" program for nation.

7—Indonesia Quits United Nations, President Sukarno declares, ". . . . since Malaysia has become a Security Council member."

12-13—Japanese Prime Minister in Washington, D.C. Eisaku Sato is President Johnson's first foreign visitor of 1965.

15—Burundi Premier Assassinated in Bujumbura. Pierre Ngendandumwe in office since Jan. 11.

16—United States and Canada Sign Automobile Pact. Lifts tariffs on motor vehicle imports.

18—New U.S. Secretary of Commerce. John T. Connor succeeds Luther H. Hodges.

20—United States Inaugurates President. Lyndon B. Johnson begins his first elected term. Vice-President Hubert H. Humphrey also takes oath of office.

21—Indonesia Formally Leaves United Nations. Submits letter of withdrawal, reducing world organization to 114 member nations.

22—New British Foreign Minister. Michael Stewart succeeds Patrick Gordon Walker.
Tiros IX Launched into Orbit at Cape Kennedy. Weather satellite to photograph entire earth once every 24 hours.

23-27—Buddhists Demonstrations in South Vietnam force out Premier Tran Van Huong.

24—Sir Winston Churchill Dies at 90 in London, great British and world statesman.
India Dedicates Sharavati Hydroelectric Project at Jog. Linganamakki and Talakalale dams and Sharavati power station completed.

26-27—Premier of Iran Dies of Assassin Bullets. Hassan Ali Mansur is succeeded by Amir Abbas Hoveida.

29-30—Burundi Cuts Diplomatic Ties with Communist China. Orders ambassador to leave Bujumbura.

FEBRUARY

1—U.S. Air Force Chief of Staff Retires. Gen. Curtis E. LeMay is succeeded by Gen. John P. McConnell, formerly vice-chief of staff.

1-12—Queen Elizabeth II in Africa. First reigning British sovereign to visit Ethiopia, spends last 4 days of visit in Sudan.

3—OSO II Launched at Cape Kennedy. Orbiting Solar Observatory designed to create artificial eclipses of sun.
105 Cadets Resign, U.S. Air Force Academy reports during investigation of cheating and theft and sale of examination papers there.

7—United States Bombs North Vietnam in Dong Hoi area after Viet Cong attacks in South Vietnam.

9—U.S. Embassy Attacked in Moscow by Vietnamese, Chinese, and other demonstrators.

13—New U.S. Attorney General. Nicholas deB. Katzenbach, formerly acting head of Department of Justice.

13-17—Violent Anti-U.S. Demonstrations Follow North Vietnam Air Attacks in capitals of Hungary, Bulgaria, Uganda, Venezuela, Malaysia, and in Medan, Indonesia.

15—Canada Unfurls Its New Flag. Red Maple Leaf replaces Red Ensign (with British Union Jack), semiofficial emblem for some 20 years.
Indonesia Seizes U.S. Information Service Library in Djakarta, third since August, 1964.

16—Pegasus I Launched at Cape Kennedy. Winged satellite to check meteoroid hazards.
New South Vietnam Regime. Phanh Khac Suu is Chief of State, and Phan Huy Quat is Premier.

17—Ranger VIII Launched on Way to Moon at Cape Kennedy.

17-18—Gambia Proclaims Independence. African country joins British Commonwealth.

20—Ranger VIII Hits Moon in Sea of Tranquillity area after sending back 7,000 photographs.

21—Negro Nationalist Malcolm X Shot to Death in New York City as he addresses his Afro-American Unity organization.
New Premier in Turkey. Suat Hayri Ürgüplü succeeds Ismet Inönü.

22—Pope Paul VI Creates 27 New Cardinals at first private consistory of his reign.

24—East German President in Cairo. Walter Ulbricht's arrival in United Arab Republic cause of breach with West Germany.

25—Chile Establishes Diplomatic Relations with Bulgaria after 17-year break.

MARCH

1—Bechuanaland Holds First Elections. Seretse Khama appointed Prime Minister.

3—British Honduras Inaugurates First Prime Minister, George C. Price, under new internal self-government constitution.

4—U.S. Information Agency to Close Libraries in Indonesia, under attack since 1958.

9—First "Great Society" Bill Signed by President Johnson, billion dollar aid program for 11-state Appalachia area.

11—Tunisia Opposes United Arab Republic on German-Israel Issues. Refuses to join Arab boycott of West Germany.

17—America's Grand Old Man of Football Dies at 102. Amos Alonzo Stagg was college coach for 70 years.

18—French Gold Purchase of $231,500,000 Reduces U.S. Stock to $14,563,000,000, lowest since Dec. 28, 1935 ($14,508,000,000).

18-19—Voskhod II Orbits Earth for 26 hours with Col. Pavel I. Belyayev and Lieut.-Col. Aleksei A. Leonov aboard. Leonov first man to float in space outside spacecraft.

1965 JANUARY 1965

SUN.	MON.	TUE.	WED.	THU.	FRI.	SAT.
					1	2
3	4	5	6	7	8	9
10	11	12	13	14	15	16
17	18	19	20	21	22	23
24/31	25	26	27	28	29	30

1965 FEBRUARY 1965

SUN.	MON.	TUE.	WED.	THU.	FRI.	SAT.
	1	2	3	4	5	6
7	8	9	10	11	12	13
14	15	16	17	18	19	20
21	22	23	24	25	26	27
28						

1965 MARCH 1965

SUN.	MON.	TUE.	WED.	THU.	FRI.	SAT.
	1	2	3	4	5	6
7	8	9	10	11	12	13
14	15	16	17	18	19	20
21	22	23	24	25	26	27
28	29	30	31			

21—**Ranger IX Launched to Moon,** last in Ranger luna photographing program.
22—**Romania Elects New Head,** Nicolae Ceausescu, as First Secretary of Workers' (Communist) party.
23—**Gemini III Flight.** Maj. Virgil I. Grissom and Lieut.-Col. John W. Young circle earth 3 times in 4 hrs. 54 min.
Honduras National Assembly Elects President. Col. Osvaldo Lopez Arellano was junta head.
24—**Ranger IX Hits Alphonsus Crater on Moon.** Takes pictures in last minutes of flight.
25—**Alabama Freedom Marchers in Montgomery.** Trekked 54 miles from Selma. White civil rightist Viola Gregg Liuzzo later shot to death on highway near Lowndesboro, Ala.
New Prime Minister in Ceylon. Dudley Sen·anayake succeeds Sirimavo Bandaranaike, world's first woman prime minister.
31—**Canada Adopts Pension Plan.** House of Commons approves federal program.

APRIL

1—**New U.S. Secretary of the Treasury.** Henry H. Fowler succeeds C. Douglas Dillon.
3—**First Spacecraft Atomic Power Reactor Launched** at Vandenberg Air Force Base, California. SNAP (Systems for Nuclear Auxiliary Power) 10A reactor put in orbit for year-long test.
4—**Coronation in Sikkim.** Maharajah Palden Thondup Namgyal and his American-born Maharani, the former Hope Cooke of New York, are crowned Chogyal (King) and Gyalmo (Queen).
6—**World's First Commercial Communications Satellite Launched** at Cape Kennedy. Early Bird is first link in global commercial communications space network.
British Budget Submitted to House of Commons. Tax levies to reduce home consumption, increase revenue, and curb capital outflow.
7—**Unconditional Talks on Vietnam Proposed** by President Johnson in Johns Hopkins University speech. Offers billion-dollar Southeast Asia (also North Vietnam) aid program, and asks Russia, other countries, and United Nations to assist.
8—**European Economic Community Agrees to Integrate Agencies:** executive bodies and ministerial councils of Coal and Steel, Economic, and Atomic Energy communities, Jan. 1, 1966.
9—**U.S. National Council on the Arts Inaugurated** by President Johnson.
Astrodome Opens in Houston. New Texas stadium world's largest air-conditioned room.
11—**$1,307,582,973 Elementary and Secondary Education Act of 1965 Signed** by President Johnson, first of such importance in 20 years.
12—**New Prime Minister in The Netherlands.** Joseph M. L. T. Cals presents new program, ending government crisis begun in February.

14-15—**British Prime Minister in United States.** Harold Wilson confers with Washington officials. Supports U.S. Vietnam policy.
15—**West Germany Completes Israeli Reparations** with final payment on $860,000,000 for millions of Jews killed by the Nazis.
19-22—**Italian Premier in United States for First Time.** Aldo Moro attends Cabinet meeting with President Johnson.
21—**United Nations Disarmament Commission Convenes** for first time since August, 1960.
23—**Russia Launches Communications Satellite.** Molniya I transmits television broadcast from Pacific port of Vladivostok to Moscow.
24—**Civil War in Dominican Republic.** Ruling junta overthrown by rebels demanding return of deposed President Juan D. Bosch.
Indonesia Seizes Remaining Foreign-Owned Enterprises. Decree signed by Sukarno.
Nepal and India Inaugurate Kosi Barrage, part of project to irrigate 2,600,000 acres in Nepal and Bihar, India.
28—**U.S. Marines Land in Dominican Republic** to protect and evacuate Americans and citizens of some 30 other countries.
29—**Council of Europe Admits Malta,** its 18th full member nation.
Explorer XXVII Launched at Wallops Island.
30—**Basutoland Begins Internal Self-Government** after 97 years of British rule.

MAY

1—**Life Peerage for Lady Churchill.** Baroness Spencer-Churchill of Chartwell will sit in House of Lords as a crossbencher.
2—**14,000 U.S. Troops Committed to Dominican Republic,** President Johnson says, "to prevent another Communist state in this hemisphere."
Early Bird Relay Links Europe and North America. European Broadcasting Union and U.S., Canadian, and Mexican networks begin regular use of initial commercial satellite.
3—**Cambodia Ends Diplomatic Relations with United States,** says Chief of State Prince Norodom Sihanouk.
5—**Formal Cease-Fire Signed in Dominican Republic,** but fighting continues.
9—**Lunik V Launched to Moon** by Russia.
11—**Israel Museum Opens in Jerusalem,** includes four separate museums.
12—**Lunik V Hits Sea of Clouds Area on Moon,** but fails to make "soft landing."
West Germany and Israel Establish Diplomatic Relations. Governments exchange letters.
12-16—**Arab States Cut Diplomatic Ties with West Germany,** except Libya, Morocco, and Tunisia.
14—**John F. Kennedy Shrine at Runnymede Dedicated** by Queen Elizabeth II, where historic Magna Carta was signed 750 years ago.
Communist China Explodes Its Second Atomic Bomb, over its western areas.

11

1965	APRIL	1965

SUN.	MON.	TUE.	WED.	THU.	FRI.	SAT.
				1	2	3
4	5	6	7	8	9	10
11	12	13	14	15	16	17
18	19	20	21	22	23	24
25	26	27	28	29	30	

1965	MAY	1965

SUN.	MON.	TUE.	WED.	THU.	FRI.	SAT.
						1
2	3	4	5	6	7	8
9	10	11	12	13	14	15
16	17	18	19	20	21	22
23 30	24 31	25	26	27	28	29

1965	JUNE	1965

SUN.	MON.	TUE.	WED.	THU.	FRI.	SAT.
		1	2	3	4	5
6	7	8	9	10	11	12
13	14	15	16	17	18	19
20	21	22	23	24	25	26
27	28	29	30			

15—**New Zealand Inaugurates North-South Islands Undersea Cable,** 354 miles across Cook Strait.

18—**U.S. Confirms 8-Satellite Launching** on March 9 by single rocket at Vandenberg Air Force Base, California.

18-28—**Queen Elizabeth II in West Germany.** First reigning British sovereign to visit there since George V visited Wilhelm II in 1913.

23—**Austria Elects President.** Franz Jonas to begin 6-year term in June.

24—**Inter-American Force in Dominican Republic,** an Organization of American States group.

25—**Pegasus II Launched** at Cape Kennedy. Begins measuring meteoroid density.

29—**IMP Launched at Cape Kennedy.** Interplanetary Monitoring Platform third of 7 designed to look for radiation storms in space.

JUNE

3-7—**Gemini IV Orbits Earth 62 Times** during flight of 97 hrs. 58 min. Maj. Edward H. White II maneuvers outside craft on 3d orbit. Maj. James A. McDivitt worked on other projects.

8—**Lunik VI Launched on Moon Flight** by Russia.

11—**Lunik VI Misses Moon** by 100,000 miles.

14—**Military Takes Control in South Vietnam,** led by Maj. Gen. Nguyen Van Thieu.

17-25—**British Commonwealth Prime Ministers Conference** in London establishes Vietnam Peace Mission headed by Prime Minister Harold Wilson.

19—**Ben Bella Deposed in Algeria** by Defense Minister Col. Houari Boumedienne.
South Vietnam Air Vice-Marshal New Premier. Nguyen Cao Ky replaces Phan Huy Quat.

21—**Excise Tax Reduction Bill Signed** by President Johnson. Urges manufacturers and retailers to lower prices.

22—**Japan and South Korea Sign Amity Treaty,** result of 14 years of intermittent negotiations.
English Parliament Septcentenary Ceremony commemorates conference called in 1265.

24—**South Vietnam Ends Diplomatic Relations with France,** charges it aids Vietnam enemies.

25-26—**United Nations Commemorative Session in San Francisco** marks signing of charter in 1945.

28—**Intercontinental Telephone Via Early Bird Satellite.** President Johnson inaugurates commercial service, calls European capitals.
Gyula Kallai New Premier in Hungary, but János Kádár still heads Communist party.

JULY

1—**Rann of Kutch Cease-Fire in Force.** India and Pakistan to withdraw troops immediately.

2—**Tiros X Launched** at Cape Kennedy.

6—**U.S. Presidential Disability and Vice-President Vacancy Resolution Passed** in Senate. Ratification by 38 of 50 states within 7 years to make proposed amendment part of U.S. Constitution.

France Recalls Permanent Representative from EEC. Boycotts European Economic Community Council meetings "for the moment."

10—**Greek Crown Princess Born in Athens** to King Constantine XIII and Queen Anne-Marie.

14—**Adlai E. Stevenson Collapses on London Street and Dies.** U.S. permanent representative to United Nations since 1960.

14-15—**Mariner IV Completes 228-Day Mars Flight.** Returns first of 22 close-up photographs.

15—**King Constantine XIII Dismisses Greek Premier** George Papandreou.

16—**World's Longest Motor Tunnel Opens in Alps.** Two-lane, 7¼-mile Mont Blanc passage links Pèlerins (near Chamonix, France) and Entrèves (near Courmayeur, Italy).
Proton I Launched by Russia. Heaviest payload (26,900 pounds) yet, put into orbit by new booster rocket. Also launches 5 Cosmos satellites with one rocket.

18—**Zond III Put into Orbit** by Russia.

20—**Zond III Photographs Hidden Side of Moon.**

23—**Coinage Bill Signed** by President Johnson. Eliminates silver from quarters and dimes. Reduces half dollar silver content from 90 to 40 per cent.

26—**Maldive Islands Proclaim Independence.** Permits Britain to retain Gan Island air base.

27—**Belgium Government Crisis Ends.** Pierre Harmel succeeds Prime Minister Théodore Lefèvre.
17-Nation Disarmament Committee Reconvenes in Geneva, first time since September, 1964.

28—**Arthur J. Goldberg at United Nations.** Succeeds the late Adlai E. Stevenson as U.S. permanent representative there.
British Conservative Party Elects New Leader. Edward Heath succeeds Sir Alec Douglas-Home.

30—**Medicare-Social Security Bill Signed** by President Johnson at Independence, Mo.
Pegasus III Launched to check on meteoroids.

AUGUST

5—**Fighting in Kashmir.** Pakistanis infiltrate India area disguised as civilians.

6—**U.S. Voting Rights Act of 1965 Signed** by President Johnson.

9—**Singapore Secedes from Malaysia Federation.** Prime Minister Lee Kuan Yew says he was forced to sign accord (August 7) by Malaysia.

11-16—**Los Angeles Riot in Negro Watts Area** set off by traffic arrest. Shops burned and looted, whites attacked, and some 30 persons killed.

12—**New U.S. Ambassador to South Vietnam.** Henry Cabot Lodge replaces Gen. Maxwell D. Taylor.

12-14—**Chicago Negroes Riot on West Side.** Accidental killing of Negro pedestrian sparks fights.

14—**South Korea Ratifies Amity Pact with Japan.** Japan to give its former colony (1910-1945) $800,000,000 in grants and loans.

JULY
				1	2	3
4	5	6	7	8	9	10
11	12	13	14	15	16	17
18	19	20	21	22	23	24
25	26	27	28	29	30	31

AUGUST
1	2	3	4	5	6	7
8	9	10	11	12	13	14
15	16	17	18	19	20	21
22	23	24	25	26	27	28
29	30	31				

SEPTEMBER
				1	2	3	4
5	6	7	8	9	10	11
12	13	14	15	16	17	18
19	20	21	22	23	24	25
26	27	28	29	30		

16—**Arthur J. Goldberg's First Formal Speech at United Nations.** New U.S. permanent representative says United States accepts fact that majority of UN members not ready to invoke penalties against Russia, France, and 11 other countries who refuse to pay for UN peacekeeping operations.

Zond III Far-Side-of-Moon Photographs Published by Russia, taken July 20.

Congo Republic Ends Diplomatic Ties with Portugal. Brazzaville also ends air and port rights, and bans Portuguese imports.

19—**Malaysia Elects New Head of State.** Sultan Ismail Nasiruddin Shah, Ruler of Trengganu, succeeds Raja of Perlis Sir Putra Ibin Al-Marhum Syed Hassan Jamalullail.

17 Germans Found Guilty of Auschwitz Murders at end of 20-month trial. Former Nazi camp staff members had part in torture and murder of nearly 4,000,000 persons, mostly Jews.

20—**White Seminarian Killed at Hayneville, Ala.** Civil rightists Jonathan M. Daniels and Roman Catholic priest Richard F. Morrisroe (critically wounded) just freed from jail.

21-29—**Gemini V 8-Day Manned Space Flight.** Lieut.-Col. Leroy G. Cooper, Jr., first to make second such flight (May 15-16, 1963), and Lieut.-Comdr. Charles Conrad, Jr., set duration (190 hrs. 56 min.) and distance (3,000,000 ground miles) records.

24—**Pact to End Yemeni Civil War Signed** by United Arab Republic and Saudi Arabia, who supported Republicans and Royalists.

30—**Natural Neutrinos Found for First Time** in South African gold mine. Case Institute of Technology Frederick Reins reports 7 such natural neutrino events since Feb. 23, 1965.

31—**Dominican Act of Reconciliation Signed.** Provides for provisional government and end of civil war.

United Nations Charter Changes in Force. United States last of Security Council permanent members (5) to deposit its ratification (plus 82 of 114 UN members). Increases Security (11 to 15) and Economic and Social (18 to 27) councils' memberships.

SEPTEMBER

2—**Manager Casey Stengel Says Farewell to New York Mets,** ending 56 years in baseball.

3—**Dominican Republic Inaugurates Provisional President,** Héctor García-Godoy.

4—**Albert Schweitzer Dies at 90** in his jungle hospital at Lambaréné, Gabon.

5-6—**Steel Strike Averted.** Workers ratify and union and industry sign 35-month contract.

9—**Department of Housing and Urban Development Created.** Act signed by President Johnson.

France to Leave NATO in 1969. President De Gaulle says his country will no longer accept North Atlantic Treaty Organization defense system.

12-13—**Labor Party Defeated in Norway Elections** after 30 years (except 3 weeks, 1963) in power.

13—**Experimental Nuclear Power Plant Dedicated** in central Idaho. Makes full use of natural uranium, not just U-235.

14—**Vatican Council II Fourth Session Opens** in Rome.

21—**United Nations General Assembly Opens.** Elects Italian Foreign Minister Amintore Fanfani President of its 20th regular session. Admission of Gambia, Maldive Islands, and Singapore brings membership to 117 nations.

New Premier in Iraq. Abdul Rahman al-Bazzar replaces Arif Abdel Razzak, now in exile.

22-23—**Cease-Fire in Kashmir.** India and Pakistan comply with United Nations resolution, but resume fighting almost immediately.

23—**New Premier in Syria,** Yussef Zayen.

24—**United States to Give Canal to Panama.** President Johnson says new treaty underway.

25—**Deposed President Juan D. Bosch Returns to Dominican Republic.** Demands billion dollar indemnity from United States for April revolt.

Greek Parliament Approves Premier. Stephanos C. Stephanopoulos third in post since July 15.

29—**National Foundation on the Arts and Humanities Created.** Act signed by President Johnson.

OCTOBER

1—**Indonesian Revolt Foiled** by loyal military forces, but resistance continues in Java.

Any Cuban Free to Go to United States. Castro widens initial offer of September 28.

3—**New Immigration Act Ends National Origins Quota System,** signed by President Johnson.

4—**Pope Paul VI at United Nations.** First reigning pope to visit Americas addresses General Assembly during 14 hours in New York City.

Supreme Court of United States Opens 1965-1966 Term. Abe Fortas replaces Arthur J. Goldberg as associate justice.

Pakistan Severs Diplomatic Ties with Malaysia for siding with India on Kashmir dispute.

Lunik VII Launched into Space by Russia.

5—**OV I Launched** at Vandenberg Air Force Base, Orbital Vehicle space satellite.

6-14—**Los Angeles Dodgers Win World Series** by beating Minneapolis Twins 4 games out of 7.

8—**Communist Party Headquarters Burned in Djakarta.** Moslem youths shout, "Long Live America."

Lunik VII Hits Sea of Storms on Moon, but fails to make "soft landing."

10—**New York Newspaper Strike Ends.** *Times* and Guild reach final agreement on 25th day.

Conservative Justice Party Wins Turkey Elections. Süleyman Demirel new premier.

12—**$10,000,000 Experimental Seismic Station Dedicated** near Miles City, Mont., for underground nuclear explosions detection.

13—**Moise Tshombe Dismissed as Congo Premier.** Evariste Kimba to replace him.

1965 OCTOBER 1965	1965 NOVEMBER 1965	1965 DECEMBER 1965
SUN. MON. TUE. WED. THU. FRI. SAT.	SUN. MON. TUE. WED. THU. FRI. SAT.	SUN. MON. TUE. WED. THU. FRI. SAT.
1 2	1 2 3 4 5 6	1 2 3 4
3 4 5 6 7 8 9	7 8 9 10 11 12 13	5 6 7 8 9 10 11
10 11 12 13 14 15 16	14 15 16 17 18 19 20	12 13 14 15 16 17 18
17 18 19 20 21 22 23	21 22 23 24 25 26 27	19 20 21 22 23 24 25
24/31 25 26 27 28 29 30	28 29 30	26 27 28 29 30 31

$2,000,000 Space Science Laboratory Dedicated at University of Chicago Enrico Fermi Institute of Nuclear Studies.

14—**OGO II Launched** at Vandenberg Air Force Base, Orbiting Geophysical Observatory.

15—**Second Molniga I Communications Satellite Launched** by Russia.

15-18—**Antiwar Demonstrations in Some 40 U.S. Cities.** Iowa State University group, Associated Student Governments, George Washington University reverse teach in, and Detroit Jaycees supports United States policy in Vietnam.

16—**British Commonwealth of Nations Admits Singapore** as its 22nd member.

16-19—**More Violence in Dominican Republic.** Santo Domingo scene of block-to-block fighting.

17—**New York World's Fair Closes.** Total 2-season attendance surpasses 51,000,000.

20—**Ludwig Erhard Re-Elected Chancellor of West Germany** by Bundestag.

20-21—**New Comet Circles Sun** and enters hairpin orbit. Ikeya-Seki, named for Japanese discoverers, has 10- to 20,000,000 mile tail.

21-26—**Organization of African States Conference** in Accra boycotted by 7 French-speaking nations because Ghana President Kwame Nkrumah aids subversives in their countries.

23—**89th Congress of U.S. First Session Ends.** President Johnson acclaims it nation's greatest.

26—**British House of Commons Installs Its First Labour Party Speaker.** Horace King succeeds the late Sir Harry Hylton-Foster.

28—**Pope Paul VI Formally Promulgates Non-Christian Religions Document.** Includes denial of Jews collective guilt in Crucifixion of Jesus.

29—**Saint Louis Completes Gateway Arch.** Inserts 19-ton apex in nation's tallest (630 feet) monument.

31—**U.S. Medal of Honor Men Support Vietnam War.** March at head of New York City parade.

NOVEMBER

2—**New Prime Minister in Afghanistan.** Mohammed Hashim Maiwandwal replaces Mohammed Yousof.
Proton II Launched into Space by Russia.

3—**New U.S. Postmaster General.** Lawrence F. O'Brien succeeds John A. Gronouski, Jr., now U.S. Ambassador to Poland.

6—**Two Congos Resume Diplomatic Relations** after two-year break.
GEOS I Launched into Space. Geodetic explorer satellite to measure earth.

8—**Canada Retains Liberals.** Prime Minister Lester B. Pearson's party wins elections.

9—**Philippines Elects New President.** Nationalist Ferdinand E. Marcos defeats incumbent Liberalist President Diosdado Macapagal.

9-10—**Electric Power Blackout in Northeast U.S., Ontario, and Quebec.** Hits New York City and other areas at evening rush hour, and remains until morning hours.

11—**Rhodesia Proclaims Independence** refused by Britain because of colony's white government.

12—**Venus II Launched into Space** by Russia. To reach planet Venus about Mar. 1, 1966.

16—**Venus III Launched** by Russia toward Venus.

17—**Communist China Barred from United Nations** for 15th time by vote in General Assembly.
France Orders Guinea Ambassador Out of Paris, after Guinea accused French of part in plot against President Sékou Touré.

24—**Britain's Princess Margaret Ends U.S. Visit,** begun on November 4.

25—**Congo Coup d'État.** Army Commander Gen. Joseph D. Mobutu deposes President Joseph Kasavubu, and takes office himself for 5 years.

26—**France 3d Nation in Space Race.** Orbits its first satellite from Sahara test center.

27—**New Kuwait Ruler.** Sheik Sabah as-Salim as-Sabah succeeds brother, Emir Sheik Abdullah as-Salim as-Sabah, who died November 24.

29—**Dahomey Coup d'Etat.** Provisional President Tahiro Congacou replaces deposed President Sourou Migan Apithy.

DECEMBER

1—**Cuban Air Exodus.** First refugees fly to U.S. under new agreement with Castro regime.

4—**Gemini VII Launched on 14-Day Space Flight** with Lieut.-Col. Frank Borman and Comdr. James A. Lovell, Jr., aboard.

7—**Lunik VIII Hits Ocean of Storms on Moon,** but Russians again fail in "soft landing."

8—**Pope Paul VI Ends Historic Vatican II Council,** adjourns its fourth session.

15—**Gemini VII and VI Rendezvous in Space,** man's first such space meeting.
Organization of African Unity Countries Act Against Britain on Rhodesia issue. Tanzania first to break relations with Britain, followed by Guinea, Senegal, and Niger.

16—**Gemini VI Returns to Earth** with Capt. Walter M. Schirra, Jr., and Maj. Thomas P. Stafford.
Pioneer VI Launched at Cape Kennedy.

17—**Great Britain Acts Against Rhodesia.** Imposes oil embargo, in force immediately.

18—**Gemini VII Returns to Earth.** Lieut.-Col. Frank Borman and Comdr. James A. Lovell, Jr., broke all previous space records.
South Korea and Japan Establish Diplomatic Relations, after each ratify Amity Treaty.

19—**Charles De Gaulle Wins Run-Off Election,** and another 7 years as President of France.

21—**Syria Government Resigns,** formed by Premier Yussef Zayen less than 2 months before.

22—**United Nations General Assembly Adjourns** its 20th regular session in 1965.
New Chief of State in Dahomey. Armed Forces head Gen. Christophe Soglo takes control.

24-25—**Vietnam Christmas Truce.** Major hostilities halted for short period.

30—**Philippines Inaugurate President.** Ferdinand E. Marcos begins his first 4-year term.

CONTENTS OF SECTION ONE

THE YEAR BOOK Board of Editors analyzes the
significant developments of 1965 and considers
their impact upon contemporary affairs. The
Related Articles list following each report directs
the reader to THE YEAR BOOK's additional cov-
erage of related subjects.

THE YEAR IN FOCUS

Portrait for THE YEAR BOOK by James Hill

Paul-Henri Spaak
ON THE WORLD

There Was an Increasing Tendency to Settle Conflicts by Violence in a Time of Tension and Crisis

It seems that the cruel memories of World War II are slowly but surely fading away. The millions of military and civilian deaths, the burning cities, the concentration camps, the unspeakable physical and moral misery of those long years has ceased to be a reality affecting our day-to-day life. Those horrors have become a memory, always less and less precise, of a receding past which is progressively losing its intensity and weight.

And now the tendency to settle conflicts between nations through recourse to violence has been redeveloping in a world of tension and crisis. The principles of the United Nations Charter have been adhered to less and less. An aggressive and often fanatical nationalism has again become fashionable. Respect for law is being replaced more and more by recourse to force. The visit of Pope Paul VI to the United Nations, and his cry of anguish and warning, was the most moving demonstration in 1965 of the fear this trend brings to responsible men.

Of all the continents, Asia was the most troubled in 1965.

"The similarity between the methods of the Chinese and those of the Nazis is remarkable."

There was war in Vietnam, war between India and Pakistan, a puzzling revolution in Indonesia, a perpetually troubled situation in Laos and Cambodia. These events were the most striking current developments in the great conflict of this century: the conflict in which communism opposes the Free World. Red China is now leading that fight.

China has adopted the most dangerous theories and tactics professed and practiced by the Soviet Union immediately after World War II. China refuses to admit the principle of peaceful coexistence. It maintains that wars of "liberation" are legitimate. This policy is typified by China's determination to foster local conflicts wherever it can do so by systematically approving all forms of nationalism and by endorsing all subversive movements, regardless of their social context.

The similarity between the methods of the Chinese and those of the Nazis is remarkable. In Europe before World War II, too few people read Adolf Hitler's *Mein Kampf*, and those who did so did not, for the most part, take the book seriously. Hitler's statements were too extreme. His aims seemed entirely unreasonable. He expressed his innermost thoughts with considerable candor, however, and he nearly succeeded in accomplishing his purpose.

The Chinese theorists are equally sincere. We would be ill-advised to minimize their intent to dominate the world and to promote the triumph of their economic and social concepts. Their tactics are not much different, and certainly not less cynical, than those of Hitler. When one learns that China, with its massive manpower, felt itself threatened because four Indian cavalrymen crossed its ill-defined border, one cannot help thinking of the so-called suffering of the Germans of Sudetenland which, in Hitler's eyes, justified erasing Czechoslovakia from Europe.

Among the various conflicts of 1965, the one in Vietnam was, of course, the gravest. Not only did it require from the United States an ever greater military effort, it also assumed all the aspects of a real war. It furthermore created a dangerous cleavage between the United States and a large segment of world public opinion. Finally, it seriously impaired the development of a policy of pacific coexistence between the United States and the Soviet Union. As recently as 1963, that policy constituted the great hope for peace among the nations of the world.

The situation which the United States faced in Asia in 1965 was very similar to that which it faced in Europe in 1948. In both instances, the question was simply this: Should the United States permit communists, either Russian or Chinese, to subjugate people refusing to accept their creed?

The United States took part in World War II partly to prevent totalitarian nationalism from overcoming the Western World. It succeeded in that aim. This very success now compels America to prevent the triumph of totalitarian communists. The United States succeeded in Europe through the Marshall Plan and the North Atlantic Treaty Organization (NATO). Will it succeed in Asia? Conditions are different and much less favorable there. Poor people, without democratic traditions and often badly governed, do not provide the basis of resistance to communism present in Europe after World War II.

Obviously, the war in Vietnam has a much broader and deeper significance than victory or defeat in one country. If America fails, or if it changes its policy in Vietnam, logically it has to cease showing any interest in Southeast Asia, and possibly in the whole of Asia. An American defeat in Vietnam would imply that no defense against Communist China could be attempted in Thailand, in Laos, in Cambodia, in the Philippines, in Formosa, in Malaysia and, tomorrow, in India.

The problem America faces is a formidable one. Its magnitude is underestimated in most of the world where public opinion—largely influenced by daily news of the war—reacts sentimentally and unfavorably. People who are well-informed try to explain the situation, but they encounter deep trends they find difficult to overcome. The Vietnamese war creates repercussions in Europe, and influences relations between the United States and its allies. Above all, it influences relations between the United States and the Soviet Union.

The relaxation of tensions between these two great powers, so hopeful a short while ago, has not materialized. It must be admitted that the position of the Soviet Union is difficult. As leader of the communist world, closely watched by the Chinese who constantly accuse it of treason, Russia cannot remain indifferent toward the situation in Vietnam. The Soviet Union is compelled, apparently against its desire, to oppose the United States. At times one wonders if China, while inciting the North Vietnamese to refuse to negotiate with the United States, is not primarily interested in preventing more peaceful relations between the Soviet Union and the U.S.

Whatever the facts may be, the conflict goes on and the chances for a reasonable solution are, for the time being, nonexistent. A broadening of the conflict remains a possibility, and the limits of this extension are unpredictable. Never since the end of World War II, has a local conflict seemed to contain such a threat to the peace of the world.

War between India and Pakistan has again aggravated the situation in Asia. The conflict over Kashmir appears quite difficult to solve, and a true peace depends upon its solution. Chinese influence in that part of the world is apparent in the unconditional support given to Pakistan, and in the senseless quarrel China picked with India. Communist China is sparking the fire, and is visibly seeking to poison present relations between India and Pakistan.

Compared to seething Asia, Africa was relatively calm in 1965. In the past few years, the newly independent countries have sought to achieve stability, and several of them have succeeded. It must be admitted, however, that in many cases their economic development remains insufficient, despite the assistance given them. The problem of these underdeveloped countries is perhaps the most important of all those the world faces. Will the rich countries have the wisdom to understand in time, and to make the effort and sacrifice needed to solve it? This is one of the biggest questions of our time.

Three other phenomena taking place in Africa are worth noting. One, which is faced by both Blacks and Arabs, is an attempt by the Chinese communists to extend their sphere of influence to the continent. Although their efforts so far have shown some small

results, notably in Congo (Brazzaville) and certain East African countries, they have generally failed to achieve a dominant role in African politics. They have, however, achieved a subtle victory of sorts. Their propaganda has prevented the development of closer, more harmonious relations between Africa and the Western World.

The second phenomena is one which finds the Blacks and the Arabs pitted against one another for domination of the continent. The Blacks, who seem to have gained a new consciousness of their individuality, have, however, successfully resisted Arab intrigues, personified in Egypt's Gamal Abdel Nasser and—until he was deposed—Algeria's Ahmed Ben Bella.

Finally, there is the problem of Rhodesia. It is humanly tragic, and politically very difficult to solve. The small White minority in that country gave clear evidence in 1965 that it was not willing to be governed by a large Black majority. The government of Ian Smith turned down hopes for settlement by pronouncing itself in favor of a policy of adventure. The decision to proclaim the immediate independence of the country from Great Britain appeared unnecessary. It created profound disquiet in Africa, incurred the opposition of many European states, and gave rise to a crisis in the British Commonwealth of Nations.

In North America, Canada and the United States enjoyed great economic prosperity in 1965, but they did not escape political problems. In Canada, the desire of the French-speaking population for autonomy, even independence, posed a problem difficult to solve. It is complicated by the fact that wisdom and reason have often been torn apart by irrational, sentimental reactions. Canadian leaders will require much tact and understanding to solve this problem. Fortunately, there is reason to believe they will succeed.

The United States also was confronted with many problems in 1965. Its position as the most powerful country in the world constantly requires it to assume heavier and more numerous responsibilities.

One is amazed by the speed with which the conditions of American external life have developed. In 1914, only a half century ago,

"America's historical role in this century becomes more and more precise . . ."

the Monroe Doctrine was still the dominant concept of U.S. international policy, and the nation had relatively little interest in the rest of the world. Today the United States is fully engaged in Africa, Asia, Europe, and Latin America. No international problem can now be solved without its assistance. Because of its involvement in world affairs, the U.S. has developed many enemies. Even its friends do not always show their gratitude for the services the United States has rendered, and the sacrifices it has made.

America's historical role in this century becomes more and more precise: it is the main obstacle to the triumph of communism and, consequently, the outstanding defender of the democratic world. Such a tremendous task is not accomplished without certain errors, but it is only fair to judge the achievement as a whole, and it is a positive one.

During World War II, the U.S. crushed nazism, fascism, and aggressive Japanese militarism. After the war, its efforts permitted Europe to heal its wounds and to protect itself against the creeping danger of Russian communism. Today, in Asia, the United States faces the dangers of Chinese communism. Thus, its historical role continues to take shape.

Latin America is unfortunately still confronted by the same problems that have plagued it in the past. In 1965, Cuba was in the throes of a serious economic crisis which the Castro regime seemed unable to surmount. Social unrest continued to provoke incidents and disturbances in Brazil, Peru, and Uruguay. Upheaval in the Dominican Republic held the attention of people throughout the world.

In looking at Latin America, it is difficult to find much evidence of stability. One receives the impression of a continent that is still groping to find itself. Troubled economic and social conditions make it a fertile breeding ground for subversive propaganda.

Europe in 1965 was least troubled of all the continents. The German problem remained unsolved. But, however great its importance, it does not, for the time being at least, seem likely to disturb the peace.

Western Europe, like the United States, has enjoyed a high degree of economic prosperity for many years. It also knows peace. It owes these two blessings to the creation of the Atlantic Alliance and to the European Economic Community (EEC, or Common Market). These two important achievements are threatened today by the policies of French President Charles de Gaulle.

The French president dislikes anything that has been done without his participation. He was out of power for 13 years and had no part in the creation of the Atlantic Alliance. The Common Market was born at a time when he was showing a marked hostility toward it. He seems bent today on destroying the Atlantic Alliance and reducing the Common Market to the status of an economic organization without any extension in the political field.

Such a policy does not stand any chance of succeeding in Europe. It may bring about the destruction, or serious disturbance of what exists, but it cannot build anything solid and endurable.

The manner in which General De Gaulle was re-elected president of France late in 1965 constituted an obvious setback for him. Some maintain that he cannot ignore what has happened, and that he will have to follow a more flexible policy. Others believe that he may react by adopting a more radical line. It may be, in view of this, that 1966 will be a decisive year for Western Europe and the Atlantic Alliance.

In the communist countries of Eastern Europe, important economic reforms have been carried out or are in prospect. The framework of communist society is being maintained, and the means of production are collectively owned. But within this framework, competition and the profit motive are now encouraged as positive elements. We are also witnessing a certain degree of liberalization in the political regimes of these nations, and an undisputed improvement of relations with neighboring countries having different political systems. Peaceful coexistence is gaining ground.

In the Soviet Union, achievements in space research remained important in 1965, but the economic situation created difficult

"The United Nations is slowly emerging from the crisis in which it found itself . . ."

problems. They were due primarily to the inadequacies of the nation's agriculture, and, secondly, to the growing desire of the Russian people for greater material well-being. The Soviet Union's ideological conflict with China, which openly challenges it for the leadership of world communism, is one of the great events in the world today. The possible consequences of this rivalry are immeasurable. China's imperialism is presently largely intellectual, but tomorrow it may assume other forms. It is perhaps even more dangerous for the Soviet Union than the United States, and there are indications that the Soviet Union is clearly aware of this fact.

The war in Southeast Asia unfortunately prevents the Soviet Union from pursuing its policy of rapprochement with the United States at the pace it desires. But in the given circumstances, its policy is moderate. Its attitude in the India-Pakistan conflict was the most recent proof of this. We can be glad that it is no longer the Soviet Union that seeks to aggravate conflicts.

The United Nations is slowly emerging from the crisis in which it found itself as a result of its extremely serious financial situation. This was caused largely by the refusal of the Soviet Union and France to contribute to the expenses for the peace-keeping operations in the Middle East and in Congo (Léopoldville).

The 1965 General Assembly session was able to follow its normal course after a compromise was reached with the Soviet Union and France on their payments. Thanks in no small measure to the good will of the United States, the organization has come back to life. It has even shown signs of vitality. In the India-Pakistan conflict, the Security Council was able for the first time in many years to make a decision which was effectively carried out, and which, at least for the time being, put a stop to the dangerous military operations that had been going on in that area.

Altogether, however, 1965 was a year in which the international situation deteriorated. It was a year in which the Chinese threat became more pointed. The responsibilities of the United States increased. Africa and Latin America groped for stability. In Europe, the economic stability that had been achieved seemed in danger because of De Gaulle's policies.

Related Articles

For a complete report on the year 1965, see Section Two, THE MIRACLE OF THE MOUNTAIN; THE SILENT STRUGGLE; and articles on the various nations in Section Three. In the same section, see also the following:

James B. Reston

ON THE NATION

It Was a Dazzling Year in "the Continuing American Revolution," Yet the People Were Troubled

Americans are funny people. They were born in rebellion but think they are conservative. They condemn "radicals," but in tinkering around to change and improve things, they are actually more radical than the people they condemn. They admire "practical" people who "live modern" and "keep up with the times," and they revolutionize more things than the "revolutionaries" they criticize.

American life is a continuing and unconscious revolution. Americans hate things that do not work. Mentally, they stick to old political concepts and institutions, but change them with their hands. America wants everybody to be happy, healthy, and useful; an idea regarded as wildly "radical" in some parts of the world. America works toward that ideal in every town, factory, school, and legislature until it changes the things that get in its way.

The year 1965 vividly illustrated this point. For many years before that, there had been conflict on a wide range of questions affecting the well-being of the American people. Then somehow in 1965, by some coincidence of time and

"Suddenly, barriers that had long divided the Congress were swept away."

atmosphere, things changed. There was a bumper crop of progressive legislation.

Even before 1965, there had been some agreement on certain basic facts. The schools had not kept pace with the growth of knowledge and population. The hospitals and doctors had not been able to provide for many old people at prices the sick and elderly could afford. And that was not all.

The universities had not been able to finance the teachers, classrooms, and other essential facilities for all the young men and women in America who had the talent to take advantage of a university education. The states had not been able to guarantee the equal voting rights promised in the U. S. Constitution to all adult citizens, regardless of race. The churches had not been able to provide adequate church-school education for the children of their parishioners without financial aid from the federal government, and the Constitution seemed to forbid such aid to church schools.

In 1965, President Lyndon B. Johnson proposed, and the 89th Congress passed, legislation dealing with all these problems. Suddenly, barriers that had long divided the Congress were swept away. Controversial programs that had lost in the past were accepted. 1965 took its place among the historic years of reform on the home front.

One of America's great historians, Arthur M. Schlesinger, Sr., who died in 1965, had long been fascinated by the patterns of American history. There were, he said, periods of innovation and periods of consolidation in the American story, and they seemed to follow a rough order. They were not, he emphasized, periods of reform followed by periods of reaction which repealed the reforms. Rather, he insisted, the movements of social and economic reform occur and progress in stages, much as a ship rises through a system of locks.

First there comes a surge forward, as society and government, feeling ready for needed reforms, move upward to higher levels. Then there follows, not a drop, not a repeal of what is new, but a level period of absorbing and tidying up the new reforms. This is what is meant by "the continuing American revolution," and 1965 was clearly

one of the creative years on history's scroll.

It created, for example, a number of "firsts." For the first time:

• The elderly in America were provided with hospital and nursing care under the federal government's Social Security system.

• The ancient church-state controversy over federal funds to church schools was set aside, and Washington was able to help finance church schools, as well as provide aid to elementary and secondary schools in areas populated largely by poor families.

• Federal scholarships—not just federal loans—were provided for poor but talented students so that they would have an opportunity to get a college education.

• Limited federal rent subsidies—not nearly as generous as the President proposed —were made available to some low-income families qualifying for federal housing.

• A new Department of Housing and Urban Development was established, with Cabinet rank, to deal with the growing problems of urban and suburban housing, community planning, and mass transportation.

• The federal government, through federal registrars, made good the 95-year-old guarantee of Amendment 15 that the right to vote should not be denied or abridged because of race or creed.

• Finally, a law was passed instructing manufacturers of cigarettes to put on each package a warning that states: "Caution— Habitual Smoking Is Injurious to Health."

In addition to these innovations, Congress made generous grants to higher education; provided $1,100,000,000 to relieve the depressed economic area of Appalachia; and added another $1,900,000,000 for the President's "War on Poverty," and $3,250,000,000 for regional development. It repealed many excise taxes; abolished the national immigration quotas system; and repealed the 25 per cent gold cover on commercial bank deposits held by the Federal Reserve Banks.

There were a number of reasons for this extraordinary record of surmounting old legislative barriers. The first was political. In the presidential election of 1964, the balance of power was upset in favor of the Democratic party, which has been the party of innovation and change since the administration of President Woodrow Wilson. President Johnson won the election by the largest margin of votes in history. In the course of this landslide, he carried his party to a two-to-one majority in the House of Representatives and a three-to-one majority in the Senate. The Democrats were also in control of most state and city governments.

The second reason for the legislative breakthrough was personal. President Johnson was not the first former United States Senator to win the presidency—Warren G. Harding had in 1920, Harry S. Truman in 1948; and John F. Kennedy in 1960—but Johnson was the first commanding congressional leader to take over the White House. He had been a prominent Representative from Texas. Later, as Majority Leader of the Senate, he had acquired the reputation of being one of the most astute political craftsmen of this century.

It was not only that President Johnson understood the psychology of Congress and the intricacies of parliamentary maneuver; he also knew the leaders of Congress intimately. He had spent over 30 years on Capitol Hill with them. He knew what things they needed to get elected in their districts, and he exploited all this experience by a persistent, determined, and resourceful personal leadership of his legislative program, in alliance with his friend, the Republican Minority Leader, Senator Everett McKinley Dirksen of Illinois.

A third consideration was at least equally, and perhaps even more, important in the enactment of the administration's legislative program. The nation was unusually prosperous and thus had the resources for new social programs. President Johnson continually pointed out that it was intolerable to have so much poverty, so many slums, and such inadequate schools and hospitals in the midst of such unprecedented wealth.

Senator Dirksen constantly quoted Victor Hugo as saying that no army could withstand the "power of an idea whose time has come." This clarifies the point. The time had come when the majority of American people were ready to do something about unequal voting laws, inadequate hospitals, and all the rest of the deprivations.

As a result, the record of the first half of the 89th Congress was being compared to

Woodrow Wilson's first term, during which the Federal Reserve System and the Federal Trade Commission were established, and the Clayton Anti-Trust Act was passed. Comparisons were being made, too, with the first two terms of Franklin D. Roosevelt's New Deal, during which the Securities Exchange Act was passed, the Federal Deposit Insurance Corporation was created, the Social Security system was established, the right of unions to bargain collectively was strengthened, a minimum-wage law was passed, and an effort was made to restore the farmer's purchasing power by controlling his production and guaranteeing his prices.

In some ways, President Johnson completed much of the unfinished business of the Roosevelt era in 1965, but the trend of reform in American political life had started well before that. President Theodore Roosevelt dramatized it with his Republican administration early in the century. Wilson followed it with his New Freedom from 1912 to 1920. Then, after a period of consolidation under the Republicans, President Roosevelt picked it up again and was followed by his disciple, Lyndon B. Johnson.

"It has been the function of the liberal tradition in American politics," the political scientist, Richard Hofstadter, has written, "at first to broaden the numbers of those who could benefit from the great American bonanza, and then to humanize its workings and help heal its casualties."

There were some striking differences, however, between the New Deal of Franklin Roosevelt and the Great Society of Lyndon Johnson. The New Deal came into being in a period of economic depression, when the people were not only willing to accept reforms, but were demanding them. The Johnson legislative program was carried out in a period of unmatched prosperity, dwindling unemployment, and social stability.

If the New Deal was experimentation and improvisation on a grand scale, the Great Society was a forehanded attempt to solve economic and social problems before they became critical. Thus, 1965 was a time of "preventive reform." It involved not only the problem of persuading a prosperous people to anticipate trouble, but also ex-

perimentation with new economic theories.

The prosperity of 1965 was assisted by economic policies that were hardly less revolutionary than the reforms they made possible. This illustrates "the continuing American revolution" in the field of ideas. The British economist and philosopher, John Maynard Keynes, had taught over a generation ago that increased government spending and reduced excise and income taxes could stimulate consumers to buy more, and producers to produce more, thus expanding the economy and creating prosperity for an ever increasing percentage of the people. This doctrine was fought for years in the Congress and in some branches of the executive, but gradually the experiment was made, and in 1965, its results won wide public approval.

The significance of this is clear enough. Just as reforms of one generation are sustained in the next, even when the conservative party comes to power, so, too, the experimental ideas of one administration tend to be accepted if they work. A conservative banker made the point at the end of the year: "After the record of the new economics in the last few years, no Republican Secretary of the Treasury in the future is likely to go back to the old system."

It would be wrong, however, even to think of the 1965 record on the home front as the work solely of one party or a politically astute President. The Congress put its stamp on that legislative program, and, as E. W. Kenworthy of *The New York Times* wrote, "it was not a rubber stamp." The Congress scaled down the rent subsidies requested by the President, for example, and made them available only to low-income families eligible for public housing. It modified the so-called "Medicare" bill in a number of ways—particularly in forcing through a Republican proposal for a voluntary supplementary insurance program to partially cover doctor bills and some other health costs for persons over 65 years old.

The impact of all these exertions in Washington illustrates just how much the federal government influences the lives of the American people. These officials and Congressmen are not distant creatures arguing about

trivialities remote from the individual lives of men, women, and children. They make the laws that tax your income; draft your sons into the armed forces; reduce or raise the prices of goods you buy, provide aid to schools, hospitals, roads; and all the rest.

Some legislation proposed by the President, of course, did not pass the Congress. Among these was a measure to repeal Section 14B of the Taft-Hartley Act, which permits the states to enact "right to work" laws banning the union shop. This was postponed for consideration in the second session of the 89th Congress in 1966. Another failure was the administration's "home rule" bill to extend self-government to residents of the District of Columbia. But these were minor misses as compared to the major legislation that became law.

In fact, so much was passed by the end of the year that the question in Washington was: what will be left to do next year and the year after that before the start of the 1968 presidential election?

The answer is that a great deal of "consolidation" remains to be done, and by the time that is finished, new problems of a rising and shifting population will demand new innovations. That is the way "the continuing revolution" works.

The Democratic Majority Leader in the Senate emphasized that in 1966 the "main concern of the Senate will be the perfection, the elaboration, and the refinement of the basic legislation which has been put on the statute books during the past three or four years." The pendulum will not swing back from reform to reaction; it will stay roughly at the point of consolidation until these reforms are digested.

What was particularly striking about 1965 was the contrast between the record of movement and progress in the field of domestic affairs and the record of disappointment, stalemate, and even retrogression in the field of foreign affairs.

These disappointments abroad sharply affected the life of the American people. At the start of the year, the United States had about 60,000 men in Vietnam acting as "advisers" and "assistants" in the war between North and South Vietnam. By the

"... a vast effort ... would have to be undertaken if order was to be restored in the world."

end of the year, the entire picture had changed. The United States had an expeditionary force of about 200,000 men engaged in the front line of an open war against North Vietnamese regular army regiments and Viet Cong guerrillas. It had three aircraft carriers operating in the South China Sea, from where American bombers attacked North Vietnam around the clock. The draft of young men had gone up from about 8,000 to over 40,000 a month. All this was the subject of debate, controversy, and even division throughout the nation.

Elsewhere, the hopes of the administration for the development of effective defensive alliances in the Western Hemisphere, the Atlantic, and the Pacific had failed to materialize. By year's end, it was widely realized that a vast effort of reconstruction would have to be undertaken if order was to be restored in the world.

Fortunately, so much had been accomplished on the home front, so many new programs had been started, and so much had to be digested and refined, that the President was able to begin this work of reconstruction in meetings with Prime Minister Harold Wilson of Great Britain, Chancellor Ludwig Erhard of Germany, President Ayub Khan of Pakistan, and later, Prime Minister Lal Bahadur Shastri of India.

Therefore, 1966 promised to be a year of concentration on foreign affairs and consolidation in domestic affairs. At home, the ship of state had risen in the locks to new heights, revealing new horizons for a nation now approaching 200,000,000 people. But abroad, the outlook was bleak, and despite the successes at home, the spirit of the people was troubled.

Related Articles

For a complete report on the year 1965 in national affairs, see also Section One, PAUL-HENRI SPAAK ON THE WORLD; SYLVIA PORTER ON THE ECONOMY; LAWRENCE A. CREMIN ON EDUCATION; and the following articles in Section Three:

Sylvia Porter

ON THE ECONOMY

*Surging Prosperity Has Given Us
Time to Meet Our Most Serious
International Economic Challenge*

As 1966 began, the United States economy entered its 59th month of strong, broad upturn to the highest peak in world history. No domestic economic event of this modern era transcends in importance this single achievement. Only once before in our history—during the 80-month boom spanning World War II—has an economic upswing lasted so long, and the unhealthily feverish, artificial, inflationary upsurge of 1938–1945 does not belong in the same class as the solid, balanced expansion of 1961–1965.

We continued to shatter virtually every record for business prosperity. We turned out well above $670,000,000,000 in goods and services, thus increasing our gross national product (GNP) by one-third since the expansion began in 1961. Industrial production, weekly earnings, personal income, and after-tax corporate profits hit new peaks.

Stock prices slipped badly in the spring, but subsequently climbed to the highest levels ever. Unemployment among married men—the breadwinners—sank to a near minimum of around 2 per cent. In many fields, employers faced

Portrait for THE YEAR BOOK by James Hill

29

shortages of semiskilled and skilled workers. Only joblessness among unskilled teen-agers, unskilled Negroes, and unskilled older workers held the overall unemployment rate above 4 per cent.

The pace of price increases quickened as 1965 rolled on, and with spending surging upward for the Vietnam war and adding heat to our already heated economy, inflation was a nagging threat at year's end. In December, the Federal Reserve Board raised the basic interest rate of the country—the discount rate—from 4 per cent to $4\frac{1}{2}$ per cent, the highest level since 1930, to slow down borrowing and thus reduce inflationary pressures on the economy.

The very "monotony" of our advance was, in fact, beginning to pose a grave danger to our economy's continuing good health. Millions of Americans—particularly youngsters—think that sustained business upturn is not "news," and that we have found the secret to perpetual prosperity. Confidence in our economy's strength is a good thing; euphoria about it definitely is not. Such an attitude could encourage excesses in spending and borrowing that would bring the upturn to an end. Sustained upturn *is* news. We have *not* found the secret to perpetual prosperity. But we have learned more about how to control the severity of business cycles. Using this knowledge, we have made the maintenance of business expansion a key national goal.

President Lyndon B. Johnson has tilted lances with businessmen and bankers several times—most notably over price and interest rate increases—but the era of "partnership for prosperity" inaugurated when he entered the White House in November, 1963, continued through 1965. Most businessmen trust Mr. Johnson as a man who understands the key role profits play in a prosperous economy and as a man "you can do business with."

Mr. Johnson, in turn, considers policies to maintain the prosperity of business so vital that when a government official was asked whether he foresaw the danger of a recession, he answered, "a recession under Johnson? 'It' wouldn't dare!"

We continue, of course, to face profound

problems. To mention only a few, we must find ways to sustain the economic upturn we have achieved, while averting inflationary wage-price increases. We must expand our trade with the European Common Market, despite President Charles de Gaulle's sabotaging activities. We must develop our trade with the Soviet bloc. We must channel funds from the federal government to the states and cities so that they can finance the staggering volume of essential projects under their jurisdiction without loading us with additional back-breaking local taxes. We must slash unemployment among teen-age, older unskilled, and Negro workers. We must get the maximum production benefits from automation and, at the same time, protect workers whose jobs are shot out from under them by technical advances. We must translate Congress' blueprints for a "Great Society" into reality and still not permit federal government spending to become a dangerous inflationary force.

Nonetheless, when 1965 ended, we were so affluent that families were spending an average of 48¢ of every $1 of income on luxuries, rather than on the traditional basic necessities of food, shelter, clothing, and fuel. We were clearly on our way toward turning upside down a necessities-dominated spending pattern which has held throughout the ages of man.

Prosperity is always a "plus," and in 1965 it was particularly so, because it bought us time in which to get our international financial accounts into a semblance of balance and to prevent our foreign creditors from staging a disastrous run on our gold reserves. Had we not been so prosperous, we could by now have lost the battle to defend the dollar. This is our biggest single international economic challenge of the mid-1960s.

"Never again will the United States be able to ignore its balance of payments in formulating domestic policies. There is no once-and-for-all solution either to the problem of maintaining balance in our internal economic expansion, or to the problem of maintaining balance in our external payments." This is the language of bafflegab

"... 1965 marked a historic turning point in the Free World's monetary system."

at its worst. But when the chairman of our powerful Federal Reserve Board, William McChesney Martin, Jr., said these words before an academic audience, he flashed a clear warning that the United States no longer will continue to flood the West with dollars in order to finance the growth of the Free World's trade. He also signaled that 1965 marked a historic turning point in the Free World's monetary system.

We have now, for the first time in the post-World War II period, taken stern, urgent actions to close the gap between what we spend abroad and what we earn abroad; that is, to slash the deficit in our balance of payments. We are curbing the outpouring of dollars that in the past two decades has helped the prosperity of nations everywhere.

We have now put the Free World's central bankers on notice that they must seek some source other than the U.S. dollar to provide the increase in money essential for the continuing expansion of world trade. The meaning of this decision to all of us is this: even a moderate slowdown in the growth of trade among Western nations because of a shortage of funds to finance the trade would be deeply deflationary. It could set off a devastating chain reaction in terms of jobs, paychecks, and profits everywhere.

We are now moving toward the first great overhaul of the West's monetary system since that system was created at Bretton Woods, N.H., in 1944. By drying up the red ink in our balance of payments, we are offering a preview of the credit pinch that could occur in the Free World's nations if their supplies of dollars stop climbing so fast. We have dramatized the need to supplement the role the U.S. dollar has played. We have thus established the background against which full-scale negotiations can be held on reform of the international monetary system. In 1965, monetary system reform actually moved from the stage of discussion to negotiation. In the rarefied sphere of international finance, the very fact that the West's top financial powers began bargaining at the highest policy-making level represented major progress.

To understand what is going on today and how much it means, you must turn back to the 1930s. At that time, manipulation of currencies by countries trying to gain a trade advantage for themselves was commonplace. Each nation's attitude was to get the most for itself, and let the devil take the hindmost. Speculation in currencies was intense, and insiders who knew the right people in a nation's government made fortunes overnight by selling one currency and buying another. There was no assurance from month to month what a currency would be worth. There was no machinery for cooperation on stabilization of currencies. As a result, nations had no confidence that the paper money they accepted in payment for goods or services would have a stable value. Because of this, the world's trade marts were in chaos, and disastrous economic depression pervaded the Western world.

On top of this came global war and even greater financial chaos. By 1944, not a currency in the world outside the U.S. dollar had a reliable value. World War II's Lend-Lease arrangements had obscured all normal trade deals and, of course, we were not trading with our enemies.

Then came the conference of Bretton Woods in July, 1944. At this conference, delegates from 44 nations created an International Monetary Fund (IMF). Its purpose was to stabilize currencies so that countries could trade with each other and have faith in the value of the currencies they were using in payment. Moreover, the delegates created an International Bank for Reconstruction and Development—also known as the World Bank—to make postwar loans to member countries for their reconstruction and development. They also made provisions for the settlement of debts among governments and central banks in gold, in such key currencies as the U.S. dollar and the British pound, and in funds borrowed by the nations from the International Monetary Fund.

There was little precedent for an international monetary system of this order. At the start, skeptics dismissed the Bretton Woods institutions as fantastically idealistic and impractical. But in the 21 years since Bretton Woods, the fantastically idealistic and impractical has become the thoroughly

"...a network of reciprocal... arrangements has been developed... to avert financial crises..."

realistic. The system created out of chaos has worked superbly well in stabilizing currencies, as well as in supporting a huge growth in international trade.

In the IMF, 103 nations have pooled their currencies and some gold to give the institution reserves to lend back to nations when their paper monies get in trouble. The IMF's reserves are now above $21,000,000,000, compared to $7,600,000,000 in 1948. And again and again in the postwar era, the IMF has used its reserves to protect currencies under attack. The World Bank has been a remarkably successful financial institution, and its loans have been of tremendous importance in developing and rebuilding economies everywhere.

Since 1962, a network of reciprocal currency arrangements has been developed, and the network has been used repeatedly by the West's central bankers to avert financial crises that could have undermined or even wrecked the economies of the entire Free World. The most recent illustration of such central bank cooperation occurred in September, 1965, when the U.S. and nine other nations—with President De Gaulle's France notably missing—made "new arrangements" to aid Britain's pound and to crush speculators against the pound sterling.

Meanwhile, the Western nations' dependence on reserves of gold, U.S. dollars, and British pounds to settle their debts with each other has been justified. The total of world trade has skyrocketed from $53,300,000,000 in 1948 to a current annual rate of about $170,000,000,000. This is a key reason why jobs and paychecks have grown so much in the West, and why Europe and the U.S. have been so prosperous.

But—and this is a crucial point—it is the U.S. that has been lubricating the monetary machinery with floods of dollars. True, we run a huge surplus in our merchandise trade with other lands, and year after year we export far more goods and services abroad than we import. But our annual spending overseas for other purposes—for military defense, economic aid, tourism, private business investments, and bank loans—has more than wiped out our annual merchandise export surplus and has splattered our

balance of payments with red ink. For 15 out of the past 16 years, we have run a deficit in our balance of payments, and this deficit has added more than $35,000,000,000 to foreign holdings of gold and dollars.

As a result of the U.S. deficit, our foreign creditors have accumulated enormous dollar claims against the United States which they can convert into our gold at any time they wish. They have drawn heavily on our gold reserves in recent years. From a high of $24,800,000,000 in 1949, our total gold reserve has sunk to under $14,000,000,000. In view of our unbroken string of balance of payments deficits, cynical central bankers began years ago to circulate "sick, sick, sick" jokes about the U.S. dollar at their annual IMF meetings. (Sample: "The U.S. is the world's poorest developed nation" with the "world's fifth strongest currency.")

In the late 1950s, when President Dwight D. Eisenhower was in the White House, it became apparent that the U.S. could not go on indefinitely priming the world's monetary pumps with dollars. But the measures we took to curtail the outpouring were only half-hearted. Then in late 1964 and 1965, time ran out on us. The deficit in our balance of payments skyrocketed to a crisis annual rate of more than $6,000,000,000; the worst ever. Simultaneously, President De Gaulle stepped-up his drive to downgrade the U.S. dollar and upgrade the French franc with a widely publicized announcement that he was exchanging almost all of France's accumulated dollars for gold. He also proposed that the world abandon the postwar monetary system and return to the long-discredited system of settling international financial accounts only in gold.

President Johnson finally opened a heavy counterattack, on Feb. 10, 1965. At the heart of the attack was a program calling for "voluntary" cooperation by U.S. bankers to slash bank loans in Europe, and by U.S. businessmen to limit direct investments in developed countries, to bring home profits earned overseas, to borrow funds abroad to finance their foreign operations, and to expand their merchandise exports. In the months that followed, the "voluntary" program worked magnificently.

"... what is at stake is nothing less than the ... future prosperity of the West."

Our balance of payments deficit shrank. There were no "sick, sick, sick" jokes about the U.S. dollar at the meeting of the IMF governors in September, 1965. But the progress was not enough to wipe out the red ink. Tighter—although still "voluntary" —guidelines for business investments abroad were announced at year's end. Yet, despite the fact that we still ran a deficit, our determination to meet the balance of payments challenge had become unmistakable.

To demonstrate to the world that we would continue to stand ready to supply gold to qualified foreign holders of U.S. dollars on their demand, Congress eliminated an obsolete requirement that deposits at our Federal Reserve Banks be backed by 25 per cent in gold. This "freed" $4,700,000,000 of the precious yellow metal for sale to our overseas creditors.

Against this background, Secretary of the Treasury Henry H. Fowler called for an IMF conference to bolster the Bretton Woods system. The deputy finance ministers of the so-called "Group of Ten"—Belgium, Canada, France, Italy, Japan, The Netherlands, Sweden, the United Kingdom, the U.S., and West Germany, plus Switzerland as an observer—began formal negotiations to find areas of agreement on various proposals for reform. The negotiations are to be broadened so that they will include representatives of less developed countries.

The bargaining will be tough, prolonged, and often frustrating. It is far too early to speculate on the precise details of the outcome. There are, however, certain fundamental points that can be outlined now. The basic Bretton Woods system will be retained. Gold and the U.S. dollar will continue as key reserves. Ways will be devised to supplement these reserves, possibly through the creation of a new currency reserve unit, backed by various major currencies and acceptable in payment of international debts.

It could take as long as three to five years before a workable supplement is built on top of the superb system we have. International monetary reform surely will assume an increasingly dominant position in the economic sphere as this decade rolls on. This is as it should be, for what is at stake is nothing less than the future of the dollar, the future of world trade, and the future prosperity of the West.

Related Articles

For a complete report on the 1965 year in economics, see Section One, PAUL-HENRI SPAAK ON THE WORLD, JAMES B. RESTON ON THE NATION, and the following articles in Section Three:

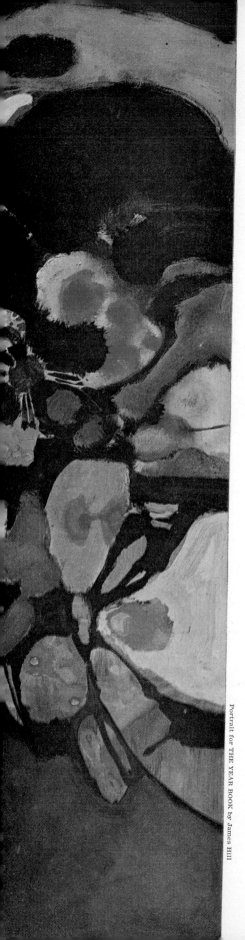

Portrait for THE YEAR BOOK by James Hill

Harrison
S. Brown
ON SCIENCE

Science Faces a Crisis in Handling
The Flow of Data It Generates;
Can It Meet the Challenge?

More than 300 years ago, a small group of men met at the Bull-Head Tavern in London every Thursday afternoon to discuss science. Although they ate good food and enjoyed each other's company, they met primarily because they found the world of science fascinating. The group, which at various times included such diverse personalities as Sir Christopher Wren, Samuel Pepys, Robert Boyle, and Benjamin Franklin, was part of the world's oldest and most famous scientific society: the Royal Society of London. In 1665, the Society published the first issue of *Philosophical Transactions*, today the oldest surviving scientific journal.

During the three centuries which separate us from these modest beginnings, the number of scientific societies has multiplied several thousandfold. Whereas the founders of the Royal Society could meet in a small room in the Bull-Head Tavern, the most recent meeting of the International Union of Biochemistry drew nearly 7,000 persons from all parts of the world and monopolized two of New York City's largest hotels. Over the same 300-year period, the number

35

"It soon became evident that no scientist could ... even scan all that was being printed."

of scientists, technical journals, and individual scientific papers have all doubled about every 15 years. Clearly, this rapid rate of increase cannot continue forever—if for no other reason, the numbers of scientists cannot become greater than the population itself! Nevertheless, it seems likely that such a rate of increase in the field of science will persist for some time to come.

In mid-1965, the first volume (A-C) of the 11th edition of *American Men of Science* (The Physical and Biological Sciences) was published. To be included in the publication, a scientist must be one "whose achievement, by reason of experience and training, is at least equivalent to that associated with the doctorate degree and who continues activity in such work." The entire set of six volumes will, when completed in 1967, contain 130,000 brief biographies of individual scientists. Comparing this with the 98,000 entries in the 10th edition, which was published five years ago, we see that the population of scientists in the United States has increased by 35 per cent in only five years. Presently, one out of every 1,500 persons in the United States is an active scientist.

During the century that followed the birth of the Royal Society and its proceedings, the number of scientific journals increased very slowly. By 1750, the number had reached 10. But shortly thereafter growth began to increase more rapidly. By 1830, there were some 300 periodic, scientific publications.

It soon became evident that no scientist could possibly read, or even scan, all that was being printed. A new invention was needed—and it soon appeared: a journal consisting of abstracts of articles which had appeared in the conventional scientific journals. Since that time, abstract journals have multiplied as rapidly as have the regular journals. The number grew from one in 1830 to 300 in 1950. And now, no scientist can even scan all the journals of abstracts.

Research is becoming increasingly difficult to follow, even for the specialist. Each year, scientific and technical work in the United States alone is described in some 300,000 articles which are published in some 6,000 scientific and technical journals. When we look beyond our national boundaries to the

world scientific community, we are confronted by a total of 35,000 journals which publish nearly 2,000,000 articles each year, written by some 750,000 scientists in as many as 50 languages. In the face of such chaotic conditions, an individual scientist cannot hope to keep track of more than an infinitesimal fraction of the flood of data.

With increasing frequency, one hears such questions as: Can we produce meaningful abstracts of abstracts? How short can an abstract be and still give the reader a useful impression of the content of the original article? Can new tools such as the computer be used to help us cope with these problems?

These are important questions, but unfortunately the size of the problem is growing more rapidly than are the efforts aimed at its solution. Clearly, we have reached a crisis in the handling of information.

We can obtain some concept of the ultimate magnitude of the communications problem by attempting to forecast how large the world scientific effort will eventually become. What will the world population of scientists be 50 years from now? How many new facts will they uncover?

Science abroad has been growing as rapidly as in the United States, even in countries that have become industrialized in comparatively recent times. We have seen the Soviet Union emerge as a major scientific and technological power. Since World War II, Japan has moved from being a nation of technical imitators to one of technical innovators. Indicative of this change in 1965 was the awarding of a Nobel prize in physics to Japanese physicist Sin-itiro Tomonaga, for his work in quantum electrodynamics.

In virtually all parts of the world, science and technology are being looked upon as vital to the development of local resources and the improvement of living conditions. To these ends, Brazil has established a National Research Council; The Philippines has set up a National Science Development Board; India has established a Council for Scientific and Industrial Research; Nigeria has formed a Ministry of National Resources and Research. It is clear that science must help feed, clothe, and house the world's burgeoning population.

It seems likely that the scientific endeavor will continue to grow as rapidly during the next half century as it has during the past 300 years. As man has moved from the world of nature into the artificial world of industrial-urban civilization, his problems —along with his pleasures—have multiplied. He has become dependent upon the smooth functioning of this new culture for his survival. Yet he is constantly presented with problems of increasing magnitude. As the problems multiply, and solutions become more urgent, our need for scientists and technically trained people will increase.

Yet the proportion of scientists in the population obviously cannot rise forever. There are other important jobs to be done. Only a small percentage of the population is temperamentally and intellectually fit for scientific careers. Nevertheless, studies indicate that the proportion of scientists in the U.S. population might grow eventually from the one scientist per 1,500 persons we find today to something like one scientist per 200 persons.

When we couple these considerations with the likelihood that the population of the United States will about double in the next 50 years, it is quite possible that between now and then, the U.S. population of scientists will increase another tenfold. Little Johnny, born today and destined to be a scientist, would by then be in his scientific prime. He would have some 1,300,000 U.S. scientific colleagues to deal with, and would be confronted, if present trends continue, by some 60,000 U.S. scientific and technical journals containing some 3,000,000 articles annually.

Looking at Johnny's position in the world scientific community 50 years hence, the picture, based on present trends, is an even gloomier one. For during this period, the proportion of scientists in the world population might grow even more rapidly than in the United States.

Fifty years from now Johnny may well have some 8,000,000 scientists with whom he can try to communicate, and there will likely be some 350,000 scientific and technical journals from which to make selections for his own working library. Such fan-tastic figures serve to emphasize that world science is indeed in the middle of a crisis with respect to the handling of the facts which it generates, and that future procedures for handling scientific information must differ drastically from present ones.

The present procedures for communicating research results have 300 years of tradition behind them and therefore cannot be changed overnight. The scientist, when he finishes a piece of research, takes pride in reporting his results to his colleagues at a scientific meeting. In addition, he feels honor-bound to present his results in the form of a journal article that describes in detail what he did, why he did it, and what his findings were. His standing in the academic community, his ability to obtain funds for his research, and his job opportunities depend in substantial measure upon the quantity and quality of his publications. Unfortunately, the quantity is often considered more important than the quality. "Publish or perish" has become an axiom affecting the destinies of many scientists.

The mechanics of producing a scientific journal are ponderous, and, as a general rule, months—in some cases years—are required for an article which has been submitted to appear in print. A few technical journals, notably *Science* and *Physical Review Letters* in the United States, and *Nature* in England, specialize in rapid publication of brief notes concerning important new research. However, the fraction of ongoing science which eventually appears in such publications is very small.

And in the interest of saving space, some technical journals now edit articles so severely that experimental procedures are given but cursory treatment, and the bulk of space is devoted to abbreviated descriptions of results. It is now predicted that details of experiments, which a scientist must know if he is to attempt to repeat another's experiment, will one day not be published, but instead will be filed in one or more central depositories, perhaps on microfilm or microcards.

Scientific meetings, like journals and societies, are also fragmenting. Most scientists admit that the days of the gigantic generalized scientific conference are numbered. Such meetings have become too large and unwieldy, and the efficiency of communication has decreased. As a result, there has been an increasing tendency for scientists to sponsor national and international meetings on highly specialized topics, thus keeping the meetings fairly small.

The thought of abolishing the existing system of journals and meetings, or even of appreciably modifying it, is extremely distasteful to most scientists. Nevertheless, changes are taking place, some of them subtle, some dramatic.

In fields of science that are particularly active, fellow scientists often exchange "preprints" or copies of manuscripts which have been submitted for publication. Modern inexpensive copying techniques have made it possible for scientists to distribute their findings in this way on a massive scale. Under such circumstances, the ultimate journal article serves the primary purpose of providing a permanent record—and, of course, ensuring some degree of personal security for the author.

These "Invisible Colleges," as such groups have been called, have begun to be organized on a more formal scale. A few years ago, under the sponsorship of the National Institutes of Health, a group was formed which called itself Information Exchange Group No. 1, composed of scientists working in the highly specialized field of "electron transfer and oxidative phosphorylation." The group was formed to improve the exchanges of information in this particular field, which happens to be an active one. It secured the cooperation of every identifiable scientist in the world working in the field. During the first four years of the program, 90 per cent of the important papers published on these and related topics reached the participants three to 12 months before the same papers appeared in the journals.

Attempts are being made to utilize the vast memories and high speeds of modern computers to aid the scientist in locating previously published research. For instance, the National Science Foundation and the American Chemical Society in 1965 initiated a two-year program that will provide quick access to information on the more than a million chemical compounds now known. The Food and Drug Administration is installing a Central Retrieval Index which will magnetically store three vital index files. The first will provide information on a given product or chemical compound. Using this file, a staff member can ask the computer to print the names of all products which contain a certain compound. A second index will give known biological characteristics of compounds. A third will describe chemical structures.

A working model-size prototype information system has been established at Massachusetts Institute of Technology (M.I.T.) to provide scientists in the Boston-Cambridge, Mass., area with a quick means for searching the literature of 21 physics journals. Remote consoles give rapid access to a time-sharing computer facility which returns information on the source of papers dealing with specific topics and other data, such as the names of authors and their institutional affiliations, citations to the literature, and the location of abstracts. At present, the library of available information exceeds 40,000 articles.

The Institute for Scientific Information in Philadelphia, Pa., has established a commercial scientific information service, the *Science Citation Index*. This computer service provides the titles, authors, and locations of all papers that relate to a particular paper.

Although it is generally recognized that these experiments are useful, and indeed may point the way to a partial solution of the problem, a great deal remains to be done before the situation can accurately be termed "under control."

Unfortunately, there is presently little international coordination of activities aimed at finding solutions to this pressing problem. The United Nations Educational, Scientific, and Cultural Organization (UNESCO) has expressed interest, but is doing very little. The International Council of Scientific Unions is also concerned and has discussed with UNESCO the possibility of establishing a world-wide program of coordinated activities. Thus far, Western Europe's Organization for Economic Cooperation and Development (OECD) has

"... if present trends continue, the current crisis ... will become a catastrophe."

established the most viable of the international programs concerned with scientific information, but its success will probably be restricted by its limited enrollment.

Certainly, if present trends continue, the current crisis in the handling of scientific and technological information will become a catastrophe. Yet, the technical competence for dealing with this problem already exists. Given a concerted international cooperative effort, the situation might be distinctly different 50 years from now. We can imagine that it might be something like this:

Visualize a World Center for Scientific and Technical Information, perhaps composed of a number of subcenters connected by wires and computers. All major laboratories throughout the world would be linked directly to these centers and would be able to obtain answers to complicated questions in a few seconds, or at the most, minutes. Small laboratories would be tied to the large ones and would be able to obtain information almost as quickly.

Technical journals as we now know them may well be important primarily as permanent records of work already reported. Following the completion of an experiment, a scientist would write a description of his experiment together with his results. This preliminary paper would be sent to a central international clearing house, which would examine it to ensure a minimum standard of quality, and then distribute copies to all individuals working in that particular specialized field. The title of the paper, together with other pertinent facts, would be placed on tape and thus would be accessible to researchers in other fields.

The experimental details would be stored in the archives, and thus would be easily and quickly accessible. The results would be submitted to a journal for publication. Once the paper and an abstract were published, the preliminary description would be removed from the tape, and the final paper, together with its abstract, would be introduced into the system instead.

Simultaneously, a group of trained evaluators would abstract data from the published paper for inclusion in special indices giving numerical data, chemical structures, biological effects, and other facts of interest to various specialists.

But enough of wishful daydreaming. Exciting as these prospects are, we are still a considerable distance from solving this tremendous problem. If such a system is actually brought into existence, it will stand out as one of the great experiments in international cooperation. If not, science may well be drowned in a sea of fact. Little did the curious and imaginative men who used to meet in the Bull-Head Tavern in London three hundred years ago realize what they were starting!

Related Articles

For a complete report on the 1965 year in science and in technology, see Section One, JOHN H. GLENN, JR. ON SPACE; Section Two, HOW FAR WILL WE GO IN SPACE?; and the following articles in Section Three:

Lawrence A. Cremin
ON EDUCATION

Education Has Truly Become "the First Work of These Times," but Many People Are Disturbed by What Is Happening

"If we are learning anything from our experience," President Lyndon B. Johnson said in the summer of 1964, "we are learning that it is time to go to work, and the first work of these times and the first work of our society is education." True to his words, President Johnson made education the first work of the 89th Congress. And in 10 months, from January to October of 1965, that Congress legislated an educational revolution.

True, certain aspects of the revolution had been set in motion earlier by such legislation as the Civil Rights Act of 1964, which required an end to racial discrimination in all enterprises aided by federal funds. Another factor in the revolution had been the Economic Opportunity Act of 1964, which established a variety of programs, ranging from Project Head Start for preschool children to the Job Corps for youths interested in improving their vocational skills. But the essence of the revolution was embodied in two laws that promised to change American schools and colleges more rapidly and radically than they had changed

"... the act ... turns out to be infinitely more than a collection of separate programs."

at any previous time throughout the entire history of the United States.

The first was the Elementary and Secondary Education Act of 1965. Looked at superficially, the various parts of the law appear to be the usual federal-aid-to-education package of the past 50 years. Each section seems to provide special money for some special phase of the school program that is of special interest to some special group lobbying in Washington, D.C.

Thus, there is assistance to school districts with large numbers of poor people (Title I). There is assistance for the purchase of teaching materials (Title II), and support for special supplementary services (Title III), both of which would reach students in private as well as public schools. There is assistance for the development of new teaching techniques and programs (Title IV), and assistance for the strengthening of state departments of education (Title V).

The act promises something to everyone. It attempts to alleviate poverty; it manages to enrich denominational, as well as public, school curricula; and it ends up aiding researchers in the universities, as well as schoolmen on the firing line of education.

When one examines the act closely, however, it turns out to be infinitely more than a collection of separate programs. Indeed, the various provisions, considered in their relationship to one another, really add up to the massive program of federal aid for general educational improvement that citizens and educators have been demanding for a generation.

Consider the sections as follows: Title IV provides money for vastly expanding the program of curriculum research and innovation that has been going on for more than a decade (see THE YEAR BOOK, 1964, pp. 37–41). Titles I, II, and III provide federal funds with which local school districts can bring the fruits of this curriculum research and innovation to their students. The *choice* of programs and materials is, however, left to state and local authorities. (Title I allocates funds on the basis of the number of poor families in a given district, but every state and almost every school district qualify for some aid.)

Title V, recognizing that the coordination and supervision of local education

programs are still state functions under the American system, provides the money with which this coordination and supervision can be dramatically strengthened where the will to do so prevails.

The second of the two laws responsible for the revolution in education was the Higher Education Act of 1965. Here, too, the various titles seem at first glance to provide for nothing more than a random collection of politically attractive programs. But on closer analysis, the programs fit together to form an intriguing whole. Ultimately, the purpose of the act is to hasten the popularization of higher education that has been going forward in the United States since World War II.

To achieve this goal, the act provides in Title IV financial aid for growing numbers of young people to gain access to two-year and four-year colleges. It assists colleges and universities in improving the instruction they offer these young people by providing library materials (Title II), and laboratory and teaching equipment (Title VI), and by encouraging pooling of academic resources (Title III). It also ensures that the colleges and universities will devote part of their resources to an attack on certain pressing social problems in the important realms of housing, transportation, health, and employment (Title I).

This last provision is perhaps the most interesting. It extends to the cities and suburbs the same relationship with the urban colleges that rural areas have enjoyed with the agricultural colleges for more than a century. The scholarship programs and the National Teacher Corps received the widest publicity when the Higher Education Act was debated in October, 1965, but it is the community service programs that may ultimately have the most profound influence.

There is no denying that the attention the agricultural colleges gave to the economic and social problems of rural America in the late 19th and early 20th centuries was crucial in improving the quality of rural life and in making the United States the greatest food-producing nation in the world. If urban colleges attack the economic and social problems of present-day American cities with the same vigor, imagination, and resolve, they may become the leading agencies for enriching the urban-industrial civilization of our time.

By definition, living through a revolution is unsettling, and there is no denying that many people—both within and without the ranks of education—were deeply disturbed by these new federal programs. True, both bills passed both houses of Congress by substantial majorities, but that should not obscure the fact that there was vigorous opposition in both instances.

The sharpest debate, of course, came in response to Titles II and III of the Elementary and Secondary Education Act, with their provisions for assistance to students in denominational as well as public schools. Interestingly enough, the National Education Association of the United States, which had long opposed *any* aid to parochial schools, endorsed the programs. The National Catholic Welfare Conference, which had led in earlier opposition to all efforts to confine federal aid to public institutions also gave its endorsement. And support came, too, from the National Council of the Churches of Christ in the United States of America, a leading federation of Protestant churches.

Jewish organizations, however, divided sharply. While Orthodox Jews tended to advocate the programs, Conservative and Reformed Jews vigorously opposed them. They argued that the programs would violate the constitutional requirement of separation of church and state by extending aid to denominational schools. Similarly, the American Civil Liberties Union warned that the participation of religious agencies in supplementary education centers was certain to dilute the principle of public control of publicly supported education.

The concern of these and other organizations did not disappear merely because the bill became law. It is probable that there will be judicial tests of the constitutionality of the act in the near future. Even if it turns out that there is no constitutional difficulty, there remains the problem of developing effective means of exercising public supervision over the new programs and the agencies that will conduct them.

The whole question of who should control the schools came very much to the fore in 1965. Profound changes were taking place in the structure and leadership of American education. In March, for instance, a group of scholars established a National Academy of Education, which, though independent of government sponsorship, followed the traditions of the National Academy of Sciences and the Royal Society of Great Britain and the French Academy.

The academy was limited to 50 members chosen for the excellence of their published writings on education. Its purpose was to serve as "a forum for conversation, debate, and mutual instruction; a rostrum for the communication of accurate information and informed opinion; a stimulus for fruitful research; and a source of counsel for such public and private agencies as require and request it." As Paul Woodring noted in the *Saturday Review*, however, the unspoken virtue of the new academy was that it provided a model of excellence and leadership in education—the model of the scholar-scientist standing beside the administrator-politician in the formulation of educational policy.

In July, 1965, President Johnson called a White House Conference on Education, under the chairmanship of John Gardner, then president of the Carnegie Corporation of New York. A great deal was written about the conference, ranging from *Time*'s judgment that the participants had explored fresh and significant policy problems, to the *New York Herald Tribune*'s verdict that the whole affair had been little more than a "prayer meeting." The most astute analysis of the significance of the conference came from Fred M. Hechinger of *The New York Times*. "The most striking fact of the White House Conference on Education," he wrote, "was the changing of the guard of educational leadership. The representatives of educational organizations who used to symbolize the Establishment seemed displaced by men and women who represent themselves and their own ideas."

In October, it was announced that James B. Conant's 1964 proposal for an "Interstate Commission for Planning a Nationwide Educational Policy" had been acted upon. Meeting in Kansas City, Mo., a group of political and educational leaders representing the 50 states resolved to set up an Educational Commission of the States, which would conduct studies, gather information, and make recommendations to its members. Interestingly enough, the chairman of the meeting was Terry Sanford, a former governor of North Carolina and a leading exponent of interstate cooperation in education, who had presided over those sessions of the White House Conference that had explored federal-state relationships.

What became increasingly clear as the year 1965 progressed was that a new educational leadership was coming into power, and that this new leadership was attacking the problems of American education through new political structures and with vastly increased funds. No one could predict what specific solutions would emerge. But change was obviously accelerating, and political conflicts were sharpening.

One serious crisis developed in October, when the then Commissioner Francis Keppel, acting under the Civil Rights Act of 1964, ordered $30,000,000 of federal funds withheld from the schools of Chicago, Ill., after protests that Superintendent Benjamin Willis had failed to act with sufficient vigor against *de facto* racial segregation. The money was released four days later after Mayor Richard J. Daley personally intervened with federal authorities. But the issue itself did not die. Several weeks later, Superintendent Bernard E. Donovan of New York City voiced the fear of many of his fellow superintendents when he asked publicly whether "the schools would be run locally or from Washington."

Commissioner Keppel expressed "sympathy" with the superintendents over some of the administrative problems occasioned by federal programs, but he insisted that the fear of federal control was not well-founded.

President Johnson himself said flatly: "I want to make clear once and for all . . . that the federal government—as long as I am President—intends to be a partner and not a boss in meeting our responsibilities to all the people. The federal government has neither the wish nor the power to dictate education."

It was this concept of federal-state *partnership* that seemed to provide a viable solution to the crisis. Yet no one really believed that a billion dollars could be funneled from Washington into the nation's schools without some measure of federal control. The problem was really one of making that control as responsive as possible to widely differing state and local needs.

One special phase of the conflict about control was the sharp controversy over a "national assessment" of education. This issue burst into the headlines after the White House Conference. Professor John Goodlad of the University of California defined a national assessment for the conference participants as follows: We are accustomed to tests that tell us how well nine-year-old Johnny reads as compared with nine-year-old Billy, or with all other nine-year-olds in the United States. But what we do not have is a quite different series of tests that indicate how a school system in Colorado, for example, measures up in its reading instruction to a school system in Idaho, or how well nine-year-olds in 1965 read as compared with nine-year-olds in 1955. Questions of this type, Goodlad continued, shift the spotlight "from the much-tested individual to the educational effort of 26,000 heterogeneous school districts, 50 states, and the nation as a whole."

Supporters of a national assessment insisted that it would give Americans a way to measure what the schools were accomplishing, and what remained to be done. "How could anyone reasonably object to obtaining additional information on the condition and progress of American education?" asked president John H. Fischer of Columbia's Teachers College.

Opponents replied with expressions of fear that national testing would lead to national conformity and a stifling of local initiative and imagination. "We have more tests than we can use now," charged Harold Taylor, former president of Sarah Lawrence College. "We test for the wrong things. The experience of the Middle East, Far East, and Europe indicates that standardized testing paralyzes thinking. Let us abolish testing and concentrate on teaching."

Arguments over federal aid to the colleges and universities were also very much in the headlines during 1965. In the realm of research, critics were perfectly ready to grant that federally supported university projects since World War II had contributed mightily to American advances in pure and applied science. But they were raising insistent questions about the difficulties that had resulted from this development.

Gerald Piel, publisher of *Scientific American*, charged, in an address to the American Philosophical Society in April, that federal research contracts were dangerously undermining the nation's major universities, turning many professors into "mercenaries of science and scholarship."

Several months later, a congressional subcommittee headed by Representative Henry S. Reuss (D., Wis.) pointed out that 54 universities out of some 2,000 institutions of higher learning receive 60 per cent of the federal funds. Likewise, imbalances occur among the various academic disciplines, with the natural sciences receiving the lion's share of the assistance, and the social sciences and the humanities much less.

Moreover, the subcommittee went on to say, federal research programs had "harmed university education in the sciences by excessively diverting scientific manpower from teaching, and by overemphasizing research to the detriment of teaching." As one scientist commented bitterly in testimony before the subcommittee, "There is no Nobel prize for teaching."

The whole problem of teaching, of course, was at the heart of a good deal of the student unrest that plagued the colleges and universities throughout the year. From Berkeley, Calif., to New Haven, Conn., there were insistent demands that more attention be given to the quality of undergraduate teaching, and that first-rate teachers be rewarded as generously as was the case with first-rate researchers.

Once again, there was no escaping the impact of federal policy. Federal research funds had already drawn some of the best professors from teaching. And now, federal scholarship funds for students promised to aggravate the situation by increasing the pressure of enrollments on facilities that were already sorely taxed. No one was ready to argue that every able American youngster should not have access to a college education. But no one really knew how to make that education truly available without incurring enormous costs on the one hand, or occasioning frightening mechanization on the other.

The problem itself was not new in 1965. What was new was the readiness of college and university authorities to face it seriously and attack it boldly. It was a readiness that had come none too soon for a society truly committed to making education "the first work of these times."

Related Articles

For a complete report on the 1965 year in education, see Section One, RED SMITH ON SPORTS; Section Two, THE NEW NEW ENGLAND; and the following articles in Section Three:

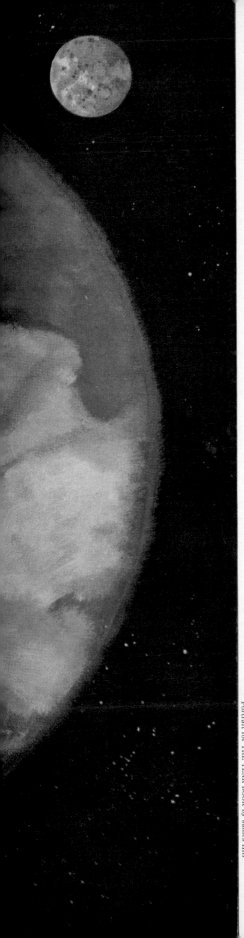

John H. Glenn, Jr.
ON SPACE

To Ensure the Continued Success of Our Space Program, We Must Soon Decide What Our Future Goals Should Be

A few months ago, my wife, Annie, and I had the opportunity to measure firsthand the effect of the United States' commitment in space exploration upon Western Europeans. At the request of the President of the United States, we visited six European countries. The warmth and magnitude of our reception established beyond any doubt that those peoples are just as deeply interested in space exploration as are Americans and Russians. We saw also that European aerospace scientists are becoming increasingly active. And, perhaps most significantly, we saw a growing —and sometimes almost prayerful—hope that the goals of space science will never be converted into instruments of catastrophic destruction.

Wherever we talked to students, scientists, or political leaders, we encountered the same knowledgeable curiosity that is so evident in America. The people of Europe closely follow our manned flights on radio, television, in the press, and in scientific journals. They are well aware of the contributions to general scientific knowledge made by our

Portrait for THE YEAR BOOK by James Hill

47

" . . . 1965 was a vigorous and dramatic year in space for the United States."

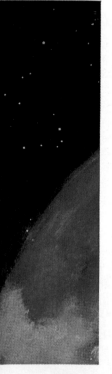

unmanned flights, such as the highly successful Ranger moon probes and Mariner IV's historic mission to Mars.

We were much impressed, too, by the growing international character of space investigation. In the beginning, space was chiefly the province of the United States and Russia. But France launched a satellite of her own in 1965, and the National Aeronautics and Space Administration (NASA) is cooperating with two European space programs. They are the European Space Research Organization (ESRO) and the European Launch Development Organization (ELDO). In addition, a number of European countries participate in the Free World's global tracking network.

This expansion of space investigation into the historic heartland of Western civilization indicates a certain maturity in man's quest to discover what lies beyond the confines of this planet. It also illustrates that people everywhere are coming to realize that they have a stake in exploring the only limitless physical frontier which mankind has ever attempted to penetrate.

In 20 European cities, audiences expressed to us the unanimous hope that space will not develop into still another frontier for human conflict. In Rome, Pope Paul VI told us that this was a subject of great personal concern to him and a matter to which he addressed his prayers. A leader of one of Europe's largest nations expressed his fear that existing control machinery in this atomic Space Age might not be adequate to ensure peace when many nations acquire the technical capabilities of the United States and Russia.

Both the apprehensions and enthusiasms, as reflected in the mirror of Europe, were indications that 1965 was a vigorous and dramatic year in space for the United States.

After approximately two years of planning, building, and testing, the United States finally set a brisk pace in manned space accomplishment that will be maintained for the next several years. Our Gemini program gave us experience in manned flights of long duration, in maneuvering, in rendezvous techniques, and in extra vehicular activity. It also produced more elaborate scientific experiments than had previously been possible. There was more room than ever before aboard the Gemini vehicles for experiments designed to test the effect of weightlessness on blood cells and the calcium content of human bones. We also had an opportunity to conduct an increasing number of experiments in the environment outside the spacecraft. There was much more time in orbit in which to perform these tests. Nothing so far discovered indicates any serious reasons why man cannot continue to function in space for extended periods as a highly qualified scientific observer, researcher, or experimenter.

New and delicate instrumented satellites and unmanned probes also operated remarkably well in the rigorous environment of space. Researchers are now extending their capabilities and potential contributions to science and society.

The value of the entire U.S. space program becomes increasingly apparent as more and more scientific experiments are carried out. To date, of course, much of the emphasis has been on solving the engineering problems of placing manned and unmanned spacecraft in space. Now that such flights are becoming more regular and more reliable, emphasis is shifting to research and exploration, which is the principal reason for the whole effort. Proof of this is the fact that in 1965 NASA selected its first group of Scientist-Astronauts. The emphasis on scientific research should reassure those who pray that the United States will employ its space capability for peaceful purposes.

The variety of progress in space exploration should be a source of national pride. Recall that in 1965, the United States orbited Tiros IX and X, meteorological satellites placed in a polar orbit that send back pictures of the whole earth; the Orbiting Solar Observatory (OSO II); Pegasus I, a meteoroid detection satellite; and Rangers VIII and IX, the probes which sent back thousands of excellent photographs of the moon. There was also the dazzlingly successful Mars probe of Mariner IV, which relayed to earth the first close-up look at another planet. The manned Gemini series, of course, helped greatly to perfect the skills

"The rate of progress in the space program is still difficult to conceive."

necessary to complete the nation's round trip to the moon via Project Apollo.

Much of the information gleaned from these programs is already being used to practical advantage. The Tiros satellites are an excellent example. Meteorologists around the world are using information obtained from them. Through an automatic picture transmission system, any nation can obtain local cloud-cover pictures, as Tiros IX and X orbit overhead, for an expenditure of only about $30,000 in equipment. The pictures provide forecasters everywhere with an immediate snapshot of the weather pattern affecting their own nation or region, and help them make more accurate short-term predictions regarding weather patterns.

During the five and one-half years since the first Tiros was launched, more than 2,200 storm bulletins have been issued by the weather bureaus of some 50 countries as a result of satellite observations. No one could even begin to estimate how many lives have been saved, or property damage avoided, through the use of this information.

The rate of progress in the space program is still difficult to conceive. Who could possibly have foreseen the benefits that would accrue from the Tiros series when our space program started in 1958? At that time, our first satellite was a small cylinder weighing only 30.8 pounds. Today we have under construction, and are testing, the Saturn V moon rocket which will be capable of placing 240,000 pounds in orbit around the earth. This same rocket has the capacity to place 90,000 pounds—roughly four times the weight of a transcontinental bus—in orbit around the moon. Saturn V is as tall as a 36-story skyscraper. It will launch our first manned lunar expedition.

I well remember the planning we did during Alan Shepard's suborbital Mercury-Redstone flight in 1961 (see THE YEAR BOOK, 1962, page 42). The total flight time of slightly over 15 minutes involved a weightless period of approximately five minutes. Al's activities during his weightless time were precisely blocked out in terms of *seconds* per task—10 seconds for certain control movements, 15 seconds for certain instrument observations. In 1965, by contrast, during the

eight-day mission of Gordo Cooper and Pete Conrad, there were some difficulties with an electrical system requiring that certain checks be made. By then it seemed quite natural to hear Chris Kraft in Mission Control at Houston, Tex. discuss the mission planning like this: "Well, I think we will run that check on Tuesday. If we don't get it in then, we'll try again on Friday." Instead of working with options in terms of seconds, we are now working in terms of days.

The international aspects of the space program have increased enormously since they were first spelled out in the Space Act of 1958. During that time, NASA has participated in the launching of 14 scientific satellites for various countries capable of building their own scientific payloads but not yet capable of putting them into space. All told, we have agreements with 59 countries. We have encouraged other countries to build payloads in this cooperative launch program because such work complements our own knowledge of space.

International cooperation in space has been extended into the field of education. To date, some 140 international research associates have visited NASA centers. One hundred and thirteen international graduate fellows have studied in U.S. universities. Two hundred and twenty-five foreign technical trainees have attended NASA centers. In addition to formal exchanges, NASA and its centers are hosts to numerous foreign visitors. By late 1965, there had been over 12,500 such visitors to the United States.

Cooperation with the Russians continues to be a question about which people are curious. An agreement was reached with the Soviet Union for extensive cooperative effort in 1962. Thus far, however, only three comparatively minor results have been achieved: (1) a one-way communications demonstration using our Echo II satellite; (2) exchanges of magnetic field data in anticipation of an agreed exchange of satellite data; and, (3) an exchange of conventional weather data over a special communications channel set up between Washington and Moscow on a shared-cost basis.

The increasing international interest in space that my wife and I witnessed in

Europe has been reflected in the United Nations (UN). A declaration of legal principles aimed at guiding space activity was unanimously adopted in the General Assembly. In the International Telecommunications Union, a United Nations agency, agreements were reached on the assignment of radio frequencies for space research and communications.

In another United Nations agency, the World Meteorological Organization, a start was made in the evaluation and planning of requirements for a world weather system (including satellite systems) which promises important benefits.

It is clear that the United States effort in space research and exploration has helped to further international cooperation. The Russian program, however, has remained almost totally secret. Thus, when we attempt to assess Soviet intentions in space, we are forced to assume the worst. Doubtless this is why in 1965 the Department of Defense decided that the Air Force should conduct programs to ensure that the United States does not lag in developing military uses of space. Experiments in the Manned Orbiting Laboratory (MOL) program remain classified, but there are obvious military advantages to be gained by just the manned surveillance of earth and near-earth space and in communications. MOL is just what its name implies; a laboratory from which experiments can be conducted that will better define future military space needs. It is regrettable that such a step has become necessary, but the United States has had little choice. Not many people realize that astronauts have never orbited over Russia, while the higher latitude and launch inclinations of Soviet manned satellites have permitted their cosmonauts to orbit repeatedly over all 50 of our states.

The problem of how we can best utilize new information obtained from the space program has received considerable attention. In the past, we had the luxury of a generation to assimilate information obtained from scientific breakthroughs and plow it back into the proper educational and industrial channels. But with the current surge of technical data cascading upon us, proper utilization of space research has become increasingly difficult.

To help solve this problem, several systems for utilizing new information have been set up by NASA and are being run on a trial basis at a number of universities. One in particular, at Indiana University, catalogs, cross references, and computerizes such information and makes it immediately available to interested parties in education, business, and industry. This is merely a forerunner of the future, for we have just begun to comprehend the importance of rapid organization and dissemination of new knowledge. Much more must be done.

The long-range future of our space program is important to all of us, but it is difficult to predict what direction it will take. We are still at the beginning of our major explorations, and their basic purpose is to probe the unknown. We must soon decide, however, what direction our space effort should take—beyond existing programs—in the years immediately ahead. The more people who participate in important national decisions, such as how far we should go in space, the better these decisions will be. Abraham Lincoln once said: "If we could first know where we are, and whither we are trending, we could better judge what to do and how to do it."

Our dilemma results partly from the splendid resources in talent, laboratories, and other facilities which we now possess. We have a large technical organization with demonstrated capability. Yet its future, once the Apollo program is completed, is not clearly defined. We face another difficulty that is rarely brought home to the public. In a world of accelerating technology, the talent of some of our best designers and innovators is not fully utilized after their brainchildren enter the long phase of manufacturing, testing, and baptism in space. This is now partly true of some of the key men who were conceptual planners in the Gemini and Apollo programs. Hence, a fundamental decision facing the nation is how soon and to what purposes we should commit this valuable and experienced man-

"Who is to say that man's destiny is entirely confined to the surface of this planet?"

power resource that we have now developed.

We could list pages of possible future space activities. They might include space stations of various sizes and differing functions to explore near-earth space, or manned missions to Mars or Venus. Many studies—some completed, some in process of completion—have been undertaken to show where we can most productively direct our efforts, and where such efforts might take us. The difficulty lies in the long lead time necessary to conduct major projects effectively, and no one can state in advance precisely what additional questions will be raised by programs now underway. One of the characteristics of any good scientific experiment is that it raises as many questions as it answers.

Hence, planning for future activities is exceedingly complex, and when we plan, we are talking about committing a good portion of our national technical capability to a particular program. The effect of any such commitment on the business community must certainly be considered, for almost 94 per cent of the present space budget is spent with private industry.

We need full public discussion and eventual concurrence on our major space goals of the future. The problem is that these areas are highly technical. It is difficult for everyone to understand, or to fully appreciate, their importance. My personal hope is that the awareness and interest of the public will be maintained, so that the new,

long-term decisions which we must reach will arise from a consensus of Americans.

In many respects, America faced a situation in 1965 comparable to our commitment to Project Apollo in 1961. Our situation may not be too unlike that which faced us, when, as an embryo nation, we wrestled with the difficult concepts and problems in exploring our western frontier. At that time, even so wise and dedicated a man as Daniel Webster expressed serious reservations about the exploration and development of the land beyond the Mississippi.

"What do we want with this vast worthless area?" Webster asked, "this region of savages and wild beasts, of shifting sands and whirlpools of dust, of cactus and prairie dogs? Of what use could we ever hope to put these great deserts or those great mountain ranges, impenetrable and covered to their base with eternal snow? Mr. President, I will never vote one cent from the public treasury to place the Pacific Coast one inch nearer Boston than it now is."

At a time when the entire earth is faced with a decrease in natural resources and an inexorable increase in population, we are not able to afford Daniel Webster's somewhat myopic view of the future. We have sent our scouts out. Who is to say that man's destiny is entirely confined to the surface of this planet?

Related Articles

For a complete report on the 1965 year in space see also Section Two, How Far Can We Go in Space? See also Section One, Harrison S. Brown on Science, and the following articles in Section Three:

Astronauts	Communications	Houston	Weather
Astronomy	France	Space Travel	

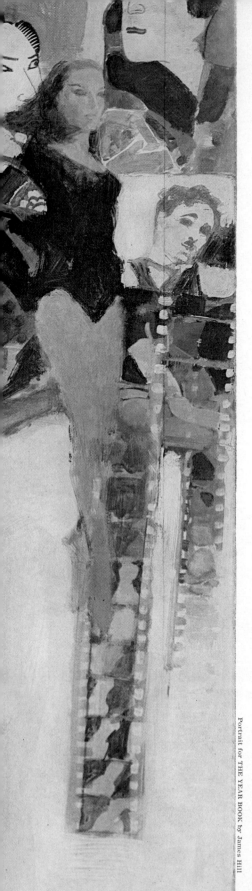

Portrait for THE YEAR BOOK by James Hill

Alistair Cooke
ON THE ARTS

*People Were Learning That an Artist
Needs a Patron, and the Lady in the
White House Seemed a Genuine One*

We never fail in this annual chronicle to remind the reader that in any of the arts it is just about impossible to chart progress, change, or innovation by the calendar. Bright boys will recall that New York City was shaken to its backbone by the Armory Show of 1913, and they will rightly argue that American painting has never been the same since.

But the now legendary importance of the year 1913 was not what it did to the painter, but what it did to the public. The Armory Show brought together in America for the first time the whole kit and caboodle of European moderns and American experimentalists. Most of the artists were, you might say, painters' painters; but they had made their mark in the art world years—even decades—before 1913. They were content, as most pioneers in the arts have to be, to be respected by their fellows at the bench and derided by the public at large.

Never did the public have such an opportunity for derision as at the Armory Show. One huge Bronx cheer, and a chorus of genteel echoes rose from Coney Island to Riverdale. The publicity that ensued rumbled through the newspapers and magazines of Philadelphia, Chicago, and San Francisco. But the mockers had the uneasy feeling, which jeering mobs often do, that they were on the defensive against something vital. Today it is almost too obvious to point out that Matisse, Rousseau, and Picasso, and William Glackens, John Marin, and Albert Ryder did have something new to say, something more durable than the roar of ridicule that met them in the New World.

Events as shattering and as neatly dated as the Armory Show happen very rarely in the arts. But that one is a useful reminder of the perils of dismissing as trash what most people instinctively *feel* is trash. Unhappily, this high-minded critical principle ("Be sure to take a long time to decide that new work is no good") is one on which quacks and charlatans flourish. Because someone told them that the first performance of Igor Stravinsky's *The Rite of Spring* caused riots in the streets of Paris, all atonalists think that if their own novelties are hooted, that fact makes them Stravinsky. Because the abstractionists (who began their first tentative daubs way back in that Armory Show) produced Jackson Pollock and Willem de Kooning, a thousand hackers come to believe that to learn to draw would be an encumbrance to the free-flowing motion of their immortal souls, and that the great thing is to drop gouts of paint on a canvas from a great height.

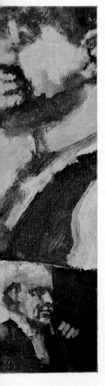

Despite our frequent warnings about the sin of denouncing new work just because it is new—and difficult—I am going to take the risk of saying that 1965 saw the positive, and to some of us very welcome, exhaustion of several fashions that have for too long been masquerading as historic advances in the art of painting. Almost everything that can be said in abstract painting seems to have been said, at least for the time being. I throw in the cautionary phrase, "at least for the time being," only because I remember, for instance, that the symphony as a form of musical expression was thought to be dead after Beethoven; but great symphonies have been written in our time by Jan Sibelius, Gustav Mahler, and others.

While we still go on hearing much about Pop art and Op art, I think both of them have passed their dizzy peak in the auction rooms where rich people risk coronaries in order to be chic. There is in New York a man who owns a collection of Pop art (corpses made of clay greet you at the door, and there is a canvas dominating the living room that you would swear was an actual monster *photograph* of a can of Heinz vegetable-beef soup) which was appraised in 1962 for just under $500,000. Today it is worth, if anything, a few thousand dollars. The reader would be wise to take heed of this example. Americans have a deep tendency to believe that what is *in* is good, and what is good is *very* expensive.

The whole field of painting in the United States is so confused by stock exchange values, and by the highly ingenious search for what might start a fashion, that it is almost impossible to write a sober survey of what has been creatively important in any given year. Let us just summarize: there is a disenchantment with abstract painting. There is a return, reported by the art schools, to the elements of drawing, especially of the marvelous, liquid complexity of the human figure. This is very cheerful news. For what has been so depressing about the myriad abstractionists of the last few years has been their shocking incompetence as painters—quite aside from the trickier question: Is It Art?

Last year, we dealt with the revolt against the pretense that the Pop and Op movements should be considered as Art. The mortality rate of Op art seems to be guaranteed by the fatal fact that the *initial* shock, or pleasure, is all there is to it: tomorrow it is amusing; the next day, it induces vertigo; the day after that, it is a bore.

The revived school of Mondrian has passed painlessly into cute, daytime dresses, which de-sex their owner by redefining a female body as an easel for the casual distribution of rectangles. A more amusing and harmless revival has been that of *Art Nouveau*, not as easel painting, but as a popular style of commercial art. Full-page advertisements for underwear and perfume appeared in the slick magazines and in the New York Sunday papers of 1965 that could have come straight from *The New York*

Times of 50 or 60 years ago. "Straight" is perhaps inaccurate. Like most revivals, this one was studied; it was more artful and self-conscious than the original. The commercial art schools have developed an odd mania for training whole classes in the decorative style of the turn of the century. The most interesting point about this trend is what started it: Cecil Beaton's set and costume designs for the movie, *My Fair Lady.*

In other days, the popular styles in the arts were encouraged by a rich patron, or enforced by a dictator. Today, a single movie can start the revival of a style that was killed off forever, we thought, by World War I. It would never have been thought of again—nor probably would the Burne-Joneses and the Dante Gabriel Rossettis have begun to fetch high prices again—if the Messrs. Loewe and Lerner had not sat down one day and decided to make a musical of George Bernard Shaw's *Pygmalion.*

Shaw himself, by the way, is said to be in a headlong decline as a well-read writer. For the time being, his ghost must comfort itself with the thought that he is guaranteed a little vicarious immortality through the loving efforts of Jack Warner and Cecil Beaton to celebrate the Edwardian costumes, the Lalique glass, the William Morris wallpapers, the "toned" oak, and the shoulder-high wainscoting of the rooms in which he lived.

A mere return to the traditions of another age is, of course, a useless method of revitalizing any art. But I have a feeling, from the work of some of the new realists, that the time is coming when rebellion for its own sake will be *passé.* I am hopeful that the best of the far-out boys will soon begin to look around the world they live in, rediscover its visual fascination in honestly new terms, and simply forget about shocking the bourgeoisie. This has been the maniacal obsession of everybody from the San Francisco Ginsbergniks and the makers of "underground" movies to the four-letter night club comics and the practitioners on the Cage piano.

In the theater, once again the end-of-year cry was: "The worst season in memory." What this means is that, in the first half of the season anyway, there was the familiar absence of either serious plays or sure-fire hits, on *Broadway.* I stress Broadway because the lamentation has no meaning once you leave what used to be called the "hardened artery" of the commercial theater.

We moaned for years about the lack of any decent alternative to the overpriced show window of Broadway, and by now we have come to take for granted the scores of little theaters in old schoolrooms, bars, stables, basement flats, and abandoned warehouses. In the last week of December, 1965, before the off-Broadway season had really got going, the hungry culture-vulture could stay a mile away from Broadway and yet see plays by Webster, Wycherley, and Robinson Jeffers. He could view a new and superior version by Arthur Miller of his "View from the Bridge"; a repertory of Gilbert and Sullivan; and readings from Shaw and Robert Frost. He could see two needling satires on racial prejudice by an unknown Negro playwright, Douglas Turner Ward; a fine first play about Brooklyn in the 1890s, by one William Alfred; and promising work by newcomers Arkady Leokum and James Broom Lynne. It would be a remarkable Broadway season which offered more. And the off-Broadway season was, at this writing, barely half over.

These comments, of course, merely reflect the theatrical situation in New York. I do not believe that elsewhere there are sufficiently powerful forces at work to enhance the theatrical situation greatly, except in one or two cities such as Minneapolis, where the Minnesota Theater Company performs to packed houses at the Tyrone Guthrie Theater, or in university towns where determined talents can maintain, for a while at least, the pretense that good theater, and/or repertory cinema is a civic necessity.

Most cities these days are oppressed by swelling populations. The cost to the theater resulting from this fact is reflected in the prohibitive prices of real estate. Added to this are the high cost of labor, and the exacting conditions labor is able to demand. Together, these factors make it ruinous for any producer, whether an old-fashioned banker or a new-style Cultural Center, to undertake the staging of work whose only prospective claim on the public's glands is that it is classic, or serious, or perhaps even possesses qualities of imagination.

The producer dare not be such an impractical idealist. He must promise something that is pretty certain to pay its way, even if it does not make a million dollars. Like the television producer who may yearn to do good work, he is an artist who must also be a successful merchant. In brutal truth, these two requirements do not necessarily have anything in common.

Let us sorrowfully admit that Broadway —which means also the commercial theater in Boston, Chicago, Philadelphia, and San Francisco—is beyond the scope of the ordinary playwright. To be staked to an appearance there, his work, like that of Alan Jay Lerner or Richard Rodgers, must promise some of the properties of a gold mine. Shakespeare would have failed to qualify; as would Ibsen, Chekov, Strindberg, Webster, Congreve, Wycherley, and Sheridan, to name but a few. That is, perhaps, why we must see their work where it belongs; off-Broadway.

The movies in 1965 did not, so far as I could see, produce any startling new talents, outside the well-known Italians, French, and British of the New Wave. If there was a characteristic of 1965, it was the moviemakers' discovery of homosexuality, loneliness, and the world of dreams. The resources of these three interesting fields are, if the 1965 film crop is anything to go on, disappointingly limited.

In 1965, the box office also discovered James Bond, and Sean Connery thereby became, in a single bound, the Number One motion picture favorite of the world. This eminence was not difficult to credit if you had the opportunity, as I did, to watch the long lines of people standing—waiting to see "Goldfinger"—in the sun in Beirut and New Delhi, in the mist in San Francisco and Istanbul, and in Tokyo and London.

The happiest trend that I could discover in 1965 was that which found all sorts of moguls, from the President of the United States to airline executives, learning for the first time that an artist needs a patron.

One of the most promising outlets for music, movies, lectures, and discussions of public affairs was the one bearing the hilarious name of "in-flight entertainment." This trend began with the projection of movies in airplanes on a single central screen—as in the old earthbound Sunday evening Methodist lantern lectures—then progressed to separate screens mounted up near the hatracks. Thereafter, the airlines installed receiving sets for almost as many channels of music and chatter as there are languages available at the elbow of listeners to debates in the United Nations.

Clearly, "in-flight entertainment" has the possibilities of an airborne Cooper Union for the culturally deprived. Clearly, it is a cultural bonanza for the harried, hurrying and successful businessman who is so busy crisscrossing the country to secure the good contract that he often has little time for the good life. The airlines now seek to repair this fault, and since they have a captive, not to say helpless, audience, their opportunities for enlightenment are many.

I myself, who am as harried and deprived as the man next to me in the window seat, have, in six transcontinental flights, seen two bad movies and a good one, heard a knowing lecture on the history of jazz piano and another on the oboe. I have listened to the piano concertos of Mozart and enjoyed the nine symphonies of Beethoven over a stereo system that gave one the illusion of having died and gone to paradise.

The passage by Congress in September of legislation providing for a National Foundation for the Arts and Humanities is an excellent gesture. The act will provide funds to create national opera and ballet companies and a national film institute. It provides for the commissioning of new works of music by American composers and the support of local symphony orchestras. But whether it will become a movement and then a force in the arts is a question yet unanswered. The type of *entrepreneur* that seems to have gained access to the ear of the White House in the last two administrations does not suggest that President Lyndon B. Johnson, any more than President John F. Kennedy, is going to burgeon

"... we saw a program ... that I am afraid ... escaped ... most of the ratings."

into Lorenzo de Medici, or even George IV. And there is no doubt that a patron by any other name is essential to any great public achievement in the arts. This is true whether the matter at hand is a series of concerts, a commission for a set of murals, the creation of a new town, or the preservation of an old street.

These things never get done by accident, or by petition on the part of a few aesthetic and public-minded men. It is not the mayor of New York City who plants trees on Park Avenue; it is the money of Mrs. Albert J. Lasker. Neither the city fathers nor the tenants of the old stretch of Park Avenue from 59th Street to Grand Central Station knew nor cared that they had there an incomparable example of American Romanesque, and a piece of Americana of unrepeatable character. The street was consequently violated and demolished by astute realtors, who wasted no time in creating a garish memorial to the steel-and-glass curtain, fluorescent picture-window school of modern architecture.

At the end of 1965, we saw a program on television done with such charming diffidence that I am afraid it escaped many of the critics and most of the ratings. It was directed with great skill and tact by the Canadian Harry Rasky. Its star was Mrs. Lyndon B. Johnson, touring Washington, D.C., and indicating, in many a quiet plea,

the good sense of caring for places and things that, uncared-for, are replaced by junk. It stirred us with the reminder that we have in the White House a genuine patron of the arts; a tireless and democratic variation of the grand tradition of the indulgent monarch.

This was demonstrated by the passage of the beautiful bill with the dreadful name —the Highway Beautification act. The final bill, it is true, was a hypocritical parody of the original. Instead of having all their federal funds withdrawn if they permit billboards within the prescribed limits, delinquent states will now receive the wrist-slap of a 10 per cent reduction in their federal bounty. Nonetheless, without the pressure of Mrs. Johnson, we should have had no bill at all.

Moreover, since the passage of the bill, she has gone around the country, sometimes scolding, more often pleading, giving heart to the garden clubs, and the city-proud, and the hand-wringing architects, and the tree-loving citizens. She has even cajoled politicians ready to lie down and be buried by the billboard lobby, one of the most ruthless and greedy groups in the history of the breed.

Such is the very human clay of our President that if Mrs. Johnson wants a beautiful America hard enough, by golly he may just insist that she get it!

Related Articles

For a complete report on the 1965 year in the arts, see the following articles in Section Three:

Portrait for THE YEAR BOOK by James Hill

Red Smith
ON SPORTS

*The Yankees Crumbled, Boxing Was Sick,
And Some People Wondered About the
Role of Athletics in Education*

On the calendar of history, A.D. 476 is circled to mark the fall of the Roman Empire. It was 1931 when Great Britain realized its sun was setting, and the British Empire became the British Commonwealth of Nations. Now 1965 has become a date forever memorable. It was the year the Yankee Empire crumbled.

Emperor Augustus "found Rome brick and left it marble." The British Empire reached its fullest flower while Dizzy Disraeli held Victoria's hand. The architect of baseball's mightiest kingdom was Babe Ruth, a fat man with a big stick.

After Ruth's arrival in New York, the Yankees won 29 pennants and 20 world championships. They opened their 1965 campaign with a record of having ruled the American League for 15 of the last 18 summers. Yet in their first full season under the ownership of the Columbia Broadcasting System, they ended with the team in the second division, a slum area they had carefully avoided for 40 years. Even worse, in the estimation of their proprietors, was the fact that their Nielsen rating plummeted.

"Was Koufax the greatest pitcher of all time? The answer is maybe."

The Yankee leaders blamed the debacle on injuries to key players like Mickey Mantle and Roger Maris. But the leaders were deluding themselves in the autumn as they had in the spring.

In a cliff-hanging finish in 1964, the Yankees had won the pennant by a single game. When they lost the World Series to the St. Louis Cardinals, they hired the St. Louis manager, Johnny Keane, to do unto their 1965 opposition as he had done unto them. But despite their 1964 ordeals, not a single, regular position on the team was open to newcomers when spring training started. This was not because every position was manned by a perfect ballplayer. It was because the Yankee management could not find one man in the whole minor league organization it considered good enough to make the team.

This had rarely, if ever, been true in the Yankee administration of general managers Ed Barrow and George Weiss. But Ed Barrow was dead, and Weiss was eased out in 1960. Weiss' last team, a pennant winner, won four more championships after he departed. In 1965, the machine he had constructed was wearing out.

Not everybody regarded the Yankees' collapse as a catastrophe. Finishing his first season as manager of the Houston Astros, a team in its accustomed position near the bottom of the National League, Luman Harris compared the performance of his nine with that of the Bronx demigods and was not displeased.

"When I took this job," he said, "I asked Paul Richards (general manager) and Roy Hofheinz (president), 'What do you want me to do?' They said, 'Build us a team like the Yankees.' So now I got a team like the Yankees, and I want a raise." Instead of more money, Luman got fired, and Richards did, too,

As the Yankees sank, the Minnesota Twins soared. This was a muscular team transplanted to the northern prairies from Washington, D.C. It was managed by Sabath Anthony Mele, who grew up as a pretty good street fighter in Astoria, Long Island. When his authority was challenged by Zoilo Versalles during spring training, Sam

Mele stopped trying to win a popularity award in his dugout and slapped a fine on the shortstop. Versalles later became the most valuable player in the league, and the Twins won the pennant.

Then their troubles started. When they met the Los Angeles Dodgers in the World Series, they encountered a left-handed pitcher named Sandy Koufax. The Twins beat Koufax once, but Koufax beat them twice. After Koufax and the Dodgers won the seventh and deciding game, only two questions remained unanswered:

When would Mele's fifth child be born? (It had been expected hourly since the start of the Series, and eventually arrived a day or so afterward.)

Was Koufax the greatest pitcher of all time? The answer is maybe. Certainly he is the best of his time.

Boxing in 1965 created more commotion than either baseball or professional football, and the publicity was not especially savory. When the year opened, the man recognized by the public as heavyweight champion of the world was a brash composer of dreadful couplets, christened Cassius Clay. In 1964, Sonny Liston, then proprietor of the title, had surrendered the championship to Clay. The new titleholder subsequently espoused the Muslim religion and changed his name to Muhammad Ali.

Because the Liston-Clay contract included a provision which, in effect, promised Liston a return bout, the World Boxing Association (WBA) unfrocked Clay as champion. The WBA is an amorphous amalgam of state athletic commissions which disapproves of return-bout contracts. The boxing public does not exactly disapprove of the WBA. It laughs at it. Thus the public laughed when the WBA declared that the real champion was a tall, inoffensive guitar player named Ernie Terrell.

Nobody had been pleased with the conclusion of the first Clay-Liston match. When a rematch was arranged for Boston, the district attorney was so displeased that he chased the fight out of town. It was held in May, in a high school hockey rink in Lewiston, Me. As the indelicate expression goes, "It smelled on ice."

This time Liston took a punch in the first round, fell down, stared thoughtfully at the timekeeper until the count had passed 10, and then got up. In spite of considerable confusion, he was declared knocked out, and Clay remained the champion.

Witnesses cried "Fake!" while politicians howled for laws to ban boxing. No such laws were passed, except for a milk-toast proscription in Connecticut, but a bill to create a federal boxing commission was widely supported. The bill may be enacted into law, but it won't cure boxing's ills. It does not create a federal authority to supersede the inept state commissions. It only sets up a national agency to duplicate and compound the maladministration which already exists in the various states.

Clay made his second defense of the title in November. His opponent this time was Floyd Patterson, who had won the championship in 1956, lost it in 1959, won it back in 1960, and lost it again in 1962. Even for Las Vegas, Nev., where remarkable things happen, the Clay-Patterson fight was a sorry travesty. The referee stopped it in the 12th round. Floyd Patterson had been defenseless since the sixth, but Clay's punches had not rendered him helpless. His trouble was a chronic ailment of the lumbar region of the back, which he had kept secret for 10 years. He had also kept the condition secret from the Nevada boxing authorities, their medical examiner, and the fans who had paid from $6, to watch on closed-circuit television, to $100 for a ringside seat.

Patterson did not do the fans a favor, but he was brave. His back popped out of plumb in the fourth round; he fell down in the sixth, then got up and was still on his feet when the referee couldn't take any more.

Clay, as ever, proclaimed himself the greatest fighter in human history. The record neither supported nor contradicted him. He had boxed three times on the championship level. Once his opponent quit in the corner; once his opponent quit in the ring; and once his opponent was a cripple.

These were the matters the sports public talked about in 1965. Fans talked also about a pain in the neck of Gary Player, a South African health faddist who was golfer of the year; about attractive Arthur Ashe, the first male American Negro to attain international prominence in tennis, and about Milwaukee's courtroom battle to keep its baseball team from moving to Atlanta.

When the major leagues, suddenly and without warning, selected a man named William Eckert, retired lieutenant general of the air force, to succeed retiring baseball commissioner Ford Frick, fans asked: "Who he? The Unknown Soldier?"

There was, however, precious little concern about a problem that bothered a few people and had been bothering some people for years. This was, and is, the question of the proper place of competitive athletics in the educational system.

As far back as 1929, an investigative body known as the Carnegie Foundation reported that the traditional ideal of "a sound mind in a sound body" had got out of joint. Many colleges seemed less interested in sound minds than in bodies that could block hard, tackle sharply, win football games, attract gate receipts, and help pay off a debt on the stadium.

The Carnegie Report made headlines, but had little visible effect in educational circles. On the contrary, colleges polished up on their techniques of recruiting athletes. Twenty-four years after the Carnegie Report, when Jimmy Brown finished high school in Manhasset, Long Island, at least 45 centers of learning competed for the privilege of preparing him to play fullback for the Cleveland Browns.

In 1952, a special committee on athletic policy reported to the American Council on Education that "serious violations not only of sound educational policies but also of good moral conduct are not uncommon." Boiled down, the committee's recommendations were: treat athletes as people, accepting no students who do not qualify for college; pay athletes nothing under the table that other students cannot get over the table; limit each sport to its proper season, with no bowl games or other post-season events.

What happened? Well, two years after the committee deplored "institutional hypocrisy," Michigan State played in the Rose Bowl. Two years after that, Michigan State was back again in Pasadena. And on Jan. 1, 1966, 14 years after the committee called for the elimination of bowl games, Michigan State's unbeaten, untied champions of the Big Ten played in the Rose Bowl for a third time, fighting for culture and the glory of the Pasadena Chamber of Commerce.

Michigan State is singled out here because the chairman of the committee that urged a firm ban on post-season football was John A. Hannah, then and now president of Michigan State. And it was Dr. Hannah's committee that said the responsibility for a sane athletic policy rested with the college president. Maybe it doesn't, though. Maybe it rests somewhere in the state house.

The American Council on Education is not a police force. Its committee recommended that the National Collegiate Athletic Association (NCAA) act as the agency to enforce compliance with the rules. This brought the following response from H. C. Willett, then president of the NCAA:

"The recently adopted athletic policy of the American Council on Education offers little that has not already been the accepted policy of the NCAA."

Since then, the NCAA has been notably active in two fields: First, in the programming and sale of college football to commercial television sponsors; and second, in the sanctioning of bowl games. These have included such cultural exercises as the Sun Bowl, the Gator Bowl, the Tobacco Bowl, the Senior Bowl, the Blue-Gray game, the Gotham Bowl, and the Liberty Bowl. The NCAA has not objected to independent promoters matching undergraduates in athletic contests for personal profit, provided the colleges get most of the swag.

In short, much lip service has been paid to the notion that "competitive athletics are an integral part of any well-rounded educational system," and mighty little has been done about the "institutional hypocrisy" that makes victory on the field an end in itself. Indeed, with the soaring prosperity of professional football, more boys than ever are entering college, not for education, but to attract offers from the Chicago Bears. More than ever before, college stadia are becoming farms for the pro teams. And if educators are disturbed about this, they seldom show it.

Somewhere near the middle stands the college coach. Generally speaking, he is truly enthusiastic about athletics and sincerely interested in young men. He is genuinely gratified when the quarterback earns a degree and goes on to a useful life. But at the same time, he makes a living from amateur sport. He knows that if his teams do not win, his children will eat sparingly.

Hence, he subscribes to practices he secretly deems repugnant. These include the "letter of intent," which is in effect a contract binding a high school graduate to the college that recruits him first. There is the athletic scholarship "subject to review," which means that if a boy doesn't make the team, financial aid can be cut off after any year. Another practice is "red-shirting," or holding an athlete out of competition one season and delaying his progress toward a degree to keep him eligible in his fifth undergraduate year.

Almost inevitably, coaching creates cynics. 'Joe,' a famous coach at one great university, was asked by a friend, "Do you have much trouble getting good boys past the dean of admissions?"

Joe scratched his head, frowned, and hesitated. "Well," he said at last, "not if they can run real fast."

Related Articles

For a complete report on the 1965 year in sports, see the following articles in Section Three:

CONTENTS OF SECTION TWO

YEAR BOOK SPECIAL REPORTS

A YEAR BOOK SPECIAL REPORT

LEAVES
FROM
OUR
LIVES

BY ROSE F. KENNEDY

A framed copy of the inaugural address of the 35th President of the United States hangs above a mantel in the home of Mr. and Mrs. Joseph P. Kennedy. The document, bearing a small oval portrait of its author, is signed simply, "To Mother and Dad, from John F. Kennedy." This address, which rings with language fully appropriate to these days, contains this challenge to all Americans: "Ask not what your country can do for you; ask what you can do for your country."

In this article, the mother of John F. Kennedy recounts how she and her husband sought to instill in their children a respect for, and a striving toward, excellence. And she suggests a course to all who would respond to the late President's challenge.

The English writer, Evelyn Waugh, has said one should begin one's memoirs when one is no longer much interested in the future. I do not quite agree. Perhaps, at 75, one should not be too concerned about the future. Yet, I find myself vitally interested in it. I am concerned about what lies ahead for our nation and what our young people are going to do with their lives to serve God, their neighbor, and their country more effectively in the years to come.

I have long been interested in these matters, and hope that the Kennedy family has helped to influence public service for the better; both on the higher levels, where comparatively few serve, and on those rungs beneath, where many thousands serve. The work of these people, as my son Jack, the late President, said, is collectively as necessary as that of the President himself.

It is quieter in my home in Palm Beach, Fla., and at Hyannis Port, Mass., too, than it used to be when the children filled the air with their laughter, their games of charades, their tennis and golf matches, and their debates. It is quieter, of course, than it was later on, when Jack was in residence with his family; not solely as my son, but also as the nation's 35th President. This is a good time for me, I believe, to reminisce—to do so with a great deal of joy, tinged with a little sadness.

The life of politics and government service came naturally to me and my children, who, it might be said, heard political lullabies as babies. Politics was in the very air they breathed. It was served to them at mealtime, so to speak. Nothing could have been more natural for our family. The children's father was United States ambassador to Great Britain from 1937 to 1940, when they were between the ages of six and 23. Their grandfather Kennedy had been an important ward leader in Boston, and had served in both houses of the state legislature. Grandfather Fitzgerald had been in the Congress from 1894 to 1900, and

The opening illustration depicts Rose Kennedy with her grandchildren at her Hyannis Port home. At right, the late President is seated beneath a shadowy portrait of his grandfather, John F. Fitzgerald, and photographs of Boston's old city hall and the White House.

Illustrations by Paul Davis

later had had the opportunity to serve three terms as Boston's mayor.

When Jack was elected to Congress in 1946—his first political office—he represented the same district my father had 50 years earlier, Boston's old 11th Congressional District. It is also an interesting coincidence that the most important action my father performed on the national level was his key role in persuading President Grover Cleveland to veto a highly restrictive immigration bill. One of Jack's last projects was the preparation of his book, *A Nation of Immigrants*. The subject was of great importance both to my father and to my son.

One of my earliest memories has politics for a background. When I was five, my father (Bostonians called him "Honey Fitz" or "Johnny Fitz") took my younger sister Agnes and me to Washington. He introduced us to President William McKinley, who gave us carnations and said that Agnes was the prettiest girl that he had ever seen in the White House. Years later, when I told Jack this story, he asked: "Why didn't he say it to you, Mother?" I had to admit my sister Agnes was the beauty of the family.

I was the first child born to John F. and Mary Fitzgerald. My father was one of nine boys. Perhaps because he had always been surrounded by brothers, he was delighted when I came into the world. He talked to me incessantly, all the time I was growing up. He told me a lot about the history of the Irish people, about their trials and their persecutions. He talked particularly about Boston and the Port of Boston and how it was nearer to Europe than New York and, therefore, he hoped, would have a greater future than New York. He took me to South America, and later tried to encourage the teaching of Spanish in the Boston public schools. He also took my sister and me to Europe, and all the time he was comparing the cities there with the cities at home and the countries there with the United States. Among other observations, he correctly predicted that Germany would become involved in a major war.

At the end of our trip in Europe, my sister and I stayed for a year at a convent in Aachen, Germany. The reason we went to a German convent was that the French convents were closed. There was a crisis between the Roman Catholic church and the French government over the question of government help to Catholic schools. The schools and the convents had been closed, and the nuns had been expatriated to other countries. There were French nuns in the convent where we went, but it was German. I had an opportunity to study German, and this was fortunate because I love music very much, and, if one knows German, one can better understand German operas and symphonies.

Awakening Important Interests

Naturally, when my children came along, I tried to awaken the same interests in them that were so significant in my life. I took them to the historical shrines in and near Boston. They visited Plymouth Rock, Bunker Hill, and other notable places. Jack went there while he was still in short pants. When the children grew older, they went to Europe, just as I had, and saw many of the landmarks of Western history and culture. Joe Junior, Jack, and Kathleen went to Russia when they were in their teens. That was in the 1930s when most people never thought of going to Russia. Later, by the time Jack went to Washington as a congressman, he had been studying the Soviet Union for many years.

I tried to keep the atmosphere in which the children were reared healthy and purposeful. At mealtime, I made an effort to interest them in something worthwhile. When they were very little, I set two tables for supper. The older ones ate at about 6:30; the younger ones an hour earlier. With the older children, we would usually talk about the news, and we had a bulletin board with important news items posted on it. As the children grew more mature, we discussed politics and government constantly. When Joe Junior and Jack went to Choate Academy, *The New York Times* was sent to them regularly, and to the girls in the convents, too. We wanted the children to be interested in the news and receptive to Mr. Kennedy's stories about Washington. When the children came to Palm Beach in the spring, I talked to them a good deal about Easter; why the feast of Easter was at a different time each year, why Lent lasted 40 days, and why we observed the custom of fasting and abstinence. Children of other religions seemed to find the conversations stimulating, too, when they were our guests at dinner.

In 1934, President Franklin D. Roosevelt appointed my husband to the newly formed Securities and Exchange Commission, and he was elected chairman. Later, he became chairman of the U.S. Maritime Commission, which was charged with administering shipping laws. Naturally, there was much talk at home about the merits and demerits of President Roosevelt's New Deal, as Mr. Kennedy saw them. But whatever conversations took place, my husband did not force his views on any of his sons.

The Virtue of Unity

I recall an incident involving Joe Junior that illustrates this, and makes a point that I have always thought interesting. When Joe Junior returned from his visit to Russia, he talked much to his father and all of us about his trip. He said that he thought there might be some merit in the Soviet ideology. His father staunchly defended the capitalistic system. Jack, who was two years younger than Joe, listened intently. He came to me one day and said he thought that Joe Junior "understood the situation better than Dad." I told Mr. Kennedy about this, half jokingly, and he replied, "I don't care what they think about my opinions. I can get along. As long as they stick together, they will be all right." He considered it a great asset for brothers to remain united.

My husband had a theory about child rearing that I believe added much to our sons' success. I dare say that it would have aided them in any field, but especially in public life where poise, a strong sense of purpose, and courage are needed.

Mr. Kennedy believed that the boys should be given responsibilities as soon as they were ready to accept them. Frequently he turned occasions at which he was to be honored into opportunities to enhance the growth of his sons. He did not eclipse his sons, as I have seen other fathers do. He did everything he could to foster their development.

An example of this occurred in 1939 when Jack was a junior at Harvard. His main interest then was in the growing tensions that would shortly flame into World War II. Indeed, this was the main interest of the Kennedy family at that time, because my husband was then serving his third year as ambassador to Great Britain.

Jack got permission to take a semester's leave from Harvard to visit the trouble spots of Europe. He stayed at the embassies in Paris, Moscow, and Warsaw, and interviewed diplomats, newspapermen, and the man in the street. He learned how deeply everybody dreaded the idea of another world war, what their relations were to the Hitler menace, and what they were doing to cope with the issue. Jack's father asked him to send him a detailed report of the political situation wherever he was, and that he did. In September, 1939, a few days after war had been declared, a Nazi U-boat sank the English passenger liner, *Athenia*, in the Atlantic. The survivors, some of them Americans, were taken to Glasgow, Scotland. My husband was deeply troubled by this tragedy, but instead of assigning someone from the embassy staff, he sent young Jack to Glasgow to interview the American survivors, listen to their stories, and assure them that they would be given all possible assistance.

When Jack returned to Harvard, he wrote his senior thesis on what he had learned at firsthand in Europe. He later turned it into a book that became the best seller, *Why England Slept*, which entailed precise and meticulous reporting on conditions in England under Stanley Baldwin as Prime Minister, as well as Neville Chamberlain.

There were similar experiences with the other children. Joe Junior (who was to die in the air over the English Channel while on a mission to destroy German missile sites in 1944) traveled in Spain during that country's civil war. He did so because he wanted to learn about the political ideologies of the two opponents in the momentous struggle which many saw as the prelude to World War II.

Building Self-Confidence

When Bobby (U.S. Senator Robert F. Kennedy) first went to Europe, my husband learned that the late Lord Beaverbrook, whom he knew well, would be on the same boat. He instructed his son to introduce himself to the English publishing tycoon and talk with him.

When the moment arrived for someone to be chosen as manager of Jack's campaign for the U.S. Senate in 1952, Mr. Kennedy did not volunteer to serve himself, nor did he advise Jack to choose a veteran of Massachusetts politics. He urged the candidate to select his brother, Bobby, who was then only 27 years old. The results of the campaign, in which Jack won the Senate seat from Henry Cabot Lodge, show how astutely and successfully Bobby met the challenge.

Experiences like these added to the self-confidence of the children in meeting people and increased their knowledge of world events. There

Joseph P. Kennedy, as United States ambassador to Great Britain, gives a reception at the embassy in London for his son, Harvard undergraduate John F. Kennedy. The year: 1938.

71

were similar incidents with Teddy (U.S. Senator Edward M. Kennedy) and with my daughters that contributed to their development.

When my husband was asked to speak at the dedication of a gymnasium he had donated to Manhattanville College of the Sacred Heart in memory of our daughter Kathleen, it was Teddy, then a law student at the University of Virginia, who made the speech, not Mr. Kennedy. Kathleen (Jack's pet name for his vivacious sister was "Kick") had died in a plane crash in France in 1948. Teddy spoke quite movingly of what a lovely, wonderful person Kathleen had been, and what a help and inspiration she had been to the family.

Mr. Kennedy gave the children many opportunities, and they responded willingly and without complaint. They tried to do what they were asked. I would like to add that it is sometimes difficult for parents of a large family to remain enthusiastic about children's interests year after year. It was monotonous for me, for instance, to tell bedtime stories for 20 years, but I did so. My husband, for his part, sustained his interest concerning the younger children as keenly as he had for the older ones, in education, and in travel, as well as in politics.

We always required our children to maintain their integrity. We were Catholics, of course, and many of the families in Boston were not of our faith. But I tried to impress the children with the importance of observing the commandments of God and of the church, and of hearing Mass on Sundays before they started off on a cruise or a picnic. Also, we tried to impress upon them that they did not need to drink or smoke just because others did. They realized, even when they were young, that they sometimes had to act independently to fulfill their obligations.

I was deeply gratified when my son Jack, realizing the importance of the day, attended Mass on the morning of his inauguration as President in order to ask God's blessing in his new and important post.

The Desire to Compete

My husband's financial resources were of great assistance, of course, to the growing political aspirations of our sons. Yet, many men of lesser means have attained political eminence. To reach the top, I believe they shared with us the desire to compete—and not to settle for second place. "Don't go for the vice-presidency," I remember my husband telling Jack one night in the library of our home in Palm Beach, "It's just as easy—or difficult—to go for the top."

Mr. Kennedy had his own way of inculcating this. When the children were small, he went to their football games to spur them on. When they raced their sailboats, he often drove near them in his motorboat. When they got home, if they hadn't done well in the race, he wanted to know why. He would make observations, discuss them in detail—the size of the sails, the preparations for the start of the race, and so forth—and become quite annoyed if the Kennedy boys had been careless.

As I look back in time from this present vantage point, I can say that these are some of the qualities we hoped to encourage in our children. But there was something more. As I have already indicated, we wanted them to have a strong sense of religious faith. Coupled with it, we wanted them to have an awareness of an obligation to do something for one's fellow man. I was always deeply impressed by the following quotation from John Cardinal Newman: "God has created me to do Him some definite service. He has committed some work to me which He has not committed to another. I have my mission. I have a part in a great work; I am a link in a chain, a bond of connection between persons. He has not created me for naught. I shall do good, I shall do His work."

Albert Einstein expressed this feeling beautifully and accurately in *The World As I See It:* " . . . a hundred times every day I remind myself that my inner and outer life depend on the labors of other men, living and dead, and that I must exert myself in order to give in the same measure as I have received . . ."

Opportunities and Obligations

Because I have always believed in these principles, I used to tell my children that they had been given unusual opportunities, and, hence, must assume unusual obligations. They must not waste their time, talent, and wealth, nor devote these gifts to their own self-aggrandizement, but to some notable work or noble achievement.

My children made this belief their own. My daughter, Eunice, who is married to R. Sargent Shriver, Jr., director of the Peace Corps and the Office of Economic Opportunity, engaged in social work in Chicago for the House of the Good Shepherd. She and her husband were foster parents for four years to three delinquent girls placed in their care by the Juvenile Court of the city. Eunice has also served as secretary of the National Conference on Prevention and Control of Juvenile Delinquency, among other posts. Jean and Patricia have worked with her in the family program to aid the mentally retarded. My sons chose politics, which can be one of the most direct ways of fulfilling such aims.

But before I proceed to the matter of politics and how it has changed during my lifetime, I would like to make two additional points. The first is that I am aware that the Kennedys do not have a monopoly on the desire to serve. They share this feeling with many people in public life. A truly notable example was the late Secretary-General of the United Nations, Dag Hammarskjöld. His writings have meant much to me lately. In his diary, *Markings*, published after his death, he wrote: "You have not done enough, you have never done enough, so long as it is still possible that you have something of value to contribute. This is the answer when you are groaning under what you consider a burden and an uncertainty prolonged *ad infinitum*."

The second point is that public careers have many tangible satisfactions. Not the least of these is the challenge of having to deal with situations that change even while one is trying to resolve them, the excitement of knowing important and interesting people who are making history all over the world, and the promise of having the tremendous power to influence for good.

The life of politics and government service has changed greatly since my father was mayor of Boston. In those days, politics, especially at the lower levels, was conducted almost entirely on the basis of intense personal loyalties. A man was frequently named to an important job, not because of his qualifications, but because he was a friend of a friend of a local boss. The lesser political leaders spent their time courting immigrant groups, listening to their stories at wakes and weddings, and helping them to find a job or a place to live. The most important city officials based their power on similar webs of personal friendship. Hence, charm and an engaging personality were essential to political success. An important part of my father's job as mayor, for example, was his attendance at hundreds of banquets and balls. Those who knew him still remember that he loved to close many such occasions with a tenor rendition of "Sweet Adeline," his political theme song.

While such characteristics are still important in politics, they are no longer among the indispensable keys to the city hall. Politics has changed greatly over the years, and most authorities agree that its sharpest turn in recent times was called by John F. Kennedy and his aides.

A New Type of Politician

John Kennedy brought into politics, and relied heavily upon, youthful men of his own generation. Like himself, they were originally political amateurs outside the regular party apparatus. But they were university-trained specialists in a variety of fields: political science, economics, public opinion, communications, history. Equally important, they had the modern feeling for efficiency. They were detached students of public affairs; they paid endless attention to detail, and used the most up-to-date techniques available. Their energy and efficiency were truly remarkable. A good example of this was the search that was carried on for Cabinet officers and other top administrative people in the 10 weeks between the election of 1960 and the inauguration.

Jack's brother-in-law, Sargent Shriver, was put in charge of finding candidates for the top posts. For the position of director of the Bureau of the Budget, inquiries were made as far away as Pakistan because one of the candidates for the job had worked there as a U.S. economic adviser. Before Mr. Dean Rusk was selected as Secretary of State, his articles, speeches, and memoranda were collected by Mr. Shriver and brought to the President-elect's home in the Georgetown section of Washington, D.C., where he read them all.

When Sargent Shriver suggested Robert McNamara as Secretary of Defense, inquiries went to bankers, industrialists, labor leaders, and educators, as one would expect. But in addition, information was collected from his friends, from friends of his wife, and even from Mr. McNamara's caddy.

"There are two things about this Cabinet," presidential aide Theodore C. Sorenson was to say later on. "First, these men are all making sacrifices to come to Washington. They are coming because they feel the same way as John Kennedy, that the country needs to move again.

The victorious clan appears at the armory in Hyannis Port to greet the nation on the morning following the election. From left, Robert, Rose, Jacqueline, the President-elect, and Edward.

*Senators Robert and Edward Kennedy sail Nantucket Sound on
a moody autumn day in a sloop that belonged to their brother, John.*

Second, they are all innovators in one way or another. Though they
may be cautious and careful, they are not afraid to try new things."

This was the kind of leader Jack was. These were the qualities he
sought to develop in himself; the qualities he required in his aides, and

encouraged in others. As his wife, Jacqueline, once very aptly said of him, "He was an idealist without illusions."

For every man elected to a high government post or named by the President to serve in a top position, there are thousands selected to work in less glamorous but vitally important roles. This need for a large number of qualified people creates great opportunities for many to fulfill themselves in exciting careers and serve their country while doing so. And the work of those in career service is, as I said at the outset of this article, as important, collectively, as that of the President of the United States himself.

I know that President John F. Kennedy felt this way, and I know that his enthusiasm, his respect for people and ideas, and his actions in office had a strong effect on the United States Civil Service. There is much public evidence to corroborate this, including his first State of the Union message, in which he wrote, "Let the public service be a proud and lively career. And let every man and woman who works in any area of our national government, in any branch, at any level, be able to say with pride and honor in future years: 'I served the United States government in that hour of the nation's need.'"

It has been brought to my attention that these words "set the tone and the stage for a new relationship between the federal career service and the presidency." So wrote John W. Macy, Jr., chairman of the U.S. Civil Service, after the tragedy of Nov. 22, 1963.

In his article, "A Legacy of Progress: John F. Kennedy and the Federal Civil Service," Mr. Macy referred to the President's State of the Union message and noted that "members of the career service were unaccustomed to such uncommon recognition between the federal career service and the presidency." He went on to describe how the new relationship between the government service and the presidency worked.

"The President frequently cited the dependence of the nation on federal career men and women. He often addressed messages of inspiration and challenge to government employees. He sought to establish ethical and professional goals at even higher levels of service. He took every opportunity to praise federal workers as individuals and as groups when achievement warranted public recognition.

"He frequently called the attention of young people to the challenge in public service and urged them to consider careers in government. He liked to recall for student groups Bismarck's remark that one-third of the students of German universities broke down from overwork, another third from dissipation, and that the other third ruled Germany —and he would ask, 'Which third is here?'"

Incentives to Public Service

To enable the government to attract the kinds of capable young people needed to make it perform best, his administration helped to pass the Salary Reform Act of 1962. This act introduced the principle that government salaries must be reasonably comparable to salaries received for similar work in private industry. Also, among his other activities that indicated his prime concern with the public service was his directive aimed at making careers in the public service as open to women as to men, wherever possible.

There was a good reason for the President to have devoted so much of his time to the federal civil service. It is not only the organization charged with carrying out the goals of any administration, it is also the largest single employer in the United States. It employs more than 2,500,000 people in more different occupations than the 12 largest corporations in the country. And, interestingly, only one-tenth of this vast force works in Washington. The rest are employed in every state in the Union, and throughout the world.

Contrary to what I suspect is a commonly held belief, the government service is *not* composed of hordes of men wearing green eyeshades and women seated at old-fashioned typewriters. Its fastest growing element is its professional, technical, and scientific personnel. In fact, the government employs more people in the physical sciences (38,100) than in general clerical positions (24,600) and more than five times as many in engineering (128,000, according to the latest survey).

Since 1960, the number of people in the physical sciences has risen 29 per cent, the number of engineers 26 per cent, while the number of typists has not increased at all. Between 1954 and 1962, professional personnel rose 40 per cent. During this period, all other types of occupations rose 17 per cent.

Jobs for Young People

As Mr. Macy has said, "The federal work force is predominantly a group of skilled specialists and trained professionals working in a wide variety of fields." This being the case, what kinds of positions are available in career government work for ambitious young people?

Your government needs astronomers to carry on the study of the sun and the planets, biochemists to help unravel the mysteries of cancer and heredity, and computer experts to track the satellites. It needs dieticians, editors, economists, foresters, foreign service personnel, and so on down the line. Indeed, in some fields, such as civil engineering and the use of computers, the government is the largest employer in the world.

Finally, it should be noted that there are similar positions available to properly qualified young people in the state and local government. Indeed, there are three times as many state and city civil servants as there are federal workers.

I have taken the opportunity here of setting down my feelings on a number of themes that are interesting and important to me. It has been indicated to me through the letters I receive from time to time that the public is interested in these matters, too. I found the role my father played in my life a decisive one and so I discussed it here. Next, I was interested in putting down my thoughts on the values that my husband and I stressed with our children. This brought me to a consideration of ways in which politics has changed from my father's time to that of the present generation. Finally, I sought to broaden the view thus presented to indicate paths of public service open to young Americans.

Perhaps I can find no more fitting way to close this article than with an aphorism that was a favorite of the late President. It is one that he often addressed to young audiences, and it sums up much that I have written here. Borrowing an ancient Greek quotation, the President used to say that true happiness can perhaps be best defined as, "the exercise of vital powers along lines of excellence in a life affording them scope."

See also, Section Three, KENNEDY, JOHN F.

A YEAR BOOK SPECIAL REPORT

By Jaroslav Pelikan

Paths to Dialogue

Protestant and Orthodox Observers, *left*, sit beside the statue of
Saint Peter as Roman Catholic prelates meet at Vatican Council II.

After Centuries of Conflict, Christians Are Moving
Toward Reunion. In This Article, a Noted Theologian
Describes the "Great New Fact" About Christianity.

The most sacred shrine in Christendom is the Church of the Holy Sepulchre in Jerusalem, located at the place where, according to tradition, Jesus was buried. It is a shocking experience for a Christian tourist to visit this shrine. Christians of many backgrounds—Copts, Armenians, Roman Catholics, and Greek Orthodox, among others—all worship here simultaneously every Sunday, but each group has its own service and even its own music. All Christians affirm that the cross of Jesus Christ is the basis of their faith, and yet they cannot pray together at the place where His crucified body was laid to rest.

This separation is not, of course, confined to the Holy Land, but is one of the most obvious and universal facts of life throughout the Christian world. During the past 50 years, Christians of many countries and many denominations have been working to remedy it. What Christians have in common is vastly more important than what separates them, but they have been more successful in showing what divides them than in confessing what unites them. The ecumenical movement is the effort to set the balance straight.

Rediscovery, reconciliation, and reunion among Christians have hit the front pages, locally and internationally. After centuries of Cold War among Christians, Roman Catholics and Protestants have found

Illustrations by Franklin McMahon

Under the twin domes of the Church of the Holy Sepulchre, *upper left*, the babel of rival sects tells of ancient divisions within the Christian Church.

**An ecumenical gesture from Pope Paul VI was his
meeting with leaders of other faiths in the Church of the
Holy Family in New York City after his historic speech to the
United Nations General Assembly in October, 1965.**

each other again. Whether in its local congregations or at its national
conventions, every Christian denomination is facing the necessity of
basically rethinking the question of its relation to other churches. This
"great new fact" of modern Christian history has permanently changed
the map of Christendom, and more changes are occurring with each
week's news.

A Roman Catholic cardinal delivered the commencement address
at the 1965 graduation exercises of a Protestant theological seminary.
A Protestant theologian (this one) has become a weekly columnist
for a chain of Roman Catholic newspapers having a circulation of
about 500,000 copies per issue. Local churches throughout the United
States regularly invite clergymen of other denominations to occupy
their pulpits. Joint services for Thanksgiving Day and joint sunrise
services on Easter Sunday are almost universal.

Christian students from various denominational backgrounds band
together on college campuses for discussion, common witness, and
social action. At Selma, Ala., and at all the Selmas, not only "black
and white together," as the freedom song goes, but ministers, rabbis,
priests, and nuns march together for freedom and racial justice. Roman
Catholic bishops in the United States have now been authorized by

The author:
Jaroslav Pelikan,
Titus Street
Professor of
Ecclesiastical
History at Yale
University, has
written widely on
many religious
topics. He is a
member of the
Commission on
Faith and Order of
the World Council
of Churches and
President of the
American Society of
Church History.

83

A leader of the ecumenical movement is the Rev. Dr. Willem A. Visser't Hooft, General Secretary of the World Council of Churches.

The late Pope John XXIII called for an ecumenical meeting soon after coming to the papacy and opened Vatican Council II in 1962.

the Vatican to permit the celebration of Mass at mixed marriages of Roman Catholics and Protestants and to allow the non-Catholic partner's minister to bless the newlyweds in their home after the Roman Catholic ceremony.

The ecumenical movement began, significantly, with the uneasiness of students in the Western World, and of converts in Africa and the Far East, over the divided state of the Church. In the case of the converts, denominational conflicts that may have seemed justifiable in Europe or the Americas were utterly remote to Christians who had just made the change from Hinduism or fetishism. It was difficult for a Bushman to understand that he was a Norwegian Lutheran or a Southern Baptist. It was even more difficult to persuade a pagan to become a Christian if he was obliged at the same time to choose from among some 300 denominations of Christianity. Thus, Christian division was an offense to the non-Christian world. In 1910, at Edinburgh, Scotland, a World Missionary Conference was held to deal with this offense. From it came, in 1921, the International Missionary Council, in which representatives of many churches worked together for the growth of the Christian mission throughout the world.

While reports of restiveness about denominational competition in the mission field and in the younger churches were coming in, Christian students in the West were expressing similar criticism. In an age when patterns of thought were determined by systems of value and belief other than those derived from the Bible and the Christian tradition, students began to recognize, far earlier than did their elders, that Christians were, relatively speaking, a shrinking minority in a world that was becoming increasingly indifferent to the pretensions of organized religion. The students knew, therefore, that the odds for the survival of Christianity at the vital centers of decision were very poor, and that they were made even worse by divisions among the churches. And so it was from the mission field and from student Christian movements that the earliest clamor came for some attempt to achieve Christian understanding in a divided world.

One concrete form that this understanding was to take was service to the needy. During World War I, Christians on both sides of the conflict did not merely content themselves with claiming divine sanction for their war efforts, as though God were fighting for either the Allies or the Central Powers. They came to see that with the end of the war, millions of Europeans, most of them Christian, would need the kind of aid that could come only from voluntary agencies. For a significant number of these Christians, the war, moreover, provoked a serious re-examination of the social structures and systems that spawn war. Christians learned that the Church could not be content to "save souls," while allowing a society to go its own way toward destruction.

The practical outcome of this recognition was the Universal Christian Conference on Life and Work, which met at Stockholm, Sweden, in 1925 and again at Oxford, England, in 1937. Nathan Söderblom, Archbishop of the Church of Sweden (Lutheran), had issued a call for this kind of a conference to be convened as early as June, 1917.

Seeking to find some Christian answers to the problems of social, political, and economic life, the Conference on Life and Work also proved that Christians could neither find such answers nor expect them to be heeded if they refused to do anything about their own divisions. It furthermore became apparent that if these same Christians wanted to work effectively to alleviate suffering, famine, and disease, their hands had to be united. Christian charity is no place for cut-throat competition. The churches simply had to find ways to cooperate, despite their religious and doctrinal differences.

Those differences would not, however, simply go away. Some of the agitators for Christian understanding have given the impression that all the differences of dogma and theology are due to the stubbornness of a few theologians and that, with a little good will, all the problems would yield to a consensus. But it is an insult to the seriousness of religious commitment to make these differences seem so trivial. Men have bled and died for their beliefs. Even if those beliefs were mistaken, they deserve to be treated with respect. The Conference on Life and Work had, therefore, to be supplemented by a Conference on Faith and Order; that is, on Christian doctrine and on the proper form of the Church and of its ministry. The Conference on Faith and Order met at Lausanne, Switzerland, in 1927, and at Edinburgh in 1937.

National Council of Churches

The Rev. Dr. Eugene Carson Blake is a former president of the National Council of the Churches of Christ in the U.S.A.

These and other meetings between representatives of various churches disclosed another unifying force that had been at work for several decades. The debates over the critical study of the Bible during the half century before World War I had divided theologians of several major communions into "liberal" and "conservative." As a result, there were, in many ways, deeper differences *within* the denominations than between them. Although these differences sometimes went so far as to produce new splits, more often they served to show that the older conflicts between churches had lost their relevance. It appeared to many, for example, that a surrender of belief in the literal infallibility of the words of the Bible made it pointless to argue whether sprinkling or immersion is the proper form of baptism.

In a positive way, too, the development of Christian thought had opened the door to better understanding between the churches. Partly through a deeper study of the Bible and partly through a growing awareness everywhere that human life is social rather than merely individual, Protestant theology rediscovered the doctrine of the Church, embodied in the Christian belief that God's gift to man in Jesus Christ creates a common bond between all those who name the name of Christ. Sometimes Protestants had spoken as though the distinctive doctrine of Protestantism was its emphasis on the freedom of the individual over and against the authority of the Church. By the end of the 19th century, however, it had become evident to most Protestant churchmen that there is no Christianity apart from the Church. It followed from this that Christians could not afford to treat the unity of the Church as an afterthought. They must find ways both of express-

National Council of Churches

Episcopal Bishop James A. Pike is coauthor of the Blake-Pike proposal for Christian unity.

85

ing the unity that already existed, and of advancing toward a unity that was both broader and deeper in scope.

Out of all these developments grew the conviction that it is the will of God for the churches to come closer together. The several ecumenical organizations—International Missionary Council, Faith and Order, Life and Work—were concerned with avoiding the ironic spectacle of overlapping and competition among groups whose purpose was to eliminate overlapping and competition. The year 1941 was set for the formation of a World Council of Churches, but because of World War

Michael Taylor

The Archbishop of Canterbury, Dr. Arthur M. Ramsey, presided at an Anglican meeting in May, 1965, that considered union with English Methodism.

II, it was impossible to establish the council until Aug. 23, 1948.

From its headquarters in Geneva, Switzerland, the World Council has helped to coordinate the work of its member churches, especially in the area of service and aid, and to inspire their discussions and negotiations toward closer unity. It is not itself a church, but an agency of about 200 churches. Through its Division of Studies, as well as through Faith and Order, it is also a source of theological insight and research. There are about 900 local and state councils of churches in the United States, together with the National Council of the Churches of Christ in the United States of America, which was formed in December, 1950, to carry out many of the tasks that had previously been undertaken by the churches themselves.

Yet, cooperation between existing denominations, which is the function of such councils, is not enough of a goal for the ecumenical movement. Separation must be replaced by true unity and organic reunion. During the past half century, there have been more than 40 reunions of bodies previously separated, or mergers of bodies that had never been united before. In 1925, for example, Canadian Methodists, nearly all the Congregationalists, and 71 per cent of Canadian Presbyterians formed the United Church of Canada. In 1947, the Church of South India was formed, uniting Methodist, Presbyterian, Congregationalist, Dutch Reformed, and Anglican groups into a new body which is now negotiating with still other churches in India. In 1961, after many years of discussion, the Congregational Christian Churches of the United States and the Evangelical and Reformed Church (both of them already mergers of previously separated groups) established the United Church of Christ. The United Church of Christ, in turn, has been engaged since 1962 in conversations with Episcopalian, Presbyterian, Methodist, Disciples of Christ, and Evangelical United Brethren churches. A continuing agency, the Consultation on Church Union, has been established.

These are only a few of the more dramatic illustrations of the ecumenical ferment throughout the Protestant world. But of the nearly 1,000,000,000 Christians in the world, only about one quarter are Protestant. Most of the rest are Roman Catholic or Eastern Orthodox. It seems somewhat foolish, therefore, to use the word "ecumenical" in the sense of "pan-Protestant." The most important new fact of the ecumenical endeavor during the past several years is that it has become fully ecumenical. Ever since the meeting at Lausanne in 1927, representatives of the Eastern Orthodox traditions have been taking an influential and respected role in ecumenical discussions. At the third assembly of the World Council in New Delhi, India, in 1961, the Eastern Orthodox churches of Russia, Bulgaria, Romania, and Poland became members. Most of the Eastern Orthodox churches in

Behind the diversity of the varied robes worn by the presidents of the World Council of Churches, shown here at the New Delhi assembly in 1961, is a unifying purpose of strengthening the Church in the world. The leaders, *left to right*, are Sir Francis Ibiam, Dr. Martin Niemoeller, Archbishop Iakovos, Dr. Arthur Ramsey, Dr. David Moses, and Charles Parlin.

World Council of Churches

the United States have become increasingly active in state and local councils and in the National Council.

But even Protestantism and Eastern Orthodoxy together represent numerically less than half of Christendom. The largest organization in the Christian world is the Roman Catholic church, in whose vocabu-

Entering the First Methodist Church of Evanston, Ill., for the second meeting of the World Council of Churches in 1954 are, *left to right*, Dr. Harold A. Bosley, then minister of the church; Bishop G. Bromley Oxnam; Archbishop Athenagoras I; Dr. Marc Boegner; Bishop Eivind Berggrav; Bishop George K. A. Bell; and Bishop C. K. Jacob.

lary the word "ecumenical" has become standard, especially since the work of the late Pope John XXIII. He created a Secretariat for Promoting Christian Unity and convoked an ecumenical council, Vatican Council II, whose closing sessions were held in the autumn of 1965. Stirred by Pope John's conciliatory spirit and charitable example, Roman Catholics have simultaneously come to look with increasing favor on the ecumenical strivings of other Christians, and have launched an ecumenical movement of their own. As in the case of the ecumenical movement among Protestants, Roman Catholic ecumenism is the culmination of a long development that must be understood, at least in its essentials, if we are to interpret the present situation properly.

Ever since the Reformation of the 16th century, the defenders of Roman Catholicism have been insisting that their cause is just, and that the Reformation and the Reformers were unfaithful to Christian truth. It was said that Martin Luther had been possessed by a demon. Rumor had it that he committed suicide. And no one could deny that he had married a runaway nun. Therefore, each time someone within Roman Catholicism called for renewal and reform, he could be tarred with the brush of Protestantism and consequently dismissed. But like the leaven in the lump, the Christian imperative for the renewal of the Church continued to work.

It was, first of all, an imperative for reform in the structure and life of the Roman Catholic church itself. But it was also a call for some real changes in the relation of the church to society—and in the relation of the church to other Christians. For in spite of the monolithic claim of Roman Catholicism to be *the* Church, it simply could not be denied that there were genuine Christians who were not members of the Roman Catholic church.

The ecumenical movement within non-Roman Catholic Christendom helped to bring all this into

**Augustin Cardinal
Bea, a member
of the so-called
"liberal" wing
of the Roman
Catholic Church,
is an advocate of
church reform.**

focus. Although there was no official Roman Catholic participation in the early conferences, there was increasing interest in them. As early as the Edinburgh World Missionary Conference of 1910, the Roman Catholic bishop of Cremona declared, in a letter to the conference, that there was a unity among Christians "great enough to warrant continuing further discussion tending to promote the union of all believers in Christ." Recently, Augustin Cardinal Bea, president of the Secretariat for Promoting Christian Unity, asserted: "We Catholics must recognize with sincere gratitude that it was our separated brethren, Orthodox, Anglican, and Protestant, who gave the first impulse to the modern unitive movement, and that we have learned much from them, and can learn still more."

The name "separated brethren" has now become the usual Roman Catholic term for other Christians, replacing "schismatic," "heretic," and other more vitriolic designations. A noteworthy factor in this change of attitude was the experience of European Christians under Nazi tyranny. In his writings against Roman Catholicism, Luther had called the pope Antichrist, and the Roman Catholics of his day had returned the compliment. With the advent of Adolf Hitler, their descendants learned what an Antichrist is really like. In the process, they found each other.

Groups of Protestants and Roman Catholics met to share in a common life of prayer and Bible study, and to consider the Christian strategy under persecution. In the concentration camps, they learned to share a common death as well. What had been learned in the time of troubles could not be easily forgotten when Hitler and his regime were dead. Even in a time of civil peace, it was unthinkable to return to the same old kind of religious war.

Not only the old ways of religious warfare, but even some of the old ways of religious thought and worship were proving just how obsolete they were. It seemed intolerable to many Roman Catholics that the central act of the church's worship should be conducted in a lan-

**Roman Catholic
women are taught
to interpret
Christian teachings
through Hindu
dances in India,
left. Pope Paul VI,
right, pushes
through crowds on
Via Dolorosa in
Jerusalem during
his visit to the
Holy Land in 1964.
While there, he met
with Athenagoras I.**

guage that no one has spoken in ordinary society for centuries. The church speaks about so central a doctrine as the sacraments in language conditioned by the centuries-old theology of St. Thomas Aquinas, with the help of the philosophy of Aristotle. This language is quite unintelligible to millions of 20th century men.

Having resisted the findings of Galileo and having established the Spanish Inquisition, the church needed to rethink its relation to modern thought and to the modern state. Meanwhile, the church had been neglecting the very resources of its own tradition, especially the Bible, from which could come the power of authentic renewal.

None of these problems could be said to be unique to the 20th century. Certainly none of them is unique to Roman Catholicism. What is unique is that on both sides of the great divide between Roman Catholicism and other churches thoughtful leaders have tackled these problems and have learned that they will have to solve them together. When Pope John XXIII announced an ecumenical council in 1961, he meant a council that would include Roman Catholics from all over the world, not, as some overly enthusiastic Protestants concluded, a council to discuss reunion with other Christians. Nevertheless, the council has transformed relations between Roman Catholics and other Christians so radically that it will be decades before we can gauge its influence. As one of the Protestant observers at the council put it, "Our presence here . . . is a miracle." Throughout the discussions and

The thrust of ecumenism cuts across boundaries of race, color, and nationality. During a European tour in 1964, the Rev. Martin Luther King conferred with Pope Paul VI, *upper left*. The next year, in a basement of the Baptist church in Selma, Ala., an Episcopalian minister addressed a mixed group during the desegregation fight. Youths, *lower right*, from 15 countries and denominations met in Wisconsin to discuss a Christian response to world problems.

deliberations of the council, delegated observers from various non-Roman Catholic communions watched and listened and prayed, and their presence helped to make the council ecumenical in fact and in spirit, as well as in name.

The decisions of the council also were ecumenical both in fact and in spirit. It reformed the liturgy of the church and opened the way for the replacement of Latin with the language of the people in large parts of the Mass. It came to terms with the contemporary world and adopted a statement on religious liberty that will make a vital difference in the relation of the church to modern society. To other Christians, both Orthodox and Protestant, it extended a fraternal hand, asking not that the prodigals return and do penance for their sins, but that Christians of all traditions work together in a spirit of mutual forgiveness for the achievement of that unity which is the will of God for the Christian Church.

Reviewing the inner life of the Roman Catholic church, the council recognized that being a layman is not a spectator sport in the church; the laymen *are* the church, priests by virtue of their baptism and therefore equipped to carry the message and mission of the church to the world. To the bishops, too, it restored many of their ancient rights that had been surrendered or usurped in an age of overcentralization, and it reasserted the principle of "collegiality" among

Against reddened skies of Old Jerusalem, doves settle peacefully on the ancient wall that divides the Holy City.

bishops. There is scarcely a single aspect of the work and thought of the church that was passed over in the deliberations of Vatican Council II. And most of its actions will certainly have a lasting affect on the whole of the Christian world.

The unspoken assumption behind many of these actions—in fact, as we noted earlier, behind much of the ecumenical movement as a whole—is the shock of the recognition that the percentage of Christians in the world is smaller this year than it was last year, and that next year it will be still smaller. When Christianity became the official religion of the Roman Empire in the 4th century, it embarked on a program of expansion that has carried it from the confines of the Mediterranean world to virtually every race and nation of mankind. Everywhere, it has come as the religion of the dominant group in the human race: European, white, Caucasian, culturally advanced, and Christian were all synonymous terms. The day of Christian-European dominance is over. The sooner Christians of every tradition recognize this fact and accept it, the better it will be for them and for the Christian cause throughout the world.

From this fact, it follows almost inexorably that the divisions which Christians could afford when they were the ruling caste have now become a luxury in which no one can indulge. If the Christian alternative to communism, materialism, and all the other ideologies competing for human loyalty is to be heard and considered, there ought to be a way of presenting that alternative that is neither sectarian nor partisan, but "catholic," that is, universal, in its appeal to all segments of human society.

To put this imperative in another way, Christians of all groups are looking for ways of continuing to emphasize their own historic values, while at the same time learning to affirm values and beliefs which other Christian groups have historically claimed as their own. The Church is what it is because of the Bible, and the Bible is what it is because of the Church. There is no need to choose between the Bible and the Church in the question of Christian authority, but Christians must learn that they cannot have the authority of either without the authority of the other. So it is with preaching and the sacraments, faith and works, freedom and authority, and many of the other antitheses that traditionally create controversy.

It is interesting, moreover, that as Christians huddle together in their new minority status, they do not wish to close their minds to the rest of the human race or even to other religions. On the contrary, one by-product of the new ecumenical spirit is a new openness to the great living religions of mankind. Such openness is not, as it has often been, the result of indifference to the deeper issues, or of ignorance about the fundamental differences. It is, rather, the result of the recognition that all those who believe that there is more to human existence than absurdity, have a stake in the preservation of the values that are an essential part of the human spirit.

A special place belongs to the new relationship between Christians and Jews. Christians have learned—through Biblical study, but even more through the nightmare of anti-Semitism—that, as Christians, they have a special affinity for the people of Abraham, Isaac, and Jacob, the ancestors and brethren of Jesus of Nazareth. Therefore, both the Vatican Council and the World Council of Churches have given particular attention to the place of the people of Israel in the plan of salvation.

As the churches have been unable to face each other without a new awareness of the place of the people of Israel, so it was perhaps inevitable that they turn their gaze also to the Holy Land, whose highways and cities have witnessed the great events that unite Christians in a common faith, as well as the scandals and atrocities that divide them. The same Palestine where sacred shrines exemplify Christian competition every Sunday has been the scene of striking demonstrations of Christian unity. When a new YMCA building was dedicated at Nazareth on April 7, 1965, it brought together Christians of many denominations, including Protestant, Orthodox, and Roman Catholic, with representatives of the Jewish faith in attendance as well. And on Jan. 5, 1964, Pope Paul VI and the primate of Eastern Orthodoxy, Athenagoras I, Patriarch of Constantinople (Istanbul), met in the first encounter between patriarch and pope since the 15th century—and their meeting was in Jerusalem. They prayed together on the Mount of Olives, where on the night of His betrayal, Christ had prayed: "I . . . pray for those who believe in Me . . . that they may all be one, even as Thou, Father, art in Me, and I in Thee, that they also may be in us, so that the world may believe that Thou hast sent Me."

There, on the mountain consecrated forever by Christian memory, these two disciples of Christ united in a prayer that symbolized the beginning of the answer to His prayer. The outcome of their prayer, and of the entire ecumenical movement, still cannot be predicted. It takes more than good will, more even than prayer, to heal the wounds of centuries. But if healing there is to be, it cannot come without good will and prayer. The rest is up to God. On this all Christians agree as they pray, separately and yet together: "Thy will be done on earth as it is in heaven . . . and forgive us our trespasses, as we forgive those who trespass against us."

See also, Section Three, ROMAN CATHOLIC; JEWS AND JUDAISM; PROTESTANT.

The ecumenical movement, about which Jaroslav Pelikan writes in this article, is an important chapter of man's religious history. But it is only one chapter. To understand the sweep and scope of earlier chapters of our religious heritage, see the Trans-Vision® on opposite page.

THE SACRED LAND

Sid Latham, Photo Researchers   O. L. Goldman, FPG

Dr. Charles Glauboch, Photo Researchers

M an is today making rapid and dramatic advances in the conquest of space, disease, poverty, and ignorance. He can look to the future with confidence and excitement. Yet, in so doing, he must not lose touch with his roots, or with the rich heritage embodied in his ideals, institutions, and character. Religion is an essential part of human heritage, and hundreds of millions of people—Christians, Jews, and Moslems alike—look to Palestine as the sacred land, the home of their faith. It is a unique land, one of many contrasts, as depicted on the left by the Jordanian camel corps, the modern city of Tel Aviv-Yafo, and ancient Nazareth. It was in Palestine that Judaism came into being. There Christianity was born. Islam, which had its origin in Arabia, found a home there, too, and became one of the world's great monotheistic faiths.

There was a time from the late Middle Ages and after it was absorbed into the Ottoman Empire in 1517, when Palestine was a land almost without a history, largely a wilderness populated by peasants and Bedouins. Finally, in the 19th century, groups of Jews came back into the area, and the Zionist movement gained momentum. Following World War I, the British ruled the land under a mandate from the League of Nations. Then came Hitlerism, and more Jews poured into Palestine. Bitter feeling developed between them and the Arabs living there. Fighting broke out and continued sporadically until after the formation, in 1948, of two separate states: Israel and the Hashemite Kingdom of Jordan. The Jews have built a flourishing, modern country, and the growth of both Israel and Jordan has been truly spectacular.

To study the development of the Holy Land from ancient times to the present, turn to the last map in this unit and lay down each of the following ones successively. To compare the modern Holy Land with previous periods, lift out the gatefold page and place it over the map to be studied.

Cover: A panorama of religious history spreads before the viewer as he gazes from the Mount of Olives toward Jerusalem. In the foreground is the Garden of Gethsemane, with the Church of St. Mary Magdalene at the right. Beyond looms the Dome of the Rock, or Mosque of Omar. The new Israeli area of Jerusalem is in the background.

COVER PHOTO: Ray Manley, Shostal

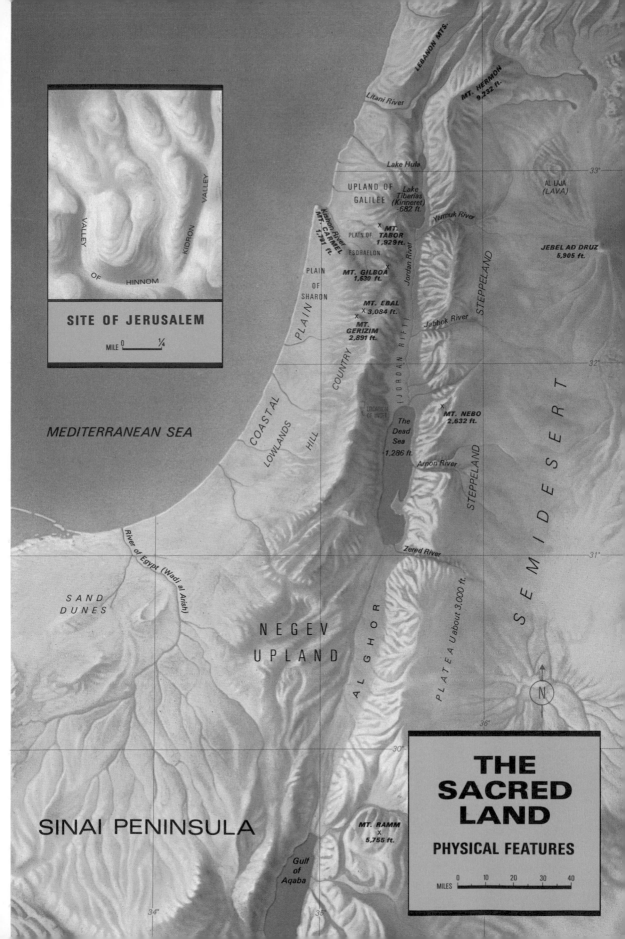

SITE OF JERUSALEM

MILE 0 ¼

VALLEY OF HINNOM

VALLEY

KIDRON VALLEY

LEBANON MTS.

Litani River

MT. HERMON
9,232 ft.

Lake Hula

33°

UPLAND OF GALILEE

Lake Tiberias (Kinneret) -682 ft.

AL LAJA (LAVA)

Yarmuk River

Kishon River

MT. CARMEL
1,791 ft.

× MT. TABOR
1,929 ft.

PLAIN OF ESDRAELON

Jordan River

JEBEL AD DRUZ
5,905 ft.

PLAIN OF SHARON

MT. GILBOA
1,630 ft.

STEPPELAND

MT. EBAL
× 3,084 ft.

PLAIN

× MT. GERIZIM
2,891 ft.

Jabbok River

32°

(JORDAN RIFT)

HILL

COUNTRY

LOCATION OF INSET

× MT. NEBO
2,632 ft.

COASTAL

The Dead Sea
-1,286 ft.

LOWLANDS

HILL

MEDITERRANEAN SEA

Arnon River

STEPPELAND

S E M I D E S E R T

Zered River

31°

River of Egypt (Wadi al Arish)

SAND DUNES

N E G E V
U P L A N D

A L   G H O R

P L A T E A U about 3,000 ft.

36°

N

30°

SINAI PENINSULA

MT. RAMM
× 5,755 ft.

Gulf of Aqaba

34°

35°

THE SACRED LAND

PHYSICAL FEATURES

MILES 0 10 20 30 40

Crusaders stormed into the Holy Land and captured Jerusalem, as shown in this medieval miniature.

A.D. 70 to A.D. 1291. After the fall of Jerusalem, Galilee became a center of Jewish learning. The great rabbinical works such as the Talmud were written there and in Babylonia. Caesarea became the seat of Christian learning and leadership.

By the fifth century, European Christians began to visit the Holy Land as pilgrims. Then, in A.D. 611, the Persians swept over Palestine and in A.D. 615 massacred most of the Christian population. In A.D. 634, an Arab army, representing the new religion of Islam, swarmed in from the desert. Jerusalem became the third city of Islam, after Mecca and Medina. The caliph Omar erected the Dome of the Rock, since known as the Mosque of Omar, on the site of Solomon's Temple.

In 1096, the crusades began, and Christians from Europe invaded the Holy Land. They captured Jerusalem in 1099, and thereafter we speak of the "Latin Kingdom of Jerusalem," though the Franks, as the Moslems called the Europeans, held power with difficulty. By 1187, Moslem invaders had regained much of the Holy Land. European power completely ended in 1291, with the expulsion of the last Franks.

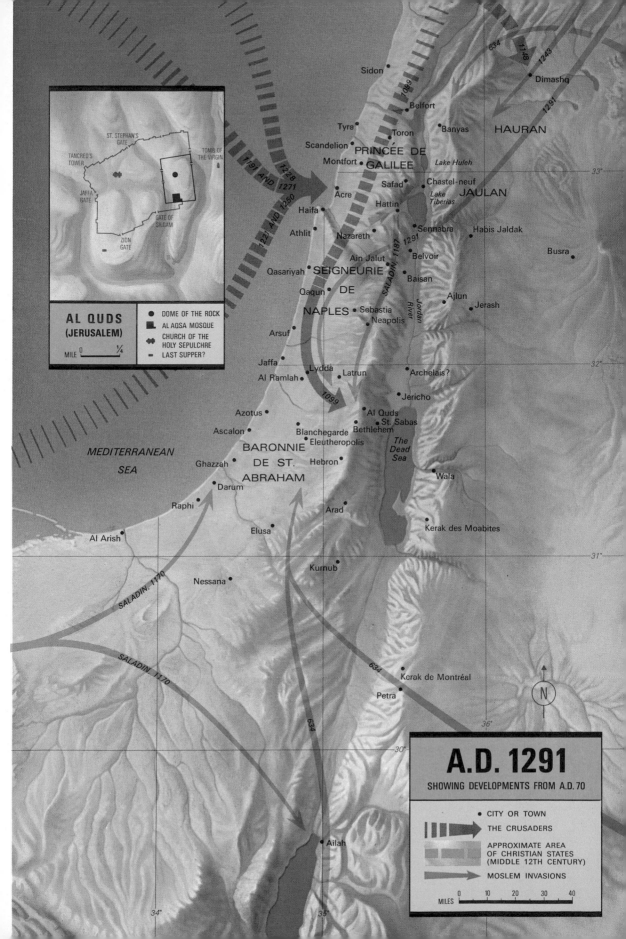

AL QUDS
(JERUSALEM)

ST. STEPHAN'S GATE
TANCRED'S TOWER
TOMB OF THE VIRGIN
JAFFA GATE
GATE OF SILOAM
ZION GATE

● DOME OF THE ROCK
■ AL AQSA MOSQUE
✠ CHURCH OF THE HOLY SEPULCHRE
– LAST SUPPER?

MILE 0   ¼

MEDITERRANEAN SEA

Sidon
Belfort
Dimashq
Tyre
Toron
Banyas
HAURAN
Scandelion
PRINCÉE DE
Montfort
GALILEE
Lake Huleh
Safad
Chastel-neuf
JAULAN
Acre
Hattin
Lake Tiberias
Haifa
Sennabra
Habis Jaldak
Athlit
Nazareth
Belvoir
Busra
Ain Jalut
Qasariyah
SEIGNEURIE
Baisan
Qaqun
DE
Ajlun
Jerash
NAPLES
Sebastia
Neapolis
Jordan River
Arsuf
Jaffa
Lydda
Latrun
Archelais?
Al Ramlah
Jericho
Azotus
Al Quds
St. Sabas
Ascalon
Blanchegarde
Bethlehem
Eleutheropolis
The Dead Sea
BARONNIE
DE ST.
Ghazzah
Hebron
ABRAHAM
Wala
Darum
Arad
Raphi
Kerak des Moabites
Al Arish
Elusa
Kurnub
Nessana

SALADIN, 1170
SALADIN, 1170

634
Kerak de Montréal
Petra

N

Ailah

A.D. 1291
SHOWING DEVELOPMENTS FROM A.D. 70

● CITY OR TOWN

▶ THE CRUSADERS

APPROXIMATE AREA
OF CHRISTIAN STATES
(MIDDLE 12TH CENTURY)

➡ MOSLEM INVASIONS

MILES 0 10 20 30 40

In this early mosaic, Andrew and Simon Peter, left, *answer the call of Jesus to join Him in His ministry.*

64 B.C. to 4 B.C. Under Roman rule, Herod the Great was placed in charge of the Jews. The people hated him because he violated their religion and despised the significance of their customs. Nonetheless, his passion for building made Jerusalem a beautiful city. Among other projects, he started a program for rebuilding the Temple, and brought water from the southern hills into Jerusalem along an open aqueduct.

Among the most striking documents we have from this general era are the Dead Sea Scrolls, uncovered in the mid-1940's at the northwest end of the Dead Sea. As a result of their discovery, we now possess a number of valuable biblical manuscripts and countless fragments of biblical books. We also possess scrolls dealing with the faith and life of a community which many believe was related to the Jewish religious sect known as the Essenes whose settlement at Qumran has been excavated.

As Herod's reign drew to a close, he ruled more and more by terror and assassination. It was he, according to the Gospel of Matthew, who ordered the "massacre of the innocents," aimed at destroying the infant Jesus. He himself died in 4 B.C.

4 B.C. to A.D. 70. Jesus, by the modern calendar born in about 4 B.C., grew up in Nazareth in Galilee. Much of His ministry was conducted in the hill country east and west of the Sea of Galilee. We know He visited Phoenicia, and He was in Caesarea Philippi. He also passed through Samaria, was active in the area around Jericho, and was crucified in Jerusalem.

The Christian religion, in fact, began in Jerusalem and from there spread in all directions across the world. From the bustling port of Caesarea, Paul set forth on his missionary journeys that carried him to Asia Minor, and into Europe. Later, under arrest in Caesarea, Paul was taken to Rome where some Christians had preceded him.

Meanwhile in Palestine, friction grew between the Jews and the Romans. Some Jews bitterly resented Roman domination, and rebelled. The Romans retaliated, and in A.D. 70, Jerusalem fell after a terrible siege. The Temple Herod had rebuilt was destroyed, and trophies from it were carried to Rome. But the fall of Jerusalem was fatal to neither Judaism nor Christianity. The Jews remained loyal to their faith, and Christianity spread to the ends of the earth.

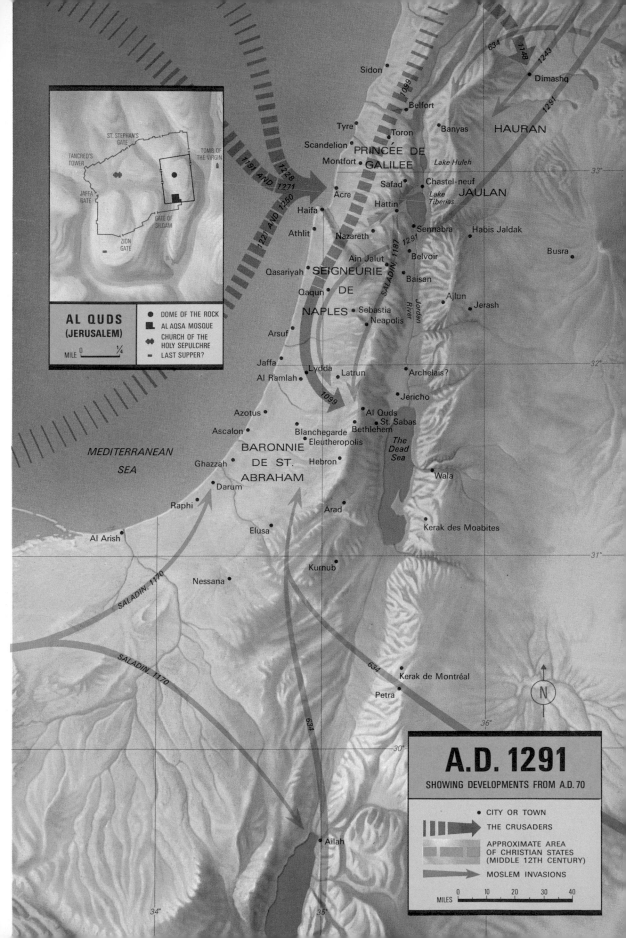

Sidon

Dimashq

634 1148 1243

1099

Belfort

Tyre   Toron   Banyas   HAURAN

Scandelion   1291

PRINCÉE DE

Montfort   GALILEE   Lake Huleh

33°

Safad   Chastel-neuf   JAULAN

Acre   Lake

Tiberias

Haifa   Hattin

1191 AND 1271

1228

Athlit   Nazareth   Sennabra   Habis Jaldak

1221 AND 1250   Ain Jalut   Belvoir   Busra

Qasariyah   SEIGNEURIE   Baisan

Qaqun   DE   Ajlun   Jerash

NAPLES   Sebastia

Neapolis   Jordan River

SALADIN, 1187   1291

Arsuf

Jaffa   Lydda   Latrun   Archelais?   32°

Al Ramlah   Jericho

1099

Azotus   Al Quds

Ascalon   Blanchegarde   St. Sabas

Eleutheropolis   Bethlehem

MEDITERRANEAN   BARONNIE   The

SEA   Ghazzah   DE ST.   Hebron   Dead

ABRAHAM   Sea   Wala

Darum

Raphi   Arad

Al Arish   Elusa   Kerak des Moabites

31°

Kurnub

SALADIN, 1170   Nessana

SALADIN, 1170

634

Kerak de Montréal

Petra

36°

N

30°

Ailah

AL QUDS
(JERUSALEM)

ST. STEPHAN'S GATE

TANCRED'S TOWER   TOMB OF THE VIRGIN

JAFFA GATE

GATE OF SILOAM

ZION GATE

MILE 0   ¼

● DOME OF THE ROCK
■ AL AQSA MOSQUE
✠ CHURCH OF THE HOLY SEPULCHRE
– LAST SUPPER?

A.D. 1291

SHOWING DEVELOPMENTS FROM A.D. 70

● CITY OR TOWN

▮▮▮▶ THE CRUSADERS

APPROXIMATE AREA OF CHRISTIAN STATES (MIDDLE 12TH CENTURY)

➤ MOSLEM INVASIONS

MILES 0   10   20   30   40

34°   35°

In this early mosaic, Andrew and Simon Peter, left, answer the call of Jesus to join Him in His ministry.

64 B.C. to 4 B.C. Under Roman rule, Herod the Great was placed in charge of the Jews. The people hated him because he violated their religion and despised the significance of their customs. Nonetheless, his passion for building made Jerusalem a beautiful city. Among other projects, he started a program for rebuilding the Temple, and brought water from the southern hills into Jerusalem along an open aqueduct.

Among the most striking documents we have from this general era are the Dead Sea Scrolls, uncovered in the mid-1940's at the northwest end of the Dead Sea. As a result of their discovery, we now possess a number of valuable biblical manuscripts and countless fragments of biblical books. We also possess scrolls dealing with the faith and life of a community which many believe was related to the Jewish religious sect known as the Essenes whose settlement at Qumran has been excavated.

As Herod's reign drew to a close, he ruled more and more by terror and assassination. It was he, according to the Gospel of Matthew, who ordered the "massacre of the innocents," aimed at destroying the infant Jesus. He himself died in 4 B.C.

4 B.C. to A.D. 70. Jesus, by the modern calendar born in about 4 B.C., grew up in Nazareth in Galilee. Much of His ministry was conducted in the hill country east and west of the Sea of Galilee. We know He visited Phoenicia, and He was in Caesarea Philippi. He also passed through Samaria, was active in the area around Jericho, and was crucified in Jerusalem.

The Christian religion, in fact, began in Jerusalem and from there spread in all directions across the world. From the bustling port of Caesarea, Paul set forth on his missionary journeys that carried him to Asia Minor, and into Europe. Later, under arrest in Caesarea, Paul was taken to Rome where some Christians had preceded him.

Meanwhile in Palestine, friction grew between the Jews and the Romans. Some Jews bitterly resented Roman domination, and rebelled. The Romans retaliated, and in A.D. 70, Jerusalem fell after a terrible siege. The Temple Herod had rebuilt was destroyed, and trophies from it were carried to Rome. But the fall of Jerusalem was fatal to neither Judaism nor Christianity. The Jews remained loyal to their faith, and Christianity spread to the ends of the earth.

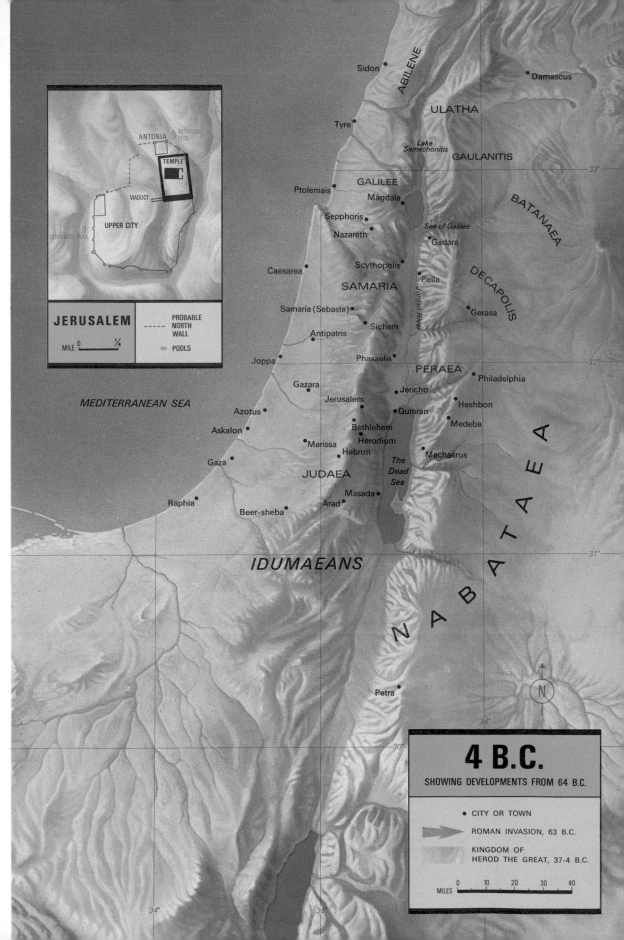

JERUSALEM

PROBABLE
NORTH
WALL

POOLS

MILE 0 ¼

ANTONIA

BETHESDA POOL

TEMPLE

VIADUCT

UPPER CITY

SERPENT'S POOL

Sidon

Damascus

ABILENE

ULATHA

Tyre

Lake
Semechonitis

GAULANITIS

GALILEE

Ptolemais

Magdala

Sepphoris

Nazareth

Sea of Galilee

Gadara

BATANAEA

Caesarea

Scythopolis

Pella

DECAPOLIS

SAMARIA

Samaria (Sebaste)

Sichem

Gerasa

Antipatris

Joppa

Phasaelis

PERAEA

Philadelphia

Gazara

Jericho

Jerusalem

Qumran

Heshbon

MEDITERRANEAN SEA

Azotus

Bethlehem

Medeba

Askalon

Marissa

Herodium

Hebron

Machaerus

Gaza

JUDAEA

The
Dead
Sea

Raphia

Masada

Arad

Beer-sheba

IDUMAEANS

NABATAEA

Petra

Jordan River

N

4 B.C.

SHOWING DEVELOPMENTS FROM 64 B.C.

- CITY OR TOWN

➤ ROMAN INVASION, 63 B.C.

KINGDOM OF
HEROD THE GREAT, 37-4 B.C.

MILES 0 10 20 30 40

The prophet Isaiah, portrayed by the medieval painter Ugolino, said that God looked for loyalty to Himself and for just social relations among men.

1000 B.C. to 587 B.C. David's son, Solomon, maintained the empire his father had created and raised its prosperity to levels it had never before known. He extended the city of Jerusalem and also built the famous Temple dedicated to the Lord. His fleet, anchored at Ezion-geber, traded with distant lands. But when Solomon died, probably in 922 B.C., his son Rehoboam was not accepted by all of the people.

Thus the kingdom split in two; that in the north became known as Israel and that in the south as Judah. The divided kingdom lasted 200 years. In the 8th century, four great prophets emerged: Amos, Hosea, Isaiah, and Micah. They told the people of both kingdoms that God looked for loyalty to Himself and for just social relations between man and man. In 722-721 B.C., Sargon II, King of Assyria, captured Samaria, the capital of Israel, and the northern kingdom came to an end.

In 598 B.C. and again in 587 B.C., Jerusalem was besieged by Nebuchadnezzar II, King of Babylonia, and its citizens were carried into exile. The city was left desolate, and the royal line of David ended.

The agony of Job is vividly depicted in this statue by sculptor Ivan Mestrovic. Despite the intense suffering Job underwent, he never lost faith in God.

587 B.C. to 64 B.C. In 539 B.C., Cyrus, King of Persia, concluded a triumphant campaign of conquest finally overcoming Babylon. This enlightened monarch decreed that all "displaced persons" in his dominions could go home. By 537 B.C., a brave and idealistic band of Jews, as they were now known, arrived at the ruins of Jerusalem.

But the city itself remained open to siege by the unfriendly people who surrounded it until, in the following century, Nehemiah built a strong wall around it. Ezra expounded the Mosaic Law, and "Wisdom" writers were active. Around 330 B.C., Judah was absorbed into the Hellenistic Empire of Alexander the Great, and Greek culture became a strong influence in Jewish life.

Thereafter, Palestine became territory disputed between the Ptolemies of Egypt and the Seleucid kings of Antioch. Judas Maccabaeus, in 168 B.C., and after him his brothers, fought the Seleucids, recovering the independence of Judah in 141 B.C. The descendants of the Maccabees, the Hasmonaean kings, then ruled the area. The last year of independence for Judah was 64 B.C. Thereafter, Rome gained control.

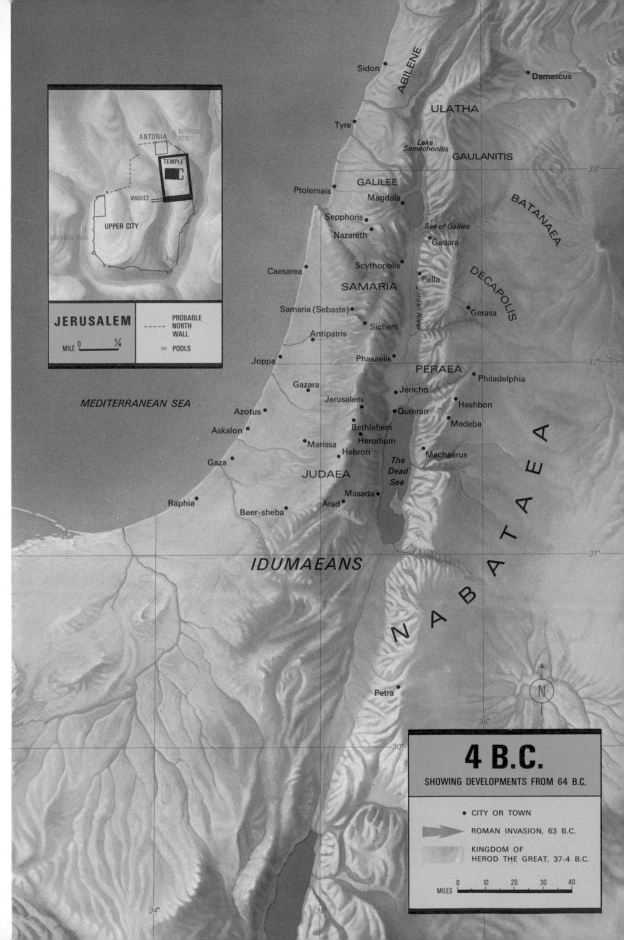

Sidon

ABILENE

Damascus

ULATHA

Tyre

Lake
Semechonitis

GAULANITIS

33°

Ptolemais

GALILEE

Magdala

BATANAEA

Sepphoris

Nazareth

Sea of Galilee

Gadara

DECAPOLIS

Caesarea

Scythopolis

Pella

SAMARIA

Jordan River

Samaria (Sebaste)

Sichem

Gerasa

Antipatris

Joppa

Phasaelis

PERAEA

32°

Gazara

Jericho

Philadelphia

Jerusalem

Qumran

Heshbon

MEDITERRANEAN SEA

Azotus

Bethlehem

Medeba

Askalon

Marissa

Herodium
Hebron

Machaerus

Gaza

The
Dead
Sea

JUDAEA

Raphia

Beer-sheba

Arad

Masada

IDUMAEANS

31°

N
A
B
A
T
A
E
A

36°

30°

Petra

N

JERUSALEM

ANTONIA

BETHESDA
POOL

TEMPLE

VIADUCT

UPPER CITY

SERPENTS POOL

MILE 0 — ¼

PROBABLE
NORTH
WALL

POOLS

34°

35°

4 B.C.

SHOWING DEVELOPMENTS FROM 64 B.C.

• CITY OR TOWN

➤ ROMAN INVASION, 63 B.C.

KINGDOM OF
HEROD THE GREAT, 37-4 B.C.

MILES 0 10 20 30 40

The prophet Isaiah, portrayed by the medieval painter Ugolino, said that God looked for loyalty to Himself and for just social relations among men.

The agony of Job is vividly depicted in this statue by sculptor Ivan Mestrovic. Despite the intense suffering Job underwent, he never lost faith in God.

1000 B.C. to 587 B.C. David's son, Solomon, maintained the empire his father had created and raised its prosperity to levels it had never before known. He extended the city of Jerusalem and also built the famous Temple dedicated to the Lord. His fleet, anchored at Ezion-geber, traded with distant lands. But when Solomon died, probably in 922 B.C., his son Rehoboam was not accepted by all of the people.

Thus the kingdom split in two; that in the north became known as Israel and that in the south as Judah. The divided kingdom lasted 200 years. In the 8th century, four great prophets emerged: Amos, Hosea, Isaiah, and Micah. They told the people of both kingdoms that God looked for loyalty to Himself and for just social relations between man and man. In 722-721 B.C., Sargon II, King of Assyria, captured Samaria, the capital of Israel, and the northern kingdom came to an end.

In 598 B.C. and again in 587 B.C., Jerusalem was besieged by Nebuchadnezzar II, King of Babylonia, and its citizens were carried into exile. The city was left desolate, and the royal line of David ended.

587 B.C. to 64 B.C. In 539 B.C., Cyrus, King of Persia, concluded a triumphant campaign of conquest finally overcoming Babylon. This enlightened monarch decreed that all "displaced persons" in his dominions could go home. By 537 B.C., a brave and idealistic band of Jews, as they were now known, arrived at the ruins of Jerusalem.

But the city itself remained open to siege by the unfriendly people who surrounded it until, in the following century, Nehemiah built a strong wall around it. Ezra expounded the Mosaic Law, and "Wisdom" writers were active. Around 330 B.C., Judah was absorbed into the Hellenistic Empire of Alexander the Great, and Greek culture became a strong influence in Jewish life.

Thereafter, Palestine became territory disputed between the Ptolemies of Egypt and the Seleucid kings of Antioch. Judas Maccabaeus, in 168 B.C., and after him his brothers, fought the Seleucids, recovering the independence of Judah in 141 B.C. The descendants of the Maccabees, the Hasmonaean kings, then ruled the area. The last year of independence for Judah was 64 B.C. Thereafter, Rome gained control.

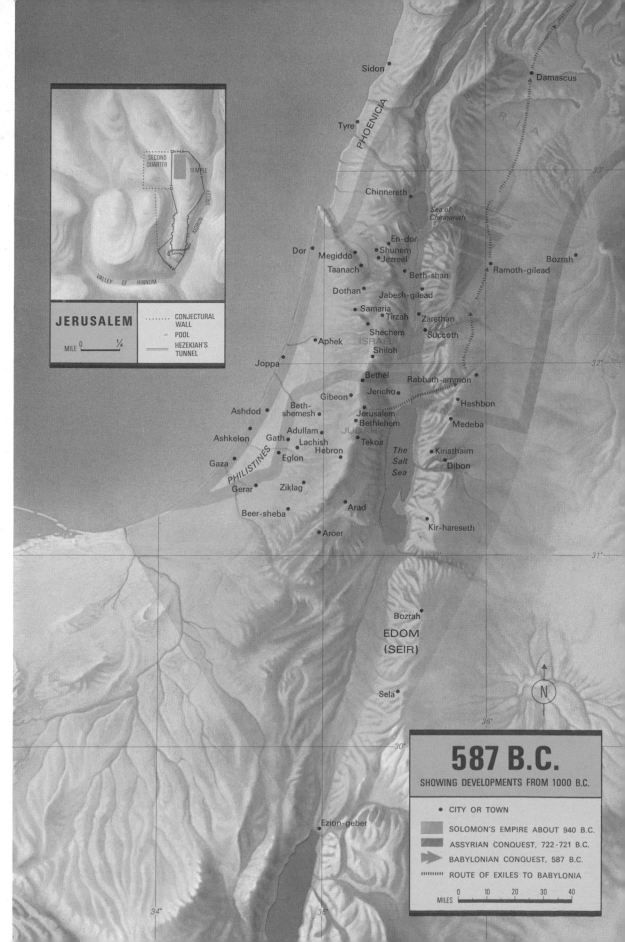

JERUSALEM

.... CONJECTURAL WALL
▬ POOL
━━ HEZEKIAH'S TUNNEL

MILE 0 —— ¼

SECOND QUARTER
TEMPLE
VALLEY
KIDRON VALLEY
VALLEY OF HINNOM

Sidon
Damascus
Tyre
PHOENICIA

Chinnereth
Sea of Chinnereth

Dor
Megiddo
En-dor
Shunem
Jezreel
Taanach
Beth-shan
Dothan
Jabesh-gilead
Samaria
Tirzah
Zarethan
Shechem
ISRAEL
Succoth
Shiloh

Bozrah
Ramoth-gilead

Aphek
Joppa

Bethel
Rabbath-ammon
Gibeon
Jericho
Heshbon

Beth-shemesh
Jerusalem
Medeba
Ashdod
Bethlehem

Ashkelon
Gath
Adullam
Lachish
JUD
Tekoa
Gaza
Eglon
Hebron
The Salt Sea
Kiriathaim
Dibon

PHILISTINES
Gerar
Ziklag
Beer-sheba
Arad

Aroer
Kir-hareseth

Bozrah

EDOM
(SEIR)

Sela

N

Ezion-geber

587 B.C.

SHOWING DEVELOPMENTS FROM 1000 B.C.

- • CITY OR TOWN
- SOLOMON'S EMPIRE ABOUT 940 B.C.
- ASSYRIAN CONQUEST, 722-721 B.C.
- ➤ BABYLONIAN CONQUEST, 587 B.C.
- ┉┉┉ ROUTE OF EXILES TO BABYLONIA

0   10   20   30   40
MILES

Baal, a Canaanite deity who was the god of growth, was denounced by the Old Testament prophets. They believed their God to be the Creator of all things.

Rembrandt's painting of Moses breaking the tablets of the Ten Commandments. Later, after his people repented their sins, Moses received a new copy of the tablets.

Before 1500 B.C. The Holy Land lies between the two worlds of the East and the West. It is part of a fertile crescent that stretches from Egypt along the coast of Palestine and then swings down the Tigris-Euphrates Valley. Archaeologists have uncovered traces of human civilization there going back many thousands of years.

Around 1900-1500 B.C., the patriarch Abraham, father of the people who were later to become known as the Israelites, arrived in this, their Promised Land, from Mesopotamia. Thus began what is often called the Age of the Patriarchs. Abraham himself met with Melchizedek, King of Salem, later known as Jerusalem, and the king, though a pagan priest, blessed Abraham. Abraham and his descendants led their flocks about parts of Palestine, or Canaan as it was then called, for several generations.

They came to know the religious ideas of the native Canaanites. These people worshiped several gods, including Astarte, Baal, and El. It was largely in protest against this worship that the religion of the Israelites later developed. As the patriarchal period came to a close, these wandering people were forced by drought to migrate to Egypt.

1500 B.C. to 1000 B.C. One of the most important events of biblical history was the exodus of the Israelites from Egypt. It probably took place around 1280 B.C. During the wandering of the Israelites in the wilderness, Moses, their leader, brought the people the Ten Commandments from Mt. Sinai, the identification of which is today uncertain. Here the Israelites became the covenant people of God.

During this period, the city-states of Philistia and the kingdoms of Ammon and Moab were established. Joshua led the invasion of Canaan and captured, among others, the cities of Ai and Jericho. Eventually, he conquered most of the areas later known as Galilee, Judah, and Samaria. After Joshua's death, individual local leaders, called judges, conquered additional areas and fought back nomadic intruders.

The scattered tribes were finally organized loosely under a monarchy. Saul was their ruler, but he did not prove acceptable to all. It remained for David to unite them. He captured Jebus, or Jerusalem, and made it his capital around 1000 B.C.

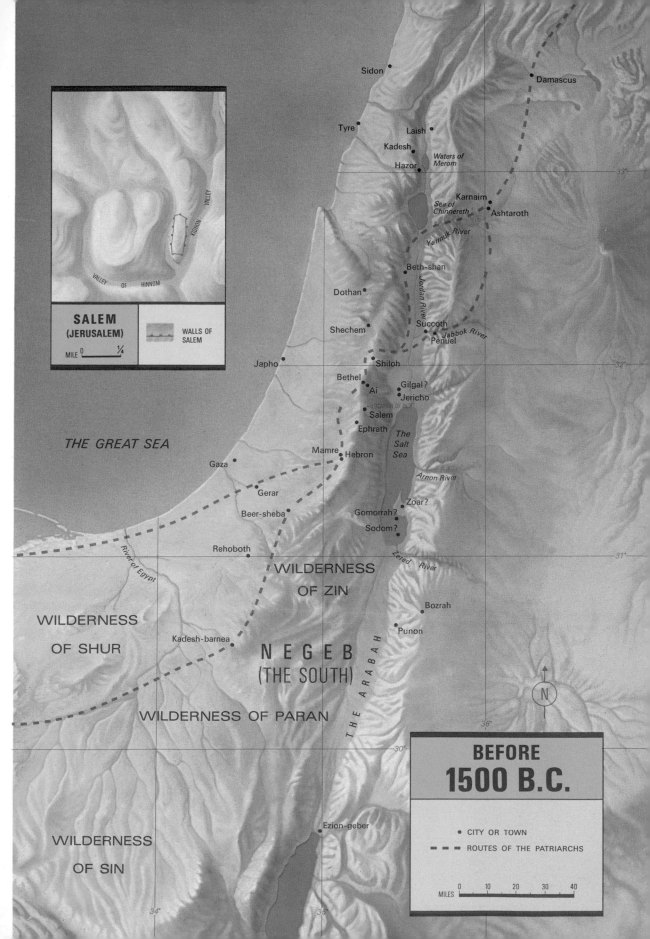

Sidon

Damascus

Tyre

Laish

Kadesh

Hazor

Waters of
Merom

Karnaim

Sea of
Chinnereth

Ashtaroth

Yarmuk River

Beth-shan

Jordan River

Dothan

Shechem

Succoth

Jabbok River

Penuel

Japho

Shiloh

Bethel

Gilgal?

Ai

Jericho

LOCATION OF LUCE

Salem

Ephrath

The
Salt
Sea

Mamre

Hebron

Arnon River

Gaza

Zoar?

Gerar

Gomorrah?

Beer-sheba

Sodom?

Rehoboth

THE GREAT SEA

Zered River

WILDERNESS

OF ZIN

Bozrah

Punon

WILDERNESS

OF SHUR

Kadesh-barnea

N E G E B

River of Egypt

(THE SOUTH)

THE ARABAH

WILDERNESS OF PARAN

N

Ezion-geber

WILDERNESS

OF SIN

SALEM (JERUSALEM)

KIDRON VALLEY

VALLEY OF HINNOM

WALLS OF
SALEM

MILE 0   ¼

BEFORE

1500 B.C.

• CITY OR TOWN

– – – ROUTES OF THE PATRIARCHS

MILES 0   10   20   30   40

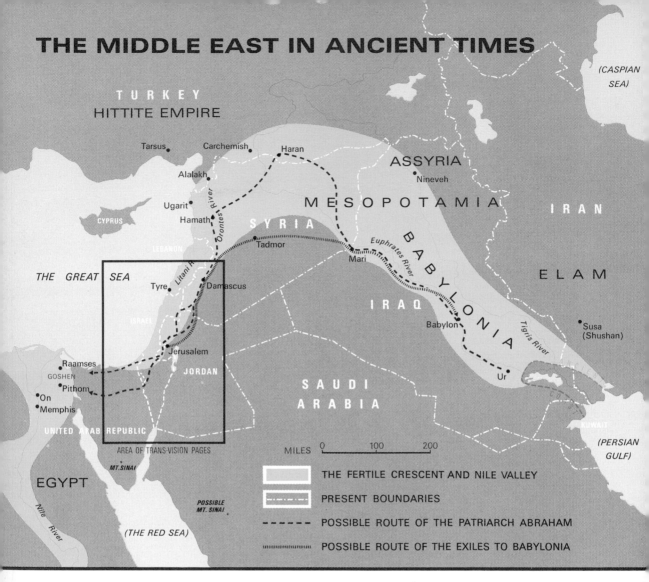

THE MIDDLE EAST IN ANCIENT TIMES

(CASPIAN SEA)

TURKEY
HITTITE EMPIRE

Tarsus
Carchemish
Haran
ASSYRIA
Nineveh

Alalakh

MESOPOTAMIA

IRAN

Ugarit
Hamath
SYRIA
BABYLONIA

CYPRUS
Orontes River

ELAM

THE GREAT SEA
Tadmor
Euphrates River
Mari

LEBANON
Litani R.

Tyre
Damascus

IRAQ

ISRAEL

Babylon
Tigris River

Susa
(Shushan)

Jerusalem
JORDAN

Raamses
GOSHEN
Pithom
On
Memphis

SAUDI
ARABIA

Ur

UNITED ARAB REPUBLIC

KUWAIT

AREA OF TRANS-VISION PAGES

(PERSIAN GULF)

MT. SINAI

MILES 0   100   200

EGYPT

POSSIBLE
MT. SINAI

Nile River

(THE RED SEA)

THE FERTILE CRESCENT AND NILE VALLEY

PRESENT BOUNDARIES

POSSIBLE ROUTE OF THE PATRIARCH ABRAHAM

POSSIBLE ROUTE OF THE EXILES TO BABYLONIA

Prepared by the editors of THE WORLD BOOK YEAR BOOK.

CONSULTANT

George A. F. Knight, Professor of Old Testament, McCormick Theological Seminary.

ART WORK

Antonio Petrucelli, and the art staff of THE WORLD BOOK YEAR BOOK.

CRITICAL REVIEWERS

E. B. Espenshade, Jr., Chairman, Department of Geography, Northwestern University;
Floyd V. Filson, Dean and Professor of New Testament, McCormick Theological Seminary;
Samuel Sandmel, Professor of Bible and Hellenistic Literature, Hebrew Union College;
Samuel Terrien, Professor of Old Testament, Union Theological Seminary.

PRINTED IN U.S.A. BY THE TRANS-VISION® DIVISION, MILPRINT INCORPORATED.

A YEAR BOOK
SPECIAL REPORT
IN TWO PARTS

CHINA

INDIA

Two principal nations on the continent of Asia are seeking to catch up with the 20th century. The means each uses, and the philosophy it follows, will influence the course of world history. Some historians, in fact, believe that the question of who will control Asia is the most important concern of modern times. In the following two articles, THE WORLD BOOK YEAR BOOK reports on the efforts of China and India to solve one of their most serious problems: feeding their teeming masses. This they must do before they can achieve the ambitious industrial goals that will bring them into the mainstream of 20th-century life.

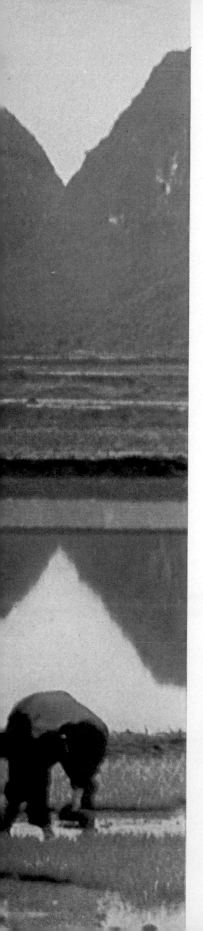

INSIDE RURAL CHINA

THE MIRACLE OF THE MOUNTAIN

BY MARK GAYN

Chou Min-shan's village, they say only half in jest, is far from anywhere. To reach it, one first takes a milk-run train from Taiyuan, the capital of Shansi province. The train rumbles south through the night, halting at every whistle stop to unload or pick up crowds of sleepy and silent peasants, soldiers, and local officials. The sun just begins to peek over the hills when one arrives at the county seat of Chin Wo. From here, after a brief nap and breakfast at a primitive inn for visiting VIP's, one pursues his journey for another two hours in an aged Russian-built automobile driven by a man who seems to be on first-name terms with every pothole in the dirt road.

I knew the Chinese countryside during the 1930's and the 1940's, and, seeing it now, after such a long time, a strange feeling comes over me. It is as if I have never been away. Everything has remained unchanged. There are the same villages with mud huts and crumbling walls that blend with the landscape. There are the same children and mongrels in the dusty streets; the same families pushing the heavy millstones. Many of the carts I pass on the road have rubber tires, but as often as not they are being drawn by human beings. And in the fields I see teams of four or five men, women, and children pulling plows. The air is filled with loess dust, and it bleaches the greenery, the faces of the peasants, and their invariable blue clothing.

After we climb what must be the hundredth hill, we suddenly come upon Chou's village. Though it is famous across the land, it is little more than a couple of dusty roads joined at right angles like a huge "L." The mud homes are strung along the sides of the "L," and Chou's office, a modest gray-brick building with an inner yard, stands where the roads converge.

I am led into a small room with a gray-white sheet hanging over the doorway to help keep out the dust and the flies. A boy brings a basin of hot water with a small towel floating in it, and I mop my face. The room is bare but for a crude table, a few chairs, and a large portrait of Mao Tse-tung, leader of the Chinese Communist party. Next to the portrait is a neatly brushed slogan, "Enhance the revolutionary tradition and strive for greater successes." There are sounds of commotion outside, and Chou strides in briskly. He gives me a happy, boyish smile, grasps my hand in both of his, and begins to pump my arm.

Chou's village of Nan Liu is at the same time a "production brigade," and it is one of the 25 such brigades that make up the *Nan Fan* (southern Fan) commune. (All that seems to be remembered of Fan is that he was a farmer who died a long, long time ago.)

As in the case of the million or so other villages of China, Nan Liu is a fragment of Mao's revolution in the countryside. Fifteen years ago,

The author:

Mark Gayn, who was born in China, is a distinguished correspondent and head of the Asia bureau of The Toronto Star. He is one of the few Western writers to view today's China firsthand.

YEAR BOOK photos by Marc Ribaud, Magnum

Older Chinese find their way of life put aside, although the new regime gives lip service to the traditions of filial piety.

the communist leaders still talked of giving the land to those who tilled it. But both reason and dogma militated against unproductive small holdings. Thus, in the fall of 1958, after trying out various types of co-operatives, Peking ordered the creation of communes. These took over nearly all the land, most of the dray animals, and what little mechanized equipment there was. Peking then proclaimed the arrival of socialism in the countryside.

But the revolution did more than merely change the ownership of the land. The country's 74,000 communes today are political, economic, and psychological tools of infinite complexity. In a typical village such as Nan Liu, the state and the Communist party join hands in directing people's minds, lives, and production efforts. From here, they govern, provide medical care, teach, exact taxes, indoctrinate, give military training, and instruct in the use of birth control devices. But Peking is 350 long miles to the northeast, far beyond the mountains, and the villagers have learned to pay heed to the whims and orders of the men closer by—the provincial bosses in Taiyuan, which is 200 miles to the north, or to the legion of officials in the county and the commune. In this multilayered hierarchy, Chou is a key figure. It is through him, as head of the production brigade, that the state and the party get the peasants to work hard, produce more, and think right.

All this emerges as hours pass, and Chou continues his recital. Chou was only 22 years old when he was elected chairman of the brigade back in 1958. He still does not look much older. His slim body, his vigorous gestures, his eagerness, and sincerity are those of a young scout-master. Now and then, he impatiently sweeps up his long black hair when it falls on his forehead.

But it soon becomes apparent that this is Chou's public image. Behind it, one discerns the shadow of the inner man. After 10 hours with him, I begin to feel that this slight youth is very much a man, with an astute mind, a measure of ruthlessness, and a great deal of ambition. Chou is the new Organization Man, one of perhaps a few million through whom the party is seeking to change the countryside.

Chou was 11 years old when a band of guerrillas walked up the hill to Nan Liu and set up a communist regime. He attended the local school, joined the communist youth organization, and in 1956 became a full-fledged communist. The party was clearly pleased with the eager youngster. Two years later, when Peking ordered the creation of village communes as part of its "Great Leap Forward," a meeting was called in Nan Liu to discuss—and approve—Peking's order. Someone stood up and proposed that the village become a production brigade in the new commune and that the peasants study Mao Tse-tung's works, for in these they would find the answers to all their problems.

I ask who this someone was. Chou hesitates, and the three or four men in the room shout with delight, "Chou, Chou; it was Chou!" Then they turn to him and say, "*Ni tai chien shu*" ("You're too modest"). Chou blushes and says, "Chairman Mao always tells us that we must guard against arrogance."

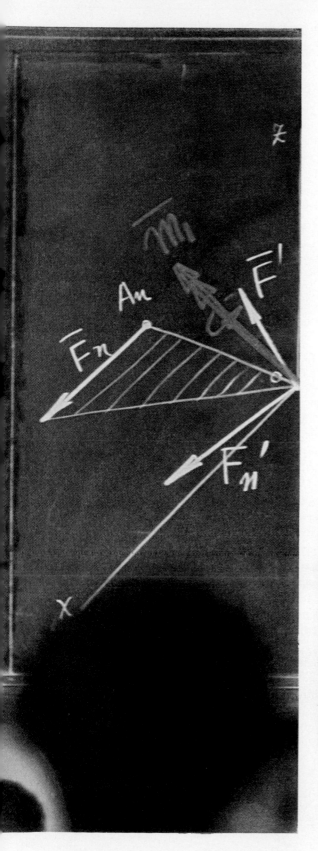

Massive programs to reduce illiteracy
and strengthen educational standards
consume more than 12 per cent of
China's state budget. About four
of every 10 persons in rural China
can now read, according to official
sources. After graduation, students
from the Peking Technological School,
left, may be assigned menial jobs
in the communes, where they are
expected to teach other workers and
also to learn respect for manual labor.

Universal primary school education is still beyond
China's reach, but four out of five children of
primary age are said now to attend school.
Secondary schools, such as the one in Nanking,
below, give high priority to scientific training.

Thirty villages were put into the commune, and among them they organized 25 production brigades. Chou was elected chairman of the brigade in Nan Liu. He has held this post since then, and, as the brigade progressed, his fame spread. In 1960, he was named an "Advanced Worker" for the province. A year later, he became a "Model Worker." In 1964, after the omnipotent *Jen Min Jih Pao* (People's Daily) in Peking twice ran full-page articles on his good works, Chou was named a member of the National People's Congress (parliament) and met Mao Tse-tung. Pilgrims by the thousands began to flock from all corners of China to see how, with the help of Mao's teachings, this youth converted a village that once needed government grain to survive into one that grew enough to feed its people, and still sell a surplus to the state.

As we sit and talk, donkeys bray beyond the wall, and the cook is noisily scrubbing the oversized cast-iron pot set into a clay stove in the yard. Now and then, youngsters bring tea or whisper into Chou's ear. Like him, they look clean, efficient, and ragged. The Chinese countryside wears cotton, and cotton textiles are tightly rationed. The annual ration in Nan Liu is four yards, just about enough for one blue suit. Chou's suit is faded and frayed, and there is a neat patch on the seat of his trousers. His cotton sandals are also in poor repair. But, somehow, I begin to feel that to Chou this is a badge of honor—a visible vow of poverty that he has taken with countless other zealots, and a vow that is expected of the Organization Man.

The sounds of the village at work come to us, and Chou tells me of the revolution in the countryside. It is a story of privation, harsh elements, backbreaking effort, and the infinite variety of methods the party has used to bend the villagers to its will.

"Up to 1958," Chou recalls, "life was very difficult here. Our fields produced little. All we had was 57 head of cattle. Of these, only 40 could be used for work in the fields. Our population kept growing, and we didn't have enough to eat. The government had to give us 70,000 catties of grain (one catty equals 1.33 pounds) to keep us alive.

"From our study of Chairman Mao's works we learned that while China is a great country, it's also a backward one. This is both good and bad. A white sheet of paper can be used for beautiful writing and painting. Thus, we decided to take part in the national revolution by carrying out reform here.

"But we had two problems to start with. Our land was poor and our livestock was meager. These were two mountains on the brigade's shoulders. So our committee studied Chairman Mao's story of Yu Kung and his mountain.* In discussing it, we realized that China has already removed the mountains of imperialism, capitalism, and feudalism. We certainly could remove our own two mountains.

---

*Yu Kung was an old man who, on discovering a mountain obstructing the entrance to his house, decided to dig it away. When the people called him a fool, Yu Kung said, "If I don't remove this mountain, my sons will. If they won't, *their* sons will." And eventually the mountain was removed.

"We didn't know, however, where to begin. So again we studied Chairman Mao's works, and we found our answer. In moving mountains, he said, people turn to God. But who's God? God is the people themselves. So we decided to call on all our people—we had 680 of them then—to move our mountains. We held a general meeting and we said, 'We must work for three to five years to convert our mountains into fertile fields.' "

At this point, I find myself wondering whether there is any connection between Chou's figurative reference to mountains and the very real mountain I already know is next to Nan Liu. Chou quickly helps me out by explaining just what did take place in Nan Liu.

"In the winter of 1958," he recalls, "we marched to the mountain outside our village. The whole area at the time was swarming with wolves. They had attacked nine persons in the preceding five years. Nonetheless, we moved into their caves, and the beasts disappeared. The mountain was badly eroded by rain. We terraced it, and shaped it so that the rain water would stay in the fields, instead of running off. The earth was frozen three feet deep, but we worked on."

As Chou tells his story, his voice rises, and his gestures become more dramatic. The work, he says, went on for six winters, through 1963. The snow fell; the cold was fierce. But Chou was always there to urge the men and women on. He would say to them, "When our people fought the reactionaries, they paid no heed to rain, storm, and snow. Why should we act differently in this revolution?" Or he would cry, "The weather is cold, but our hearts are warm. The earth is hard, but our will is harder."

Chou was the organizer, the driver, the cheerleader, the slogan-maker, the spinner of tales. From a communist song, he borrowed a phrase which he told me had become a village saying: "There are many lovely and precious things, but the loveliest and the most precious are our government and Chairman Mao." Or, borrowing from another song, he would say, "Our parents took good care of us, but no one is doing as much for us as the party and Chairman Mao." In the end, he made many peasants feel that Chairman Mao had no greater preoccupations than the affairs of Nan Liu, and that the villagers simply had to do well or they would be betraying Mao's confidence.

In his unceasing efforts, Chou was aided by the other 25 communists in the village that by now had some 800 people. One of the 25 was a 68-year-old man, to whom revolution brought literacy. Now he was able to read newspapers, study Chairman Mao's essays, and even write a poem which he delivered at the drop of a hat:

> At night I study Chairman Mao's works
> And keep them in the recesses of my heart.
> My debt to Chairman Mao is so great
> I shall never be able to repay it.

Nan Liu suffered repeated calamities. Despite the careful terracing, heavy rains periodically washed away parts of the mountain, so that it

China's 74,000 communes differ in size and affluence. This one near Peking is one of the best. Its 55,000 persons live in 110 villages and farm 22,000 acres. Average income is about $11 per month. Building at right is the machine shop. Commune boasts a total of 64 tractors.

had to be reterraced. There were devastating droughts. The worst began in 1959 and lasted through the spring and early summer of 1960. When no rain came by May 13—the traditional rain deadline in China's country lore—the old men shook their heads and called it a disaster. The villagers were summoned to a meeting, and Chou recalled Chairman Mao's statement on "learning from the experience of the elders." An oldster was consulted. He said there might be water in a patch of grassland a mile or two away. (Why the older peasants remained silent until that point was not explained.) Teams of peasants dug for three days and nights, and 30 feet down they found enough water for drinking and irrigation. One of the communists in the brigade won some renown by carrying four buckets of water suspended from his shoulder pole, instead of the usual two buckets. "The slogan we adopted," Chou now recalls, "was that each man must sow 1,000 seeds of corn, and then make sure they were irrigated." The rains broke the drought on the 257th day, in July. Despite the drought, the brigade, under Chou's leadership, was able to produce a surplus of grain.

There was also a memorable insect invasion that threatened to destroy the cotton crop. To meet this danger, the village sent its 250 youngsters into the fields. They stayed there for seven days and nights, examining each leaf of each plant. They did not return until they had liquidated 70,000 bugs.

In the face of all such trials, Chou says, there has been a steady improvement in the yield of the reluctant earth. The production of wheat per *mou* (one-sixth of an acre) has gone up 60 per cent. The output of cotton has risen 24 per cent. The livestock—cows, oxen, donkeys—has multiplied almost fourfold to 210 head. ("This," Chou notes, "has given us more manure for fertilizer and more animals for field work.")

The income of the peasants has also risen, Chou tells me. In a year, an average adult toiled 300 workdays, for each of which he was paid the equivalent in cash or grain of 60 cents in American money. (Having visited other communes in China, I suspect that Chou exaggerates. The annual income of each working adult in Nan Liu is probably much closer to $100 a year than to $180.) This compares with the $250 to $300 earned by the average factory worker, who, however, has no pork or cabbage of his own to help enrich his daily menu.

With all the added money in their pockets, Chou contends, the peasants have gone on a shopping spree. Over a period of "a few years," they have bought 75 bicycles and 83 sets of farm tools (hoes, rakes, and such) for private use. The brigade's funds have also gone up, enabling it to buy a small power plant to operate the two new milling machines, eight small rubber-tired carriages for moving anything from potatoes to an ailing grandmother, and, inevitably, loudspeakers. In Nan Liu, as in most villages of China, loudspeakers are as much a part of the landscape as the dust. A person standing in a field a mile or two from the village can still be reached by the sound of a militant song, news broadcasts, Chairman Mao's sayings read by a schoolgirl, or Chou's exhortations.

After lunch, while Chou is talking to the latest busload of Chinese visitors, I leave his office and wander across the road to the village store. The sun is beating down on the dry earth, and the thick dust lies unstirred except when a cart, drawn by three mules, goes by with a heavy load. The cart stops, and three men jump off to pass the time of day with the few villagers in sight. Nearby, despite the heat, a group of young men in trousers and undershirts are tossing a ball.

The store is small, dark, and relatively well-stocked. It has rationed

Tools for commune peasants are made in the tool and die shop, which also serves as a classroom in which peasants are exposed to industrial work.

cotton socks, face cream for the village lovelies, and the red tin dragon images that parents put around the necks of newborn sons to bring them good luck. The store offers rationed cooking oil and two sewing machines, the latter selling at $65 each. (Chou says 30 of these were sold in the preceding two years.) Two girls are pricing a length of flowered cotton. The material for a jacket and trousers would cost them the equivalent of 15 workdays, and they look undecided.

As I come out, I see two youngsters writing on a blackboard by the roadside. What they are writing is a news item announcing that another four planes of the American aggressors have been shot down by the patriotic forces in Laos (regarded in China as an important battleground). Next to the blackboard, two squatting men, looking wholly unconcerned, are reading three-day-old copies of the provincial newspaper. For the first time, I notice that an outside wall of Chou's office is covered with a large mural. It shows young people with eager faces following an older peasant. The inscription says, "Learn from the older peasants." In this village, run by such a young man, there is a touch of irony in the mural.

And then I suddenly realize that although the village looks much as it must have 30 years, or perhaps even a century, ago, it has really changed to a remarkable degree. The peasants still know no condition but poverty. They still live in mud huts and still use primitive tools. The older ones among them, at least, still worship their ancestors. But the bonds that once held the family together are under a powerful strain, and the old virtues and values are being replaced.

Filial piety is still strong, but the young are taught that devotion to the state, the party, and to Chairman Mao is an even greater virtue. Go-betweens still help to arrange marriages, but, more frequently, the youths find their own mates. This is definitely the era of the young, who are impatient to wreck and to rebuild, rather than of the aged, who want to hold on to the accustomed ways. The old social structure, topped by the landlord, the usurer, and the old headman, is gone. Instead, there has come the new breed of communist Organization Men, young, able, and hard-driving. They have seemingly taken monastic vows, use Chairman Mao's works the way the old-time revivalists used the Bible to inspire and to silence all doubt, and they are dedicated to carrying out Peking's policies.

Chou's mission is twofold—to increase production and to change men's souls. His prime tools are political. The party's Central Committee in Peking organizes vast campaigns that sweep across the land like wildfire. In no time at all, they reach Nan Liu. When, for instance, Peking ordered a campaign of support for "the democratic people of Vietnam," Chou had the villagers march through the dust carrying red banners and posters. There was fiery anti-American oratory, and children put on a dance in which they chased a frightened President Lyndon B. Johnson.

Politics in Nan Liu is a serious matter. It is pursued by the Communist party branch, by the communist youth organization, by something called the Poor and Lower-Middle Class Peasants' Association, by the production brigade's propaganda section, and by the women's federation. When the peasants take a break in the fields, they may have to listen to a party agitator, or to a reading of excerpts from Chairman Mao's works. When they return home, they may be visited by a party worker or summoned to a lecture or a public meeting. Chou recalls a recent meeting at which a peasant, taking his cue from one of Chairman Mao's essays, recited his own poem:

> We're now in Nan Liu village
> But our eyes are on the Tien An Men.*
> We toil in the fields,
> But our minds think of all the world.

A meeting that starts with poetry may easily turn to condemning the laggards or to exposing internal enemies. I have visited communes elsewhere in China in which as many as 6 per cent of all the adults were described as being hostile to the system. Nan Liu is fortunate. It has only two former landlords whom Chou describes as enemies, and they are being given huge, daily, soul-saving doses of indoctrination.

As with all other villages and towns in the land, Nan Liu also has its militia detachment. It includes nearly all of the able-bodied men and women in the village. With their rifles or Tommy guns, they drill after work in the fields, lying in ambush behind a hillock, or storming the unseen imperialist foe. The task of the militia, Chou explains, is to resist aggression from without and to be vigilant against enemies at home.

Not far from Chou's office stands the village school. Here, the youngsters begin their indoctrination at an early age. At five, they break into a merry song such as this:

> There is in Peking a golden mountain,
> And on it there is a golden sun,
> And that sun is Chairman Mao.

At the age of seven, their dancing instructor is likely to put them through the motions of bayoneting the "American bandit aggressors in Vietnam." The little books they read usually carry colored pictures of soldiers and airplanes, or boys with guns. They extol revolutionary gore and heroes. In nonpolitical subjects, schooling is severely practical. Indeed, under a new reform, the pupils may be spending half their time in the next few years in the classroom and the other half in the fields or cow barns. This is expected to make them better workers and better citizens. Some people grumble that this would also make the children "half-students." Chou scoffs at such criticism.

The sun is beginning to set, and deep shadows fall on Nan Liu when Chou suggests that we see his mountain. We drive up the dirt road that has sunk so deep into the soft loess that one is sometimes below the level of the fields. The road is lined with young trees, and Chou says, "Someday we shall cut these down and build new homes with the

---

*Peking's Gate of Heavenly Calm, from which Mao Tse-tung customarily reviews parades on national holidays.

Despite its effort to catch up with the 20th century, China still has large areas little changed from former times. These Yunnan province women are hoeing in a rice paddy.

A peasant family is permitted a small vegetable garden, perhaps 30 x 50 feet in size, which provides much of its food and profit. The government abolished these plots in the late 1950's, causing a food crisis in the country. Later they were returned. This family plot is in a commune near Shanghai.

Loess soil of north China is fertile, but quickly erodes in wind and rain. Terraces, therefore, are essential, even in wheat fields such as these in Shensi province.

lumber." Not far from the top of the mountain, we turn off the road and suddenly I see the miracle that Chou and the villagers have performed. What had been a bare, rain-scarred mountain, similar to those I view across the valley, has now become a 420-acre field—a succession of terraces of grain and cotton. The wind runs through the field of wheat, ruffles the top-heavy stalks, and keeps on descending until it raises a whirlpool of dust in the village below. Each terrace is perhaps 60 feet wide, and is slanted inward toward the face of the mountain to retain the moisture. The back wall of each terrace is freshly trimmed.

I have seen such terraces from Korea to Indonesia. But this is still an impressive sight, and one suddenly realizes why Peking honors this young man and why pilgrims come to see what he has done. Yet, one is also startled by the primitiveness of this tiny fragment of the new China. Just below me, on a terrace chosen for cotton planting, perhaps a score of men, women, and children are at work, with only two horses to help them. The seeder, the harrow, all the tools are crude and ancient. Some are being dragged by the villagers. Chou's village may be the hope of Peking, but it must also be Peking's despair, for, despite the miracle it has accomplished, this village is still barely emerging from the dark ages of land tilling.

We come down the mountain, and I see some of the small plots— each about 30 x 50 feet—the peasants can call their own. Here, they raise the vegetables needed to supplement whatever grain is allotted to them by the brigade for their "workdays." Here, too, they grow the feed for their animals and fowl. No peasant can own a cow or a mule; these animals belong to the brigade. But he can have two or three pigs to sell to the commune or for his own table (a luxury few can afford).

During the late 1950's, communist zealots abolished the private plots, and the result was suffering. The government in Peking soon ended that practice, as it also ended occasional efforts to house all the peasants in barracks.

Discontent, however, persists. Many peasants still remember the acre or two they received soon after the communist takeover, only to have them confiscated, first for the so-called "co-ops" and then for the communes. Still more peasants object to having commune officers from another village decide what is to be done with the grain and cotton grown in Nan Liu, and how much each peasant is to get as his share. Whether the field is his or not, the peasant feels that the harvest he helped to grow belongs to him, and he wants to see it and feel it and have a say in its division. This is a source of sharp friction between the peasant on one hand and Peking (and Chou) on the other hand. The villagers, finally, feel the new party overseers are sometimes getting too much of their grain for too little work. They also resent the young upstarts who tell the older men what to do, and how to do it. The discontent presents no threat to Peking, but it is there.

Toronto Star photo by Mark Gayn

Chou Min-shan is typical of the new Organization Man in Red China. He is young, energetic, and dedicated to the communist program.

The people of Nan Liu live in acute poverty, but they are not starving. Even in the cruelest years from 1959 to 1962, there was enough food to sustain life, and it was divided equitably. By contrast, the old villagers remember that in a famine in the 1920's, ten people died of hunger in Nan Liu.

The fuller rice bowl is not the only symbol of advance, however. The usurers are gone, and the officials, such as Chou, are honest. The school gives a modicum of learning, and illiteracy among the older people is rapidly declining. The public health system has virtually ended epidemics. I see no children with trachoma or running sores, and no oldsters begging for a few coppers. But Nan Liu is still desperately short of fertilizer, and it woefully lacks modern equipment. (The entire commune, with its 30 villages, owns only four tractors.)

There are still no trained agronomists attached to Chou's brigade, and only now and then will one visit Nan Liu to offer hasty counsel. An observer looks at this famous village and realizes that progress in the Chinese countryside is spotty and heartbreakingly slow. It must be counted not in years, nor even in decades, but in generations. Chou's grandsons will be living in the 21st century when Nan Liu may still be approaching the 20th century. The meaning of Nan Liu for China is plain. No modern industry can be built atop a backward countryside without creating harsh problems for tomorrow. China's atomic plants and new industries to the contrary, the country's advance must continue to be held back by its Nan Liu's.

We drive down to the village and leave the car. On the dusty road, we meet peasants returning from work or going on their errands. No one smiles at Chou. No one greets him. Can it be that the villagers who appreciate the miracle on the mountain have no love for this very hard, young miracle man?

See also Section Three, ASIA; CHINA.

INSIDE RURAL INDIA

THE SILENT STRUGGLE

BY KEKI R. BHOTE

Among the 550,000 villages of India, two of the most typical are known as Alande and Utroli. These dusty hamlets nestle in the foothills of the Western Ghats in the county of Bhor, more than 100 miles by road southeast of Bombay. Here, in the dim past, was the proud home of Sivaji, the "Mountain Rat King," who led his rugged Mahratta warriors down from their mountain hideouts to turn back the ancient Mogul hordes.

The glories of Sivaji still raise a flicker of pride in the people of Alande and Utroli. But until recently little else—surely nothing subsequent to Sivaji's 17th century accomplishments—stirred the villagers from their usual lethargy and their blind repetitions that for hundreds of years made yesterday like today, and today like tomorrow. Only a few years ago, the two villages were just a collection of mud huts plastered with cow dung. They had no roads, no wells, no schools, no self-government.

Lalita Mhasavade, a village level worker in India's Community Development program, teaches a group of women in Utroli how to read and write.

The villagers—trampled for centuries by local maharajas, victimized by the excesses of the caste system, immobilized by a rigid family structure—slumbered on in medieval oblivion. Indeed, when independence dawned on India in 1947, Alande and Utroli were scarcely aware that the sun had begun to rise.

Since then, however, a new spirit has swept these villages. Under the guidance of the national government in New Delhi, Alande and Utroli are attempting to catch up with the 20th century. If this is a race for survival against the Red giant to the North of India—and perhaps it is—then China is the hare and India, plodding, flexible, undogmatic, is the tortoise. The outcome of this race will be felt around the world.

India is the second most populous nation on earth. Of its 490,000,000 people (about one out of every seven persons in the world), more than 360,000,000 live in farming villages much like Alande and Utroli. Seven of every 10 workers are engaged in agriculture, and account for about half the national income. Even so, India today cannot feed itself because its crop yields per acre are among the lowest in the world. Because of his primitive methods, the Indian farmer grows only one-fourth as much rice per acre as a Japanese farmer; one-fifth as much cotton as an Egyptian.

India's leaders, heirs to the nonviolent traditions of Mohandas K. Gandhi, believe that progress in their country will be permanent only if it reaches the grass roots of their society, the farmer.

India failed in its first attempt after independence to increase agricultural production. The Grow More Food Campaign, as that initial program was called, was little more than a national campaign of exhortation. A few placards appeared in a few villages. There were some programs to demonstrate modern farming techniques. But the farmers did not respond. By 1951, the program was called off.

After India's first general elections in 1952, the government decided

The author:

Keki R. Bhote, who is now a citizen of the United States, is a foreign correspondent for Jame-Jamshed, a leading newspaper in Bombay, and is a widely known lecturer and author. He has made four world tours, interviewing leaders in Asia and Europe.

YEAR BOOK photos by Baldev, Pix

Under a pipal tree in the village of Alande, lower right, G. B. Bandal presides at a meeting of the village council.

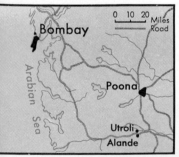

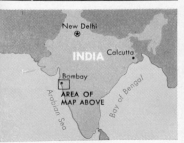

on a new course. It was based on the belief that, given the proper initial help and encouragement, India's villagers had sufficient individual initiative to become the main architects of their own progress. This is the essence of India's new village Community Development program. Community Development, in some form, now reaches most villages.

Because so much of the future of Asia is at stake in this program, I recently revisited my homeland for a firsthand look at how it was proceeding. Even by jet, India is a long way from the United States. When I got behind the wheel of my jeep in Bombay and headed into the hills of the Mountain Rat King, it seemed that the distance surely must be measured not only in miles, but in years as well. I wondered if I might not be received something like a Connecticut Yankee in King Arthur's Court.

It was my hope that I could slip casually into the village, meet the key people, mingle with the villagers, and slip away again. I wanted to escape government handouts, official receptions, and the usual red carpet treatment for visitors from abroad. I wanted a realistic view of village progress, without the rose-tinted glasses of the Ministry of Community Development. My scheme was working out well until my good friend and colleague, photographer Baldev, unslung his camera. People everywhere like to have their pictures taken, and rural Indian villagers are no exception. Baldev became the Pied Piper of Alande and Utroli, and a crowd of delighted children followed him throughout our visit. Notwithstanding, we saw rural India as few outsiders could have hoped to see it.

To understand the Community Development program, one must know a little about its general plan of organization and administration. The basic unit is the block, an area roughly equivalent to a U.S. county. Each block contains about 100 villages and is administered by the Block Development Officer (BDO).

Under the BDO is a team of specialists in agriculture, public health, village industries, and women's programs. The key man on the BDO's staff—indeed the cornerstone of the entire Community Development program—is the village level worker (VLW, or *gram sevak*). Each VLW serves an average of about 10 villages. The VLW is selected from among the villagers and is then trained for two years at one of four national Community Development training centers. He maintains day-to-day contact with the villagers, calling in the specialists when necessary. He must win the confidence and respect of the people. He, along with a *gram sevika* (a woman village level worker), who concentrates on the welfare of the women and children, is the instrument for change.

The male VLW for Alande and Utroli is V. L. Shrotri, a lean, shy man about 30 years old. When I set out to find Shrotri, I soon learned that he shied away from publicity and would slip into crowds whenever I got near him. After considerable persistence, however, I caught up with him as he was standing in a field with two bullocks in the background, discussing rice cultivation with three farmers.

To outward appearances, Shrotri seemed incapable of shouldering

S. K. Dey, minister for Community Development, was graduated from the University of Chicago. Dey left industry to work for the government.

C. S. Subramaniam holds the important post of minister for food and agriculture in the Shastri cabinet. He was born in the same south Indian town, Coimbatore, as was the author.

his responsibilities. A thin man, with bushy black hair and a scar on one cheek, he was a *Matric fail*, a polite term for a high school drop-out. He had had only four months of training for his job, instead of the prescribed two years. *Karma* (the wheel of destiny) had not smiled upon him. With a salary of just $22 a month, he had to support a wife and four children. He traveled on a bicycle between three villages assigned to him, except when he could hitch a ride on a jeep. These hardships seemed to leave him with little ambition to move to a higher position.

Despite his personal problems, Shrotri has helped to change the face of Alande and Utroli. Since he took over his job in 1962, the villages' approach road, once just a cow path, has become a *pucca* (firm road) that can handle jeeps, or even the Chryslers of visiting dignitaries. The road is the villagers' window to the outside world. They built it after they had voted in their own village council to volunteer their own labor. The community well, the council building, and the schoolhouse were built in the same way. The villagers have also erected poles for electricity. Ironically, the poles stand naked today, pointed reminders to visiting government officials to hurry up with electricity from neighboring Phatgar Dam. The school, which once contained only four grades, now has seven. Instead of almost total adult illiteracy, Alande and Utroli now have 225 enthusiastic literates out of an adult population of about 3,000. They are graduates of adult classes started by Shrotri and his female VLW.

But it is in agriculture that these villages are writing their best chapter. With Shrotri's help, the farmers are learning the benefits of fertilizers, hybrid seed, and water conservation. They can now obtain supplies and farm implements at their tiny service cooperative. The

Demonstration plots show how greatly rice yield can be increased by the use of hybrid seed and chemical fertilizer. Plot in foreground was planted in the traditional manner.

Village Level Worker V. L. Shrotri explains to farmers the superior yields obtained from hybrid rice seed containing both Indian and Japanese strains. Pure Indian seed will not stand up to chemical fertilizers and heavy irrigation.

co-op also furnishes them with credit at 8 per cent interest, a lot less than the 40 per cent formerly charged by the moneylenders. These changes have brought a 50 per cent increase in rice yield in Alande and Utroli. Food shortages plague India's big cities, but until the drought of 1965, there was no longer a food problem here.

How has the seemingly mediocre Shrotri managed this change? His success can be partly explained by the sheer need for his services. But much credit is due Shrotri himself. He is of the soil. His approach is low-key; his tools are patience and persuasion. Gradually, Shrotri convinced the skeptics that he knew how to grow more rice per acre than they did. Then the program took hold.

I first met Lalita Mhasavade, Shrotri's female counterpart, in Alande's wooden community building. Lalita's dark complexion set off the flashing whiteness of her teeth and sparkling eyes. Her white sari swayed gently as she led a dozen young girls in a primitive Indian ballet. As I watched the dancers' expressive hands and bodies, and saw the lights in their eyes, I knew that this dance—as most primitive Indian ballets—was intended to convey a message. And the message, I soon learned, was intended for me: "The village has a water shortage and the govern-

Two Peace Corpsmen were assigned to Bhor county. Here, Corpsman Phil Vroman visits a poultry farm he set up in Utroli village.

137

A student recites her lesson in a private school run by the wife of a well-to-do Bhor farmer. Students work in her home with materials sent by the United Nations Children's Fund. Their tuition is only 63 cents a month.

Girls picking peas in a field after their lessons in the classroom learn to perform tasks that are necessary to everyday village life. Their training is based on Gandhi's belief that schooling should not be solely theoretical.

ment must do something about it." Lalita's dance came through loud and clear, but she had made one miscalculation. She thought I was a a visiting government official, and she had devised her dance to nudge me into doing something about the water shortage.

I could scarcely have had a better introduction to Lalita, the dynamic, outgoing girl who is the gram sevika for the villages of Alande and Utroli. No shy, retiring drop-out was this girl. She had graduated from high school, spent two years taking the full Community Development training course, and was now infusing the women of the six villages for which she has responsibility with enthusiasm and faith in the Community Development program.

As I talked with Lalita, other women crowded about us, eager to tell their own story about special village projects. What a contrast this was to my memory of Indian village women, who habitually drew their saris across their face to avoid the gaze of a male stranger! The loss of shyness, Lalita explained, was perhaps the women's first important step toward the 20th century.

"They have come out of their homes to become educated, to form societies, and even to become members of the village council," Lalita said. "They run their own preschool activities for children and they attend tailoring classes and handicraft sessions. The women weave cloth and make paper dolls that they soon will begin to sell in city markets."

Lalita thinks her greatest success has been in setting up a rural radio forum in an area where there is only one radio to a village. The women who attend the forum listen to broadcasts together and then discuss the topics among themselves. They also meet with officials of All India Radio to plan future programs on subjects close to their own needs.

A usurious local moneylender, a breed that is disappearing, studies his books. The government instituted co-ops to end their power. Some villagers are in debt to moneylenders all their lives.

One of the most talked about subjects at these meetings is birth control. The city of Buffalo, N.Y., is a long way from Alande and Utroli, but urban Buffalo and rural India are linked by a most important recent development. It is the invention only five years ago by Dr. Jack Lippes of Buffalo of a simple, inexpensive, and reliable birth control device, called the Lippes Loop. The loop is an inexpensive twist of plastic which a physician can easily insert into a woman's uterus. It will remain in place for years but can be removed anytime. Since India's population has a net increase of 12,000,000 people a year, Indian leaders are speaking of the loop as the medical miracle of the century. (In a sense, it is a miracle, since doctors are not yet sure just how it prevents conception.)

In Alande and Utroli, I talked about the loop with Usha Deshpande, a trim, white-saried field-worker of the public health department. She is responsible for covering 40 of the surrounding villages under the auspices of Community Development.

"Until the Lippes Loop," Usha confessed, "our efforts at birth control got nowhere. In my territory, 154 women have now been fitted with the loop. Alande has none yet, and Utroli has only four. But these figures are misleading. When our doctor came here for the first time, most of the women were busy with the harvest. For the doctor's next

World Diet

*Calories Per Person
Per Day*

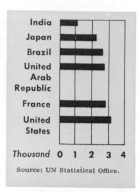

	Thousand 0	1	2	3	4
India					
Japan					
Brazil					
United Arab Republic					
France					
United States					

Source: UN Statistical Office.

Symbolic of India's poverty is this woman cooking chapatties, a flat, unleavened bread, which she and her family will eat with a vegetable stew as their big meal of the day.

visit, we already have signed up 50 women in Utroli and 155 in all of Bhor county, though still none in Alande."

One problem will remain, however. Indian women have no religious taboos against birth control, but they will not practice it until they have had two sons. As a father of five girls told me somewhat ruefully: "I have yet to begin."

In addition to implementing birth control, India's Community Development program is designed to attack another great problem of community life: the caste system. K. N. Kadam, Community Development's social welfare officer for Bhor county, is a veteran of many conflicts between caste Hindus and the untouchables, of whom there are more than 60,000,000 in India.

"We have a three-point program for the so-called untouchables in Bhor," he explained. "We grant them economic subsidies for wells, houses, farm implements, and seeds, as well as interest-free loans up to $100 without security. As has been the practice throughout India since 1955, we give them free scholarships to schools in the towns and cities. Surprisingly, about 100,000 untouchables throughout the country have taken advantage of this opportunity. It is in our social uplift program that we try hardest and succeed least. Untouchables and caste Hindus, you see, have nothing in common culturally. In social matters, we cannot force the pace."

Usha Deshpande, a public health worker in the Community Development program, holds the Lippes Loop as she explains aspects of birth control to women of Alande and Utroli. She is paving the way for the doctor's visit.

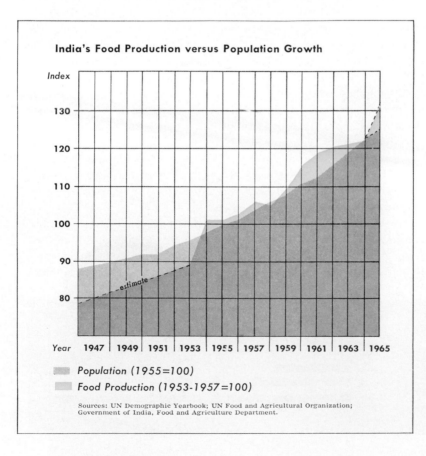

India's Food Production versus Population Growth

Index

130

120

110

100

90

estimate

80

Year 1947 1949 1951 1953 1955 1957 1959 1961 1963 1965

Population (1955=100)

Food Production (1953-1957=100)

Sources: UN Demographic Yearbook; UN Food and Agricultural Organization; Government of India, Food and Agriculture Department.

Despite the drought of 1965, India appears, in the long run, to be winning the grim struggle between a soaring population and hunger. Between 1947 and 1965, population increased from 345,000,000 to 490,000,000, but food output was at last keeping pace.

I asked if caste Hindus and untouchables ever exchange visits. "Yes," he said, "on formal occasions, such as meetings, fairs, and marriages." Then he added: "Also at vote-getting time." The power that grows out of the ballot box may yet prove to be the most potent weapon the untouchables have in their struggle for first-class citizenship.

The most notable political achievement of the villagers of Alande and Utroli is *panchayati raj* (village self-government). In Alande, G. B. Bandal, president of the village council, explained its origin. "In 1959," he said, "Jawaharlal Nehru, India's late Prime Minister, became convinced that village India would lie in the sleep of centuries unless real political power was put in its hands. And so panchayati raj was born. Under this system, we villagers run our own local affairs, elect our own representatives, and spend funds allocated to us as we see fit."

Panchayati raj is a three-tiered democratic system. At the village level is the *gram panchayat* (village council), elected by members of the village. Above this, at the block, or county, level, is the *panchayat samiti*, consisting largely of village council presidents. At the district level is the *zila parishad*, composed of panchayat samiti presidents and members who represent the district in the national parliament and the state legislature. The only government employees in this political structure are the village level workers, the block development officers, and their superior at the district level, the Special Development Officer.

Bandal took me to a village council meeting. He made a rambling speech about the shortage of drinking water, grew indignant about the shortage of monies received from the panchayat samiti, threw the Kashmir crisis in for good measure, and then opened the meeting for discussion. I watched the council members in their turbans, sitting expressionless as they listened to Bandal. One by one, they got up to speak. They began slowly, but soon warmed to the point they wished to make. There were no tidy solutions to the shortages Bandal had spoken of, but the villagers were talking in democratic fashion. Their remarks made me recall an old saying of Chester Bowles, U.S. ambassador to India: "The Indian villager may be illiterate but because of the richness of his traditions, he is far from uneducated."

To broaden my sampling of rural India, I traveled across the subcontinent on planes that were seldom on time, on railways so crowded I sometimes had to enter the coaches through the windows, in autos that frequently broke down, in jouncing jeeps, and on a pair of tired

Farm Productivity

Productivity of Farm Labor Measured by Number of Pounds of Grain Produced by Each Farmworker Annually

Source: UN Food and Agricultural Organization. Figures are latest available for each country.

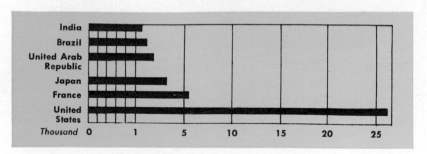

"May you drink of the water of 10 wells!" This was an old Indian saying which meant, "May you be a well-traveled man." That saying indicates how scarce wells were two decades ago. Now every village has water, as does Utroli.

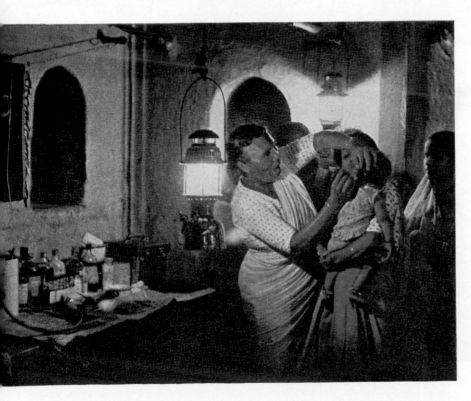

The dai (midwife), is the nearest thing to a doctor in much of rural India. Many are being given modern training by the World Health Organization. Here, the dai examines a child in Utroli.

feet. The heat was oppressive; the monsoons played cat and mouse with schedules; the flies usually beat me to the food in the villages; and the village water was undrinkable. But despite these inconveniences, it was an exhilarating experience.

I traveled to the villages of Tudyalur in south India and Butana in north India. I interviewed cabinet ministers in the government of Prime Minister Lal Bahadur Shastri, as well as university professors, economists, and U.S. aid officials. Most revealing of all was a visit to the Nilokheri National Community Development Training Center, where I interviewed block development, agricultural extension, and social education officers. Their experience, insight, and criticism based on intimate contact with several hundred villages gave me a broader base for some final conclusions on the present state of India's silent struggle. It is these conclusions—tentative, incomplete, and perhaps fallible—which I shall attempt to summarize.

India is so big, so complex, so exciting, and so frustrating that an observer might justifiably draw almost any conclusion he wants from what he sees. He can, for example, draw dire conclusions from the food crisis that developed late in 1965. The monsoon, which customarily drenches the country during the summer, failed to materialize. Rainfall was from 30 to 40 percent below normal. This fact, plus hoarding, confronted India with its worst food shortage since the country won its independence in 1947. An observer can point to the prolonged debates within the government over the use of fertilizers, a delay that has left Indian fields gasping for growth-producing chemicals. He can look at these things and conclude that bungling India will never move ahead.

The government's plan to upgrade rural India entails, in part, bringing water, electricity, and fertilizer to the farms. Here, laborers and modern cranes work to build Nagarjuna Sagar Dam in the state of Andhra Pradesh.

Or, conversely, he can go out on the farms as I did and see how India is beginning to evaluate programs and policies in terms of results. The government now recognizes that water, fertilizer, and electricity are three essentials that it must provide to the villager if he is going to play his part in the nation's development. It has begun to construct dams and irrigation canals. In Madras state, 85 per cent of the farms have been supplied with water and electricity, but this is admittedly the exception. Nonetheless, if India can step-up its output of livestock, poultry, and fish, and increase its storage facilities and marketing outlets, it should be able to feed itself by 1972.

Coupled with the nation's drive to increase its food production, is the program to reduce its soaring birth rate. The goal is to reduce births from 20,000,000 to 13,000,000 per year. The Lippes Loop is the breakthrough that India has been waiting for. The government hopes to give away 5,000,000 loops each year.

Community Development is an educational enterprise in the broad sense, but in the actual matter of schooling, criticism centers about the educational standards. The educational system is still patterned after the British model, geared to turning out a nation of clerks. It does not provide the basic farm education visualized by Gandhi. The present-day village teacher, moreover, lacks the community respect enjoyed by the *guru* (religious teacher) of old. Ceaseless squabbles continue among the proponents of regional languages versus the proponents of Hindi, and those who would retain English as the national language. This foments national disunity, and lowers educational standards.

The tyranny of the caste system, as mentioned previously, still reigns

A symbol of progress in a highly technical field is the atomic power plant in suburban Trombay, which supplies electric power for much of urban Bombay. But the principal fuel throughout India is still dried cakes of cow dung.

in most villages, but there are signs of progress. The story of the two wells is typical. In one village, the caste Hindus refused to share water from a newly constructed well with the untouchables. The latter were forced to dig a well of their own, but the caste Hindus lent their bullocks and moral support. Shocking? Of course. But 10 years ago, the untouchables would not have dared to think of digging a well of their own, nor would the caste Hindus have aided them. The untouchables would have had to beg for water. The evils of the caste system will disappear only as more and more untouchables get off the land to seek the anonymity of the big cities, or as their improved educational and economic status wins the respect of the skeptical caste Hindu, with the nudging of the ballot box.

The political system of grass-roots democracy appears to be developing. The criticism most often voiced against it is that the members of the village councils are conscious of their rights, but not of their responsibilities. Yet, as recently as 1959, they were conscious of neither.

It was hoped that the development of farm cooperatives would help to teach individualistic farmers to work together for mutual benefit, but progress has not been encouraging. This is because the management of the cooperatives is still largely in the hands of the government, and because laws sharply limit their size.

In the government apparatus, the village level worker—the pivot of Community Development—is frequently underqualified and overworked. His boss, the block development officer, often retains the revenue official's patronizing attitude. There appears to be less change in the lower and middle echelons of government than in the people the government is attempting to change. Even worse, many middle level government functionaries display an abject servility to higher authority that muzzles the dialogue of progress. But change is occurring at last in village India, and the most important change is in the villager himself. S. K. Dey, minister for Community Development, told me: "Fifty years ago in the village where I grew up, the sight of a government official would cause the villagers to flee. Today they come into my office; they argue; they demand; they are not afraid."

The Indian peasant—for centuries asleep, mute, fatalistic—has awakened. The distant government which he once viewed as an overpowering tax collector is now his partner. It is this change that is the most promising part of India's development. Throughout hundreds of thousands of its villages, the silent struggle to become a part of the 20th century goes on, unknown to the outside world, unknown even to a large number of India's city dwellers. Few countries have started with less, or attempted more. Despite all the problems and frustrations, the nation's Community Development program is the greatest group dynamic laboratory in the world. In the words of the British historian Arnold J. Toynbee, if it proves successful, "next to the American revolution, India's Community Development will be mankind's greatest achievement."

See also Section Three, ASIA; INDIA.

How Far Will We Go In Space?

BY ISAAC ASIMOV

**From the Facts and Capabilities
Now at Hand, a Noted Science
Writer Projects the Future
Accomplishments and
Limits of Space Exploration**

In 1965, man for the first time "walked in space."
Moreover, he remained in orbit longer than he ever
had before.

In 1965, we could look at our television screens
and watch (live!) close-up pictures of the moon
sent back to us by Ranger IX.

In 1965, after a journey of 134,000,000 miles,
Mariner IV flew past Mars, and from a distance of
6,000 miles sent back 22 photographs of the
planet's surface.

Yet 10 years before that, not a single object had
been placed in orbit about the earth. The Space

The author:
Isaac Asimov is
associate professor
of biochemistry
at Boston University
School of Medicine.
He has written
many articles and
books on science,
among them *The
New Intelligent
Man's Guide to
Science.* Dr. Asimov
has been a member
of THE YEAR BOOK
board of editors, and
with this edition,
he becomes a
contributing editor.

Age had not begun and very few people, except scientists and science-fiction writers, even dreamed it was about to begin.

What lies ahead of us now? If mankind can advance so far in space in less than 10 years, where will he go in the next 10 years? In 20? In a century? Is there anything we *cannot* do in space by 2100, for instance?

It is difficult to predict the future. Yet, our success in 1965 was so heady that we should, for the sake of our own perspective, look at the practical limits of our explorations into space. We should do this hard-headedly, basing our judgment on facts at hand, capabilities we have, and solutions we can reasonably predict.

We can begin by asking where we stand on the matter of unmanned exploration of space. There, the greatest barrier was overcome in 1959, when, for the first time, a rocket was hurled upward by man at a speed of more than seven miles a second. At such speed, a rocket is not confined by gravity to an orbit about the earth. It "escapes," and goes into orbit about the sun. The faster a rocket is hurled, the larger is its orbit about the sun. If it is made to slow down, it will drop closer to the sun. By carefully adjusting a rocket's speed in a mid-flight maneuver, we can place spacecraft close to Venus or Mars, even though these planets at their closest are many millions of miles from us. Mariner II executed a passage within 22,000 miles of Venus in 1962, and Mariner IV passed even closer to Mars in 1965.

It would not take much more refinement to plot the course of an unmanned probe to Jupiter, Saturn, and beyond. This is something that could be done now if our space scientists were not committed to other tasks of greater importance.

It is not enough, however, simply to send a piece of metal toward Jupiter. If a planetary probe is to be useful, the ship must send back signals. The signals tell us its position and provide us with other vital information. From how far out in space can we reasonably expect to be able to receive such messages?

Already space scientists have sent radar waves to Jupiter and have detected the reflection. The distance of such a round trip to Jupiter is about 800,000,000 miles. This is quite an advance over the time, a mere 20 years ago, when it was a great feat to bounce radar waves off the moon—a round-trip distance of less than 500,000 miles. It seems possible that within 10 years or so, our techniques will have developed to the point where we could produce a radar beam that could bounce

The opening illustration depicts a spaceship as it nears the vicinity of a neighboring planet. Inside the roomy cabin, the astronauts, unencumbered by heavy space suits and helmets, tend the banks of flashing lights and switches that control the interplanetary vehicle. Throat mikes and earplug receivers provide the necessary communications. The ruby glass in the ports protects the crewmen from damaging glare as they scan the surface of the planet. Once the spacecraft has completed its mission, a metal screen will slide up to protect the window area of the ship from the impact of meteoroids.

Illustrations by Arthur Lidov

off a body 4,000,000,000 miles away—the distance to Pluto, which is the most remote planet in our solar system.

We will soon be in a position, then, to explore the entire solar system with unmanned probes. By the year 2000, we might well have launched one or more probes to every one of the planets in the solar system. The results of these probes will not, however, all be known by then, for trips to the outer reaches of the solar system take a great deal of time. Mariner IV took more than eight months to reach the vicinity of Mars. If it were traveling to Pluto, many years would be required for the flight.

BEYOND THE SOLAR SYSTEM

Can we explore beyond the solar system? After all, if we propel a rocket at a speed of more than 26 miles a second (escape velocity from the sun at our distance from it), it will no longer remain in orbit about the sun. It will leave the solar system forever. If we aim it correctly, it will eventually approach Proxima Centauri, the nearest star next to the sun, or any other object toward which we might send it. Unfortunately, even the nearest star is almost 7,000 times as far away as Pluto. The flight of an unmanned probe to Proxima Centauri might take many centuries. Nor does it seem that we will be able to develop communication beams of sufficient power to track a probe all the way to the stars. Certainly we will not in the next century or so. In 1965, there was some speculation by the Russians concerning radio signals that might be reaching us from intelligent beings on the planets of stars other than our sun. The Russians had to admit, though, that such signals would have to be sent out by "super-civilizations," intelligent beings with technical know-how vastly exceeding ours.

We must conclude, then, that although we will soon have the ability to explore the entire solar system by instrumented satellites, we will by the year 2000 already have gone about as far as we can in that direction. We do not have the ability to explore far beyond the solar system. We may not have that ability for many centuries, if ever.

And what about manned flight? A lunar probe taking pictures of the moon does not compare in excitement with a man landing on the moon. And will reaching the moon be the end? Can we expect human beings to land someday on the surface of Mars or Jupiter? Where can we draw the line and say: "Here man is not likely to go in the next century and a half?"

Man can explore space in four stages: in journeys that last days, or months, or years, or centuries. The first stage, a trip of a few days, will take him to the moon. We hope to have a man on the moon by 1970. Is there anything to stop us from achieving this goal, with the exception of mechanical failures?

There are two hazards that are being thoroughly studied. First, an astronaut would be exposed to weightlessness for as long as a week. Is this dangerous? Well, during 1965 men were kept weightless for extended periods while in orbit and fulfilled their missions well. That seems to take care of that. Secondly, astronauts will be exposed to

THE INNER SOLAR SYSTEM

|← —————————— ONE BILLION MILES —————————— →|

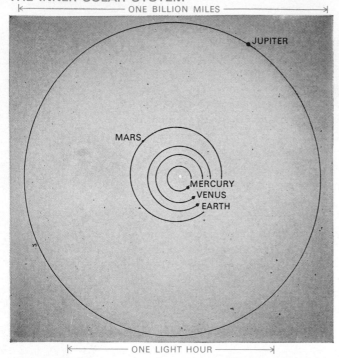

|← —————— ONE LIGHT HOUR —————— →|

Distances to the inner planets of the solar system, *above,* enable them to be reached in a matter of months. But voyages to the outer planets, *below,* would take many years.

THE OUTER SOLAR SYSTEM

BILLIONS OF MILES 0   1   2   3   4

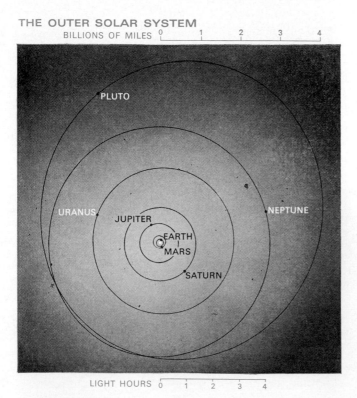

LIGHT HOURS 0   1   2   3   4

radiation in the Van Allen belt about the earth and to bursts of high energy particles from the sun, as well as to cosmic rays from beyond the solar system. Can they be protected from this? Dozens of satellites have been sent out by the United States and Russia to study the nature and effects of radiation. Nothing has been reported so far that would make a lunar flight impossible.

The only obstacle, then, that is keeping us from a flight to the moon right now is the need to work out the engineering details necessary to be reasonably certain that we will not only send an astronaut there, but also bring him back alive. Once we reach the moon, there seems to be nothing to prevent us from ferrying machines and supplies there to build a permanent base. The moon, it is true, has no water or atmosphere. It gets unbearably hot during the day and unbearably cold at night. It is subjected to a never-ending rain of tiny meteors and dangerous radiation. An underground cavern could be gouged out, however, and sealed. With material obtained from the surrounding rock and from the earth, conditions could be made quite comfortable and almost identical, except for the low gravity, to those in an air-conditioned enclosure on earth.

By 1980 or 1985, such a base may exist. From an astronomical observatory on the moon men could see the universe much more clearly than on earth. (If the moon is ever highly colonized, it may also be used as a launching site for spaceships.)

The second stage of space exploration—trips of a few months—will place the inner solar system within our grasp. This includes the planets Mars, Venus, and Mercury. Of these, Mars is the least forbidding. Despite its extremely thin and arid atmosphere, Mars just possibly may have simple life-forms on its surface. The main difficulty in reaching Mars involves the length of the journey. Before men can reach Mars, they must spend six months or more in space. Can they remain in isolation that long? Can they carry sufficient supplies? Can they endure weightlessness that long?

Let's consider these problems. Isolation need not have serious effects. Four or five centuries ago, men made voyages that lasted several months across wide oceans under conditions almost as dangerous for them as a flight to Mars would be today. They were even more isolated then than a space traveler would be now. They were truly cut off from home, whereas an astronaut would be in radio communication with the earth at all times—with the encouragement of all humanity constantly in his ear.

The problem of supplies is one for which solutions are being found. First of all, it will not be necessary to pack aboard a spacecraft to Mars the several tons of water and oxygen each man would need during the trip. Instead, the spaceship would carry a miniature chemical plant which would distill and purify waste water and process carbon

The future may see the moon being used as a launching site for spaceships heading out into the solar system. Because of the weak gravitational pull of the moon, only a single booster will be needed for escape into space. Once in flight, the propulsion unit will be dropped away and the retractable wings extended.
The pointed nose of the spacecraft is designed to counteract the effect of radiant heat transfer which becomes dominant at very high re-entry velocities. The sleek, shape of the craft will provide maximum maneuverability when it enters a planetary atmosphere.

dioxide to recover oxygen for breathing. It is not contemplated, how-ever, that food would be produced aboard ship. Food would be brought along in freeze-dried packages. Unless this were done, the weight would be excessive for take-off.

What about weightlessness? It would seem that a man in a state of weightlessness for six months or more would suffer some physical harm. If, however, a specially designed spaceship, or part of it could be spun slowly, a centrifugal effect would be produced within it that would push the astronaut out toward the walls. This would have the same effect upon him as a gravitational field. It would take no energy to keep the ship spinning once it was put into such motion, and the effect might well be to keep the astronaut healthy and comfortable.

If these problems are solved, astronauts may land on Mars by 1985, and there may be a permanent station there by 1995. Stations might also be established on the two tiny Martian moons, Deimos and Phobos, which have no atmosphere and virtually no gravity.

THE DANGER OF RADIATION

Nothing has been mentioned here about the danger of radiation on a trip to Mars. The principal danger would come from high-energy particles emitted at unpredictable intervals from flares on the sun. Although spaceships to Mars would be moving away from the stronger radiation of the sun, radiation shields would have to be provided to protect the astronauts during periods of intense solar activity. Mars itself has no detectable radiation belts to worry about once the space-ship nears the planet.

Trips to Venus and Mercury would take no longer than the trip to Mars, but those to Mercury would take considerably more energy because of the orbital mechanics involved. Neither Venus nor Mercury is expected to have any radiation belts to speak of. Both are, however, in the direction of the sun whose radiation increases dangerously as it is approached. If the radiation danger can be overcome, and, in all probability it will be, Venus and Mercury can be reached before 2000.

Establishing permanent bases there is another matter. The surface temperature of Venus, as measured by Mariner II, is about 800° F. This is the temperature all over the planet's cloud-shrouded surface, both day and night, so it must be at least that hot under the surface. There would be no escaping the heat by burrowing underground. Un-

The planets nearest earth—Mars, Venus, and Mercury—will be the first visited by man. Here an advanced re-entry vehicle approaches the surface of Venus, its cloud cover shining in the sun. The spaceship is about the size of today's jetliners. Out in interplanetary space, its propulsion system might be an advanced ion engine that would be capable of continuous acceleration. As the ship approaches Venus, it would switch to a system producing greater thrust. Radar signals recently bounced off the planet suggest that Venus has mountainous surfaces beneath the cloud cover. But unless data from unmanned probes indicate temperatures much lower than the 800° F. now envisioned, man will probably be content to study the hot planet from a safe distance, perhaps occasionally ducking under the clouds for a somewhat closer look.

manned probes could reach Venus's surface, and a manned expedition might make a temporary flight beneath the clouds, but it seems unlikely that a permanent base will be established on Venus in the foreseeable future.

Mercury is a better prospect. Until very recently it was thought that Mercury presented only one side to the sun, so that one side was always unbearably hot, while the other was almost at absolute zero, or $-459.69°$ F. If so, we could land on the cold side. It is simple to establish an artificially heated base, whatever the cold. Now, however, we know that Mercury rotates, so that each part of its surface has a day

Improved observation of the sun might be accomplished by placing an unmanned solar observatory on the asteroid Icarus. This small planet—probably between three and eight miles in diameter—has an elongated orbit which takes it from midway to the orbit of Jupiter to within 19,000,000 miles of the sun. The implanting of the solar station would have to be accomplished in a fairly short time while Icarus is nearest the earth and relatively cool. Weightless conditions would necessitate the manned vehicle being lashed to the asteroid. An excavation would be made in its moonlike surface, probably by means of a controlled explosion. Assisted by astronauts attached to the parent ship by booms, the observation station would be lowered into the crater and covered with debris. Then the spaceship would depart, leaving the capsule buried safely underground, with only its sensing devices projecting through the surface. As Icarus neared the neighborhood of the sun, the observatory's sensing devices would take measurements of the sun's magnetic field and its particle fluxes.

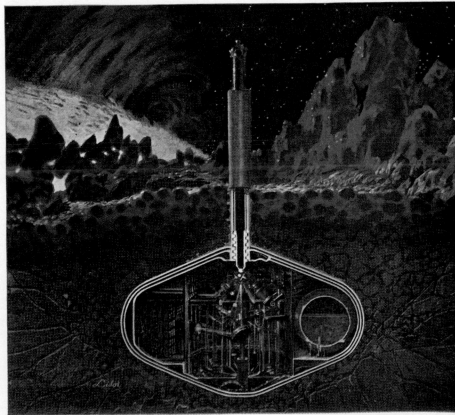

and a night about 59 days long. This means that any expedition landing on Mercury would have to do so at a point far enough into the night shadow for the surface to have cooled down. An underground base would then have to be dug before the landing point had circled into sunlight again.

Mercury approaches to within 28,000,000 miles of the sun. Can men ever expect to approach even closer? One possibility exists. There is a tiny asteroid named Icarus, which at times passes within a few million miles of the earth. It has a very flattened orbit. At one end, it reaches halfway to the orbit of Jupiter, but at the other it falls in toward the sun, speeding about it at a distance of only 19,000,000 miles. If an expedition could reach Icarus while it was passing near the earth and implant the proper instruments there hastily, marvelous observations could be made of the neighborhood of the sun, the charged particles it emits, and the magnetic field it produces.

Any closer approach to the sun by man than Icarus would seem unlikely. Spaceships, manned or unmanned, could be made to skim about the sun at closer distances, but the heat and radiation would very probably be fatal not only to men, but even to instruments, unless they were particularly well-protected. It seems doubtful, therefore, that in the next century and a half, men will succeed in approaching the sun more closely than does Icarus.

VOYAGES LASTING FOR YEARS

The third stage of space exploration—that which will involve voyages lasting years—will carry us to the vast outer solar system. This can be done in graduated steps. Between the orbits of Mars and Jupiter circle thousands of asteroids. A few of them are a hundred miles or more in diameter. Ceres, the largest, is 480 miles in diameter. Once we get to Mars, we will be able to reach the asteroids without too much additional trouble. Perhaps as early as 2000, man will have landed on Ceres. Step by step, other asteroids may be reached. One of the most interesting is Hidalgo. It has a very elongated orbit. At one end, it approaches to within 24,000,000 miles of the orbit of Mars. At the other end, it recedes as far from the sun as does Saturn. Hidalgo's orbit is quite tilted as compared to the orbits of the various planets, so it comes nowhere near Jupiter and Saturn. Still, if an expedition could land on Hidalgo when it was near Mars, men could remain in space for years, studying conditions in the outer solar system at their leisure, knowing that they would eventually return to the neighborhood of the orbit of Mars.

Astronauts could tackle the outer planets one by one, establishing themselves firmly on one, then progressing to the next one. To make these trips, however, even under the best of conditions, astronauts would have to spend many years in space, if spaceships are equipped with chemical rockets of the kind used today. Unless a new kind of rocket is developed, it may well be that man will never pass beyond the asteroids.

The use of nuclear rockets is a possibility. Rockets might be driven by a series of atomic explosions or by exhaust gases expelled by the heat of a nuclear reactor. In either case, rocket ships could be kept under acceleration for longer periods, and would attain higher speeds.

Then, too, there is an ion rocket now being developed by scientists. Ordinary rockets achieve their thrust by hurling large quantities of heated gases backward. This brute force is necessary to lift the spacecraft above the atmosphere and push it into an orbit around the earth. Once in orbit, however, and surrounded by a vacuum, a ship might make use of electrically charged atoms (ions) instead. These can be hurled backward by the action of an electric field. The thrust of the ions is very weak, so the rocket's speed increases very slowly. The ion engine is, however, much more efficient in the long run than an ordinary rocket. Acceleration can be continued for indefinite periods, and speeds approaching that of light itself (186,282 miles per second) could, in theory, be attained. By 2000, when men will have reached Ceres, both nuclear rockets and ion rockets may be in operation. If so, it may be with these that the outer solar system will be explored.

HOW FAR IN A CENTURY?

A generation later, say by 2025, we may well have landed on one or another of Jupiter's satellites. A century from now, a landing may have been made within Saturn's satellite system, with plans in the making for reaching the satellites of Uranus and Neptune. By 2100, perhaps, man will stand on Pluto, at the very limits of the solar system.

Notice that I mention the satellites of Jupiter, Saturn, Uranus, and Neptune. What about those planets themselves? These four planets are giants. Conditions there are far removed from those on the earth. They are frigidly cold and have deep, thick, poisonous atmospheres that have incredible storms, and winds of unimaginable violence. Pressures at the bottom of these atmospheres must be thousands of times greater than ours. Nor are we certain as to the kind of solid surfaces they have.

If astronauts ever did reach the solid surface of the outer giants, they would be subject to gravitational pulls much stronger than those we experience on earth. These pulls would largely immobilize the astronauts, and make the problem of getting off the planet almost insuperable. The difficulties in sending manned expeditions to the surface of the giant planets are so great that for a long time space scientists will be satisfied to send unmanned probes spiraling toward Jupiter, Saturn, Uranus, and Neptune. Manned exploration of these planets will not take place in any forseeable time, but small Pluto can be landed upon.

The fourth stage of space exploration—voyages lasting centuries—will take us to the planets of the nearer stars. As was said previously, the nearest star is almost 7,000 times as far away as Pluto. Why bother?

Well, nowhere in our solar system is there another planet on which man could live comfortably. He would have to huddle underground or beneath domes. Nowhere else in the system, outside the earth, can there be anything more than very primitive life-forms. Out there among the stars, however, there are sure to be other earthlike planets, which may very likely bear life. Some of them might even bear intelligent life. Unfortunately, we cannot detect them until spaceships can get fairly close to the stars that these planets circle.

But can other solar systems be reached?

Certainly the task of reaching even the nearest ones is many times as difficult as that of reaching even the farthest planet of the solar system. A major problem in making such a trip would be to ensure protection against the lethal, high energy particles that would collide with a spaceship, endangering its passengers and instruments. No solution to this problem is yet known. Moreover, even the most advanced rockets we can imagine cannot go faster than the speed of light, and, at the speed of light, a round trip to the nearest star will take nearly nine years. Round trips to more distant stars would take hundreds or thousands of years.

Even by 2100, when mankind may well be in occupation of Pluto, it seems doubtful that any serious attempt would have been made to send out an expedition to the stars. Does that mean, though, that men will *never* reach the stars? "Never" is a pessimistic word. Scientists have speculated on several means of reaching the stars. The first necessity,

of course, is the ability to reach speeds approaching that of light. These may be reached by means of ion rockets or some other technological developments not yet visualized.

Einstein's theory of relativity explains that all internal motions slow down in objects moving at great speeds away from the earth. The faster the speed, the slower the internal motions. All clocks on board a spaceship would slow down. So would every other motion that might be used to measure time. This is the same as saying that time itself would slow down. All atomic motions within human beings would slow down, too. Astronauts would metabolize more slowly, live more slowly, age more slowly.

Such slowed-down individuals would be unable to detect this change. To themselves, they would seem to be living normally. Still, while life seemed to pass in the usual way, they would reach a star in what might seem to them to be about five years. Time on earth would, however, have continued in the ordinary fashion and when the astronauts returned, while they might think only 10 years had passed, they might find that on earth a century had gone by.

If it turns out speeds near that of light are not practical, it may be possible, nonetheless, to live long enough to reach the stars. To achieve this, astronauts could be frozen and put into a kind of suspended animation for decades or generations until their destination was in view. We cannot say as yet, however, whether such suspended animation by low temperature hibernation will ever be possible.

There is a third way out. In place of the small ships used for exploration and colonization of our solar system, a huge ship might be built for voyages to the planets of the stars. Actually it would be a small "planet" itself. On such a "starship," there might be hundreds, or thousands of men; plus room for agriculture and for herds of animals. Whole generations of men and women might be born, grow old, and die while the starship traveled from one star to another.

Would men be willing to spend their lives and the lives of their children and grandchildren on a journey through space? It seems hard to believe that earthmen would choose to do this. Perhaps, though, we will not need earthmen. Once our solar system is colonized, there will be men and women who may never have seen earth; who may have been born on Mars. They will not know earth's blue skies and spacious fields. Their underground home on Mars will not be too different from that on a starship, and the change from one to the other may be quite

Voyages beyond our solar system might take centuries, and thus would require vehicles that could sustain space colonies. The day-to-day activities of this Ferris wheel-type spaceship would take place in the outer ring. The ship would accommodate some 100 passengers, providing each with 5,000 cubic feet of living space. The large wheel, about 300 feet in diameter, would rotate at about four revolutions per minute, producing gravitational effects similar to those on earth. Once put in rotation, the wheel would keep on rotating. The right end of the central shaft is the front of the spaceship, and it would contain the navigational center and a celestial observatory. The four spokes would serve as passageways to the living chambers. The propulsion system, probably of a nuclear type, is located at the rear of the ship.

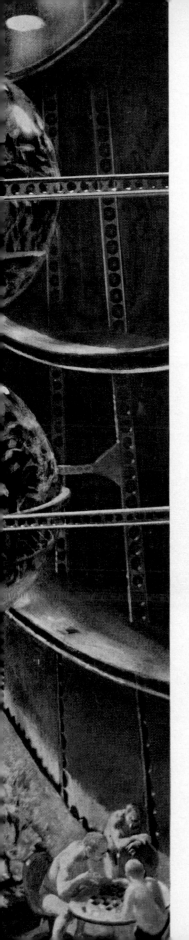

One section of an interstellar spaceship might be devoted to *hydroponics*, the growing of plants in a chemical solution instead of soil. The food produced in such a system would only be supplemental, but the fresh fruits and vegetables would provide the space families with a welcome change from a diet of prepared foods. Some plants needing a humid atmosphere would probably be grown in closed pods. By taking up carbon dioxide and giving off oxygen in photosynthesis, the garden would also contribute to the purification of the spaceship's air. This hydroponic section would require an ample supply of light and water, and thus it could also be used to provide a parklike area for the space travelers. Diversions of all types would be needed to relieve the tedium of a lifetime spent in space. And as on earth, young men would probably seek the company of young women, old men would play chess, and little boys would have trouble keeping their swimsuits up.

possible for them. The stars may not be explored by earthmen at all, but by colonists from Mars and other worlds.

What would these colonists be like? One can't help wondering. They will undoubtedly be accustomed to the lower gravity of the moon and Mars and will also be accustomed to maneuvering under gravity-free conditions. They may be more slightly built than earthmen because of having less gravity to contend with, but they could well be of greater mental stability, since only the most stable would have endured the transplantation from Earth to a life under the difficult conditions of worlds not really fit for human beings. Frightened neither by the confinement of a spaceship nor by the limitless reaches of space, they may be humanity's true answer to the Space Age.

When expeditions are sent to the stars, we need not expect to see them come back. Even a successful expedition to any but the very nearest stars, cannot possibly return to earth in the same century, as we count time. Nor will it be possible to communicate with any human colonies that may be established on the planets of other stars. Even if we develop the ability to transmit communication beams intense enough to reach other stars, it will take dozens of years, even centuries, for such beams to reach the colony. It will take an equal amount of time for the colony to answer.

Let us summarize then. A reasonable guess is that by 2100, mankind will have explored our entire solar system and will have landed on the surface of any planet, satellite, or asteroid he wishes, except for Jupiter, Saturn, Uranus, Neptune, and Venus. He will have studied the sun from close range, but not more closely than from a distance of 19,000,000 miles. Mankind will *not* have made any attempt to reach or colonize planets outside our solar system.

After 2100, a long pause may be enforced on mankind. He will probably have gone as far as he can go without developing technical abilities far beyond what he will possess even then. Those space feats which mankind will not have accomplished by 2100 (a landing on the giant planets, a very close approach to the sun, a voyage to the stars) may not actually be impossible, but they are so difficult that mankind may not even attempt them for many centuries after 2100.

See also Section One, Focus on Space; Section Three, Astronauts; Astronomy, Space Travel.

Polluted America

BY BROOKS ATKINSON

*A Pulitzer Prize-Winning Critic and Lifelong
Naturalist Looks at the Land He Loves and
Issues a Stern Warning to All Americans That
They Are Endangering Their National Heritage*

Pennsylvania Dept. of Health

When the English pioneers settled in Jamestown and Plymouth in the early 17th century, none of them imagined that in the 20th century Americans would poison their environment. No one could then foresee a time when Americans would pollute the air, the water, and the land as if our natural resources were inexhaustible and worthless.

But that is what we are doing, and we can destroy our civilization this way. No species can exhaust its resources and endure. Nature elimi-

YEAR BOOK photo
by Wes Kemp

The author:
Brooks Atkinson,
foreground above,
*was long a foreign
correspondent and
drama critic of* The
New York Times.
*Atkinson has
written many
books and is a
Fellow of
The American
Academy of
Arts and Sciences.*

nates the species that overtax their environment. Highly developed nations like ours invite reprisals from nature.

The three and one-half centuries during which the original immigrants and their descendants have prospered in America are only a minute fragment of the life span of the continent. For millions of years, there has been organic life on the land. Between 35,000 and 40,000 years have passed since the first Asiatic tribes crossed over into what is now Alaska and made use of the rivers, forests, prairies, and minerals.

To the earliest immigrants from England and other European countries, America seemed fabulous. No one knew where this vast land ended. The early settlers took everything for granted. Everything seemed to have been waiting for centuries for the use of free men who could casually mine and plunder the land without exhausting it and who felt they could progressively consume the capital of land and stream that the centuries had so lavishly provided. Regarding trees as weeds, the pioneers destroyed them and burned them in heaps to make arable land. Suddenly released from the restraints of life in Europe, they hacked at everything that stood in their way.

By 1910, much of the forest was gone. The beavers and fur seals were nearly exterminated. Vast herds of buffalo were reduced to the few that were protected (a million buffaloes were killed every year from 1872 to 1875). The last of 5,000,000,000 passenger pigeons was in a zoo in Cincinnati. Now as we look back on those early centuries, when so much that was politically good was accomplished, we are stunned by the speed and the callousness of the destruction. But man is the Giant Predator—that "pervasive and destructive vertebrate," as William Vogt, the ecologist, once called him.

After ravaging the land and slaughtering its wildlife, the American is now going even further: he is pouring untreated sewage and industrial wastes into lakes and rivers. He is defiling the skies with smoke and exhaust gases. He is contaminating the land with pesticides. The United States Department of Health, Education, and Welfare, which is deeply involved in all these problems, has said, "We are running out of safe, clean, usable water, partly because we are dumping so much of our refuse into our main water sources—our streams. So, too, we appear to be running out of clean air in many of our more populous and industrialized areas, and for similar reasons."

Conservation Vital

Land, water, and air are limited resources. Although our population has increased from 31,000,000 to 195,000,000 in 100 years, the supply of land, water, and air has remained the same. The increase in population automatically puts increased pressure on our resources. But we use them as if they were waste products, to which we contribute the additional wastes of home and industry. Unless we change our whole concept of the environment, and unless we conserve our natural resources and use them intelligently, we cannot pass our civilization on to future generations. Only when a nation accepts responsibility for its natural resources can the momentum toward destruction be retarded.

During the 19th century, the great adventure of settling the prairies, building cities and industries, laying the transcontinental railroad tracks, and constructing beautiful ships gratified and paralyzed the American imagination. The myth of inexhaustible abundance was still the folklore of the land. Yet, even in that distant time, a Yankee named George C. Whipple made a statement that we would do well to heed now. Speaking for the first Board of Health of the state of Massachusetts, he declared: "We believe that all citizens have an inherent right to the enjoyment of pure and uncontaminated air and water and soil; that this right should be regarded as belonging to the whole community; and that no one should be allowed to trespass upon it by his carelessness or his avarice or even his ignorance." This statement is even more pertinent now than when it was made.

A Danger to Health

Pollution of the environment endangers the health of the population from a wide variety of sources. No one had thought very much about air until the last two decades. Most of us were brought up to think that if we opened the window at night, we would be invigorated by fresh air. But it is no longer fresh in most of the settled parts of the continent. It is so polluted from the combustion of coal and oil (known as "fossil fuels") that clean air has become an increasingly serious problem for about 60 per cent of the population.

Looking out of the 19th story window of my New York City apartment as I write this article, I have just counted 11 smoking chimneys. One is belching thick, black smoke that billows above a loft building. Another emits a blue haze that sweeps across the rooftops for several blocks. Two of the four soaring stacks of a power plant emit streams of brown smoke that drift into the upper atmosphere. A flake of oily ash blows through a crack below the window I have left partly open and smudges the paper on which I am writing. The 11 smoking chimneys I see are, of course, only a minute fraction of all the chimneys that are contemptuously tossing waste into the New York air. Moreover, massive and more destructive waste is coming from the exhaust pipes of automobiles—carbon monoxide, sulfur compounds, and nitrogen oxides.

Wherever there are cities, there is air pollution that affects our health. A long cloud of polluted air hangs in the sky all the way from Washington, D.C., to Boston in the eastern United States. In the West, Los Angeles, which lies in a basin surrounded by mountains, has had a long and increasingly alarming experience with smog. (Strictly speaking, the word "smog" means a combination of smoke and fog, but it is commonly used to describe the haze that air pollution creates.) The geographical location of Los Angeles prevents the "ventilation" needed to disperse the polluted air. The city has been variously referred to as a "bay of smokes" and a "gas chamber."

Since 1930, Los Angeles commissions have tried to diminish, if not eliminate, smog by prohibiting the burning of trash in household incinerators, and by compelling oil refineries and industrial plants to install devices for controlling the emission of waste products into the

167

A jet airliner coming in for a landing in New York City is cloaked in smog that shrouds the towering skyline. A cloud of polluted air hovers in the sky all the way from Washington, D.C., to Boston.

air. But the smog has increased. Although the smog in Los Angeles is the most notorious in the United States, similar situations exist in many cities. Vivid examples of air pollution can be seen in the inferno of smoking stacks between Gary, Ind., and Chicago, Ill., or along the New Jersey Turnpike where a complex of plants discharge smoke and gases that blow across New York City when the wind is from the west.

Pollution of the air is estimated to cost the nation between $11,000,000,000 and $20,000,000,000 a year in damage to property, houses, furnishings, and clothing. It contains caustic elements that rot building stones and eat holes in metal roofs. Among its eccentric minor effects, it damages the pipes of church organs. In New York City, the sheep-

YEAR BOOK photo by Don Stebbing

Exhaust fumes from motor vehicles, above, are a major source of air pollution. Open burning of garbage and trash, below, also discharges pollutants into the atmosphere of many communities.

Pennsylvania Department of Health

skin valves that let air into the pipes deteriorate rapidly. A valve that would last 20 or 30 years in a clean atmosphere lasts only above five years in New York City.

This is the air we breathe. Where the air is dirty, there is evidence which suggests that the incidence of respiratory diseases, ranging from chronic bronchitis to cancer, increases. Among older people, there is evidence that air pollution accelerates diseases that include hardening of the arteries, heart trouble, asthma, and emphysema.

The Threat of Air Pollution

Under extreme circumstances, multiple deaths have occurred during periods when temperature inversions intensified pollution. A temperature inversion occurs when a layer of warm air lies above a layer of cooler air and acts as a lid that prevents the rising and dispersion of ground pollution. There are a number of classic instances of deaths during temperature inversions. In five days in 1930, for example, 60 people died during a temperature inversion in the heavily industrialized Meuse Valley in Belgium. They had breathed excessive amounts of sulfur and hydrocarbons. In 1948, a temperature inversion in Donora, Pa., that lasted four days produced an accumulation of fumes from steel, acid, and zinc plants. Forty-three per cent of the population became ill. Twenty persons died.

In 1952, a London fog filled the ground level of the atmosphere with sulfur dioxide and additional contaminants. There were about 4,000 deaths. In 1953, between 65 and 250 New Yorkers may have died from air pollution when a stagnant weather system captured a high concentration of toxic elements that entered the lungs. In two weeks in the winter of 1963, air pollution was reported as a major factor in 647 more deaths than normal in New York City.

Air pollution poses another threat; one that is almost unbelievable.

Major Sources of Air Pollution

*The three largest U.S. cities are all plagued by air pollution,
but the major sources of it vary, relatively, to a marked degree.
Chicago and Los Angeles use modern methods to control incineration.*

YEAR BOOK diagram

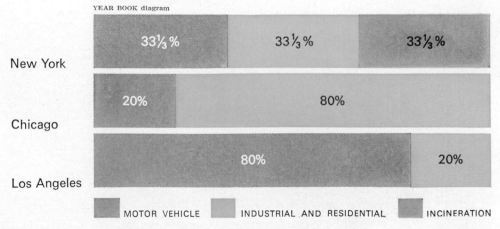

Cool Upper Air

Warm Desert Air

Cool Sea Air

Polluted Air or Smog Is Trapped
by Warm Air Blanket

Edward J. Blood

Smog-bound Los Angeles, above, has been called a "bay of smokes"
and a "gas chamber," as pollutants are frequently trapped by
thermal inversions. In such cases, cool air from the ocean
stagnates beneath a blanket of warm desert air, preventing
normal dispersion. When the warm air is finally blown away,
the ground air is able to escape, and the smog disperses.

It can change the physical nature of the planet. Exhaust gases from the burning of fossil fuels increase the carbon dioxide content of the air, which, in turn, increases the temperature of the atmosphere. Unlike some other pollutants, carbon dioxide cannot be washed out of the air. The temperature increase affects life in the oceans. During the 20th century, "there has been a well documented warming of the oceans in the Northern Hemisphere," says a report by the Conservation Foundation. "The changes in marine life of the North Atlantic have been very noticeable. . . . The abundance and distribution of a number of commercial fish have shifted northward."

But this is only a minor result. If the carbon dioxide content of the atmosphere were doubled, the average temperature of the earth would rise 3.8° F. The glaciers in the north would then begin to melt, and the level of the oceans would rise and inundate coastal cities. "It is almost inevitable that as long as we continue to rely heavily on fossil fuels for our increasing power needs, the atmospheric carbon dioxide will continue to rise, and the earth will be changed, more than likely for the worse," the foundation concludes. It is also possible that high-flying jet aircraft may help to increase the atmospheric temperature by spreading a layer of haze through the atmosphere in the form of ice crystals that will not melt. In the United States, there are more than 1,000 jet planes continuously in the air. They, too, burn fossil fuels and leave residues in the atmosphere.

Those of us who remember the anxiety over fallout from nuclear fission a few years ago may have some difficulty in accepting the idea that nuclear energy used for industrial purposes is on the whole cleaner than the energy derived from burning fossil fuels and is, therefore, more desirable. Nuclear energy, as such, is not an air pollutant, but it has one tremendous disadvantage: it produces large quantities of radioactive waste—"radioactive garbage"—that cannot be carelessly flung into the air or water, or onto the land, but must be disposed of with extreme caution.

As long as we require energy to drive cars, manufacture goods, and heat houses, there is no easy solution to the problem of air pollution. The simple process of being alive creates wastes and contaminants. Nature itself contaminates the air with volcanic eruptions, forest fires, and dust storms. Absolute purity is absolutely impossible, but this does not justify massive contamination of the air over cities in the United States which are being increasingly polluted by man with toxic wastes dangerous to the health of all.

Our Natural Glory Degraded

Since rivers and lakes occupy an exalted place in the natural glory of the United States, it is depressing that we are degrading them. We treat water as if it were "a discarded piece of trash," in the angry phrase of an Alabama state conservationist. The history of America is inter-twined with its rivers. This is one of the grandest facts about America. The voyages of De Soto, Marquette, Joliet, and La Salle on the Mississippi are an example of this. In 1608, a year before Henry Hudson explored the river now named for him, Captain John Smith expressed himself as astonished by the abundance and the quality of the fish in the Potomac estuary. In 1804, Lewis and Clark began their epochal penetration of the new continent by ascending the Missouri, which, like the Hudson and Potomac, is now heavily polluted. Audubon drifted down the Ohio, and Thoreau rowed up the Merrimack—both of them polluted rivers now.

Our love of America derives to an important degree from the lore of its rivers. Their names have a mystical resonance—Bitterroot, Chatta-hoochee, Colorado, Columbia, Green, Monongahela, Penobscot, Rac-coon, Rogue, St. Johns, Snake, Susquehanna, Yellowstone. There is something almost hypnotizing about all bodies of water. People are drawn to them and gaze at them as if under some spell. As Herman Melville, the author of *Moby Dick*, put it: "They must get just as nigh the water as they can without falling into it."

People also have a less admirable trait on the shores of rivers and lakes. They use water as a dump. They throw things into it. They find rivers convenient places in which to get rid of junk. Probably the people who sail on the Potomac near Washington, D.C., love the river and find the sensation of being on it, or close to it, an idyllic experience. But some admirers who recently volunteered to help clean it picked out of it old automobile tires, mattresses, boxes, discarded automobile batteries, and a sewing machine. When the skipper of a small boat tried to retrieve a wrench he had dropped into the river, his magnet brought up nothing but beer cans. The bottom of the Potomac is lined with rubbish. Although human beings love rivers, they also use rivers contemptuously.

A Grave Water Problem

Municipalities and industries putrefy rivers on a massive scale. A century ago, when the population was small and industries were few, clean water did not seem to be a serious problem. It is one of our gravest problems now. In addition to the needs of our increasing population, the uses of water have increased with the installation of more bathrooms, washing machines, garbage disposal units, and lawn sprinklers. By the year 2000, our requirements for water will be about 1,000,000,-000,000 gallons a day. Since the available water supply is expected to be about 650,000,000,000 gallons a day, it is readily apparent that most of the water will have to be used at least twice. If it is used more than once, treatment methods will have to be more efficient than are the methods in common practice today. Sewage treatment plants that remove 80 per cent of the contaminants from water are currently regarded as good. Seventy per cent is as much as many modern plants remove.

Despite the size of the problem and the attention paid to it by government officials and responsible citizens, a lot of today's sewage is not treated at all. "It is an astonishing fact," says the United States Department of Health, Education, and Welfare, "that of the 11,420 U.S. communities with sewers, 2,139 still dump their sewage raw into local streams and watersheds."

One-third of New York City's sewage (500,000,000 gallons a day) flows raw into the Hudson and East rivers. The sewage from Detroit passes through a primary cycle of sewage treatment but not a secondary cycle. It pollutes the Detroit River so heavily that the federal government is demanding an improved treatment plant that will cost the city $100,000,000. Although Chicago treats its sewage in modern plants, the surplus effluent that is finally discharged into the Chicago Sanitary and Ship Canal contains wastes equivalent to the untreated sewage of 1,000,000 people and contains solid wastes, suspended in solution, amounting to 1,800 tons a day. Lake Michigan is an "industrial cesspool," in the phrase of U.S. Senator Gaylord Nelson of Wisconsin. Along its shoreline, it receives wastes from Illinois, Indiana, and Wisconsin cities and industrial plants. Some experts doubt that this portion of Lake Michigan can ever be cleaned. During the summer of 1965, one quarter of Lake Erie was so heavily polluted by adjacent

U.S. Department of Health, Education, and Welfare

Discharge from a paper mill flows into Lake Erie and covers several acres of the water's surface. The lake has been described as the worst case of large-scale pollution that has ever been known. One observer has said that it is "dying."

cities and farms that its oxygen supply was virtually depleted. Lacking oxygen, fish were unable to breed and feed. "A dying lake," someone called it. Someone else has described it as the worst case of pollution on a large scale that has ever been known.

This heavy contamination is not a transient problem. At the present rate of construction, treatment plants will not keep pace with the expanding population. By 1970, the total discharge of wastes will be considerably greater than today. In 1963, it was estimated that the treatment projects then needed would cost $2,200,000,000—a sum that startles people concerned with the problem.

Water pollution consists of organic wastes from domestic sewage and industrial plants, plant nutrients that breed algae and water weeds,

U.S. Department of Health, Education, and Welfare

Municipalities and industries putrefy rivers on a massive scale, as shown by waste material flowing from a steel mill, above. *The lovely Potomac,* left, *is so polluted even the fish die.*

175

oil, acids, chemicals, alkalies, dyes, detergents, pesticides, and sediments. It also consists of radioactive residues from the mining of radioactive ores, nuclear testing, and intrusions of salt water. Heated water discharged from power plants is also a pollutant. Pollution kills fish on a colossal scale. Since polluted water can and does cause typhoid, dysentery, and hepatitis, clean water is not just a matter of aesthetics. It is also a matter of public health. Shellfish can transmit many diseases. The condemnation of shellfish because of contamination from sewage can also be extremely costly. When the oyster beds at the mouth of the Mobile River were condemned in 1960, the loss of income to the industry was estimated at $4,880,000 a year according to the Alabama Conservation Department.

The debasement of our rivers is an appalling sight. Take the "lordly Hudson," or the "great river of the mountains," as it has been called. Because of its romantic beauty, it has been traditionally compared to the Rhine. The comparison, unfortunately, has another aspect. The Rhine, too, is grossly polluted. Beginning as fresh water from the Alps, it picks up chemicals, potash, minerals, and oil as it flows through Germany. When it emerges in The Netherlands, visibility in the water is limited to 16 inches.

The Hudson is much the same. At Troy, it picks up sewage, pesticides, oil, and other pollutants from cities and farming areas along the Mohawk River. (One stream that empties into the Mohawk is said to be so full of oil and grease that its water cannot be used to fight fires.) From Albany south to New York City, the lordly Hudson is a long sewer. It is a little less polluted at the middle section near Poughkeepsie, but heavily polluted in the north and south sections where municipal

Home Sewage Disposal

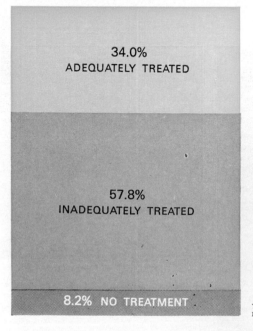

Thousands of communities still dump raw human waste into rivers and waterways. Of all sewage discharged from American homes, only 34 per cent is adequately treated.

YEAR BOOK diagram from U.S. Public Health Service estimates and *Chemical Week*

and industrial waste is large. Even the middle section is so contaminated that it cannot be used for drinking or for swimming without heavy chlorination. It was a joyous river a hundred years ago. Unfortunately, it is a filthy river now.

In the spring of 1965, I rode up the river from New York City to Glens Falls and back again in a helicopter with a director of the New York State Regional Development Office. From a helicopter, the configuration of the Hudson is a natural masterpiece—broad bays of open water shining in the sun, the dramatic stone wall of the Palisades, the narrow trench of the Highlands, the noble mound of Storm King across the river from the steep pitch of Breakneck Ridge, the green hills, the smooth croplands, the charming islands. No wonder Henry Hudson admired it. When he was there, the bays contained whales and bred shellfish, and the river was full of sturgeon. Sturgeon still abounded in the 19th century and were known as "Albany beef" because of their food value. It has been said that men first settled along the Hudson, not because of its navigability, but because of the abundance of fish that could be found there.

A helicopter journey today, however, discloses the negative aspects of this glorious waterway. It is a sewer and a dump. One sees oily scum, garbage dumps, sewage outlets that stain the water along the shore, long, ragged plumes of smoke from industrial plants, white and yellow waste fluids pouring out of factories and spilling into the river, decaying piers, capsized barges, abandoned buildings without roofs or windows. Each generation leaves its rubbish along the Hudson River to infect and corrupt the future. Given time, the Hudson will be a wasteland.

On the west shore across from Poughkeepsie, a large, rambling boathouse in a gay design is slowly crumbling. It is a relic of the days when boating on the river, swimming in it, and picnicking beside it were common forms of pleasure. The river is sparingly used for pleasure now. The water is green or brown and opaque in many places. It has a disagreeable odor. Much that takes place along the Hudson tends to degrade it. It has degenerated into a commercial waterway, used largely by tankers that discharge oil at the many tank colonies on the shore. The festive Hudson River Day liners with their great American flags, their streams of fluttering pennants and their holiday travelers no longer ply the upper reaches of the Hudson. Civilization has corrupted this great river.

The Plight of the Potomac

The history of the Potomac is similar. In the early 19th century, in the warm months of the year, John Quincy Adams, a gloomy Yankee, used to begin his day as President of the United States by walking from the White House to the Potomac, laying his clothes on the bank, and swimming in the water. Few things during the rest of his day seemed so clean and tonic. Modern Presidents have to swim in the White House pool which is filled with filtered and chlorinated water. The Potomac estuary in the District of Columbia is contaminated with the residue from sewage plants, sediment from upriver, sludge, trash, litter, logs, and other forms of debris from a modern city. Someday, swimming may be pleasant and safe in the Potomac if people now concerned about the river can persuade others to share their hopes. But the dirty water is far from inviting today.

In view of the history of the Potomac, and the loveliness of the parks on both shores, the filthiness of the water is particularly discouraging. George Washington, in a mood of pardonable pride, called the Potomac "the finest river in the world." When he was farming in the Mt. Vernon region, it was certainly different than today. Now 2,000,000 people

We Can Meet The Challenge

By J. I. Bregman
and
Sergei Lenormand

If no sizable effort is made to reduce and control the massive contamination of our vital resources, the nation's health, wealth, and beauty will continue to erode at an even more catastrophic rate than in the past. Although the situation is critical, it is not hopeless. Effective methods are available to deal with the problem.

The major sources of air pollution can be attacked in five basic ways:
• A relatively simple approach, already adopted in some communities, is the elimination of all open burning of garbage, leaves, trash, refuse, and junk. At a modest cost, such wastes can be collected and disposed of in modern municipal incinerators that emit far less exhaust gas than does open burning. Often garbage and trash can also be used for land fill.
• Because sulfur dioxide is one of the most noxious and damaging of the air pollutants, all heating and industrial plants can be required by municipal ordinances or state laws to burn only fuels containing a low sulfur content. If this is not possible, ways can be provided for removing or dispersing the resulting gas.
• New combustion equipment can be designed to burn fuel efficiently.
• Filtering devices can be installed to collect soot, ash, and other solid particles discharged by heating systems and industrial plants.
• Pollution caused by automobiles can be minimized by installing devices, or redesigning engines, to reduce exhaust gases. California has already passed a law requiring exhaust reduction systems on all automobiles sold in the state beginning in 1966.

Methods for eliminating the major portion of pollutants from water have been known for many years. Techniques such as filtration, aeration, settlement (in which solids are allowed to sink to the bottom of polluted water), and dilution (in which polluted water is cleansed by mixture with fresh water) can be used for primary treatment.

Chemical methods, such as chlorination, can be employed for secondary treatment. When applied to both municipal sewage and industrial wastes, a combination of these techniques can eliminate almost all objectionable materials. Most communities already have some kind of water treatment facility, but in many instances, such facilities are inadequate.

An urgent need exists for the construction of separate storm and sanitary sewerage systems. The two systems should not be combined as they so often are at present. In the first place, storm run-off does not require treatment. It can drain directly into a waterway. More important, when combined with sewage in one system, storm run-off frequently overloads treatment plant facilities. This causes much of the sewage to flow directly into nearby waterways.

To use the water available to us in the most efficient manner possible, we must conserve as much as we can. Already, in some industrial operations, water is treated in the plant and reused, cleansed, and reused many times before finally being evacuated. Hopefully, this practice will become much more widespread in years ahead.

The reduction of water and air contamination is clearly a problem that is more political and financial than technical. Some 32 states and Puerto Rico had approved some air pollution laws by 1963. Of these, however, only 15

live around the estuary. In 1985, there will be 3,000,000; in 2010, 5,000,000. Contemplating the rapid expansion of the future, Gordon E. McCallum of the United States Public Health Service says: "Our job will never end." It will be virtually impossible to keep ahead of the problem. If John Quincy Adams dipped into the Potomac every morning now, he would require medical attention. The water of the lovely river that washes our beautiful capital city is not clear, not blue, but "soupy green," as one of its custodians describes it. Although the Potomac estuary may look romantic, its contamination is real.

actually carried any enforcement authority. Among the states that now have control programs, the average expenditure is only about four cents per capita per year—less money than schoolchildren spend for candy or ice cream in a single week.

To a large extent, the problem consists of overcoming fears of federal intervention and resistance to appropriating sufficient funds for the control of the major sources of pollution.

The first federal air pollution control program of any consequence was established in 1955, with the passage of Public Law 155. This act provided for government research, as well as for grants and contracts to research organizations and universities.

In 1963, a major implementation of this act came with the enactment of Public Law 88-206, popularly known as the Clean Air Act. The act laid the foundation for interstate agreements, and the establishment of a commission with legal authority to curtail or prevent one state from polluting another. It also made substantial funds available to develop control agencies on state, county, and municipal levels. In addition, the federal government for the first time was able to take legal action when it could prove an interstate health hazard existed.

Another big step forward was the passage late in 1965 of a law giving the federal government authority to establish emission standards for motor vehicle exhausts. This means that by 1968, all new automobiles will probably be equipped with devices to control exhaust fumes.

Federal jurisdiction over water pollution advanced appreciably in 1965 when President Lyndon B. Johnson signed a bill that requires the states to establish clean water standards by 1967. Thereafter, the federal government will have the power to set standards for states that have not done so.

Residents of New York state have already given evidence that they intend to solve their own problems without pressure from the federal government. In November, they overwhelmingly approved a proposition authorizing the state to raise $1,000,000,000 through a bond issue to assist the financing of sewage treatment and other anti-pollution facilities throughout New York.

The issue of state versus federal jurisdiction—either with regard to water or air pollution—is not really the crux of the matter. The crucial issue relates to individual concern and commitment. Are we willing, for example, to spend as much to combat pollution as we spend on smoking?

The funds essential to this massive task in the coming decade may be more sizable than those needed for almost any other government program. The expense, however, may be no more than the approximately $50,000,000,-000 spent for tobacco during the past 10 years, and certainly less than the roughly $100,000,000,000 expenditure for alcohol during the same period. Moreover, the longer we wait to mobilize against pollution, the more it will eventually cost. The total clean-up bill substantially increases each day we delay making a total effort to restore our environment and maintain the integrity of our natural resources.

While we may not be able to eliminate it, we have the means to control pollution. It is now imperative that we get on with the task.

General pollution of the environment will continue until the public puts a stop to it. Municipalities will economize on the treatment of sewage until the citizens assume the responsibility themselves. Industries will continue to dump their wastes into the air or the water until citizens make a public issue of it.

In this, as in all aspects of life, we need an ethic. In the legal sense, people can own land, but they do not own it in the moral sense. They are custodians of a land that each generation passes on to the next. In *A Sand County Almanac*, an inspired and pioneering book published in 1949, the late Aldo Leopold defined the land ethic: "A land ethic changes the role of *Homo sapiens* from conqueror of the land community to plain member and citizen of it. It implies respect for his fellow members and also respect for the community as such." Our natural resources are not adversaries to be conquered, nor raw products to be squandered. They are rich and wonderful parts of our inheritance. They are to be loved, respected, and wisely administered by all of us.

Since human beings have minds, they do have certain advantages over what we call dumb animals. We can reason from facts. We can

YEAR BOOK photo by Don Stebbing

"In three and one-half centuries of expansion and an increasing productivity," author Brooks Atkinson recently remarked, "Americans have had to exchange the old myth of unlimited abundance for the sobering reality of a polluted continent. We think of ourselves as intelligent beings, and in many respects we are. But we have also behaved irresponsibly, as if each generation owned the total environment and could carelessly dispose of it without any obligation whatever to the next."

save life by obeying abstract knowledge and doing some of the things that do not come easily. But in the last analysis, we are mammals. We flourish or fall, live or die, by the same natural laws that govern the wild creatures of the earth, as well as the grains in the meadow and the roses beside the house. As a nation, we acquired a beautiful land three and one-half centuries ago. We have created a civilization that is in many ways as beautiful as the land because its sovereign principle is freedom of the body, mind, and soul.

But freedom can degenerate into anarchy. Having been carelessly used, the land has lost its original grandeur and exultance. "The air we breathe, our water, our soil, and wildlife are being blighted by poisons and chemicals which are the by-products of technology and industry," President Lyndon B. Johnson said in 1965 in his "Message on the Natural Beauty of Our Country."

We are wasting and poisoning the shining green land that Americans have loved since the day they first saw it.

See also Section Two, *Water for a Thirsty World;* Section Three, WATER AND FLOOD CONTROL.

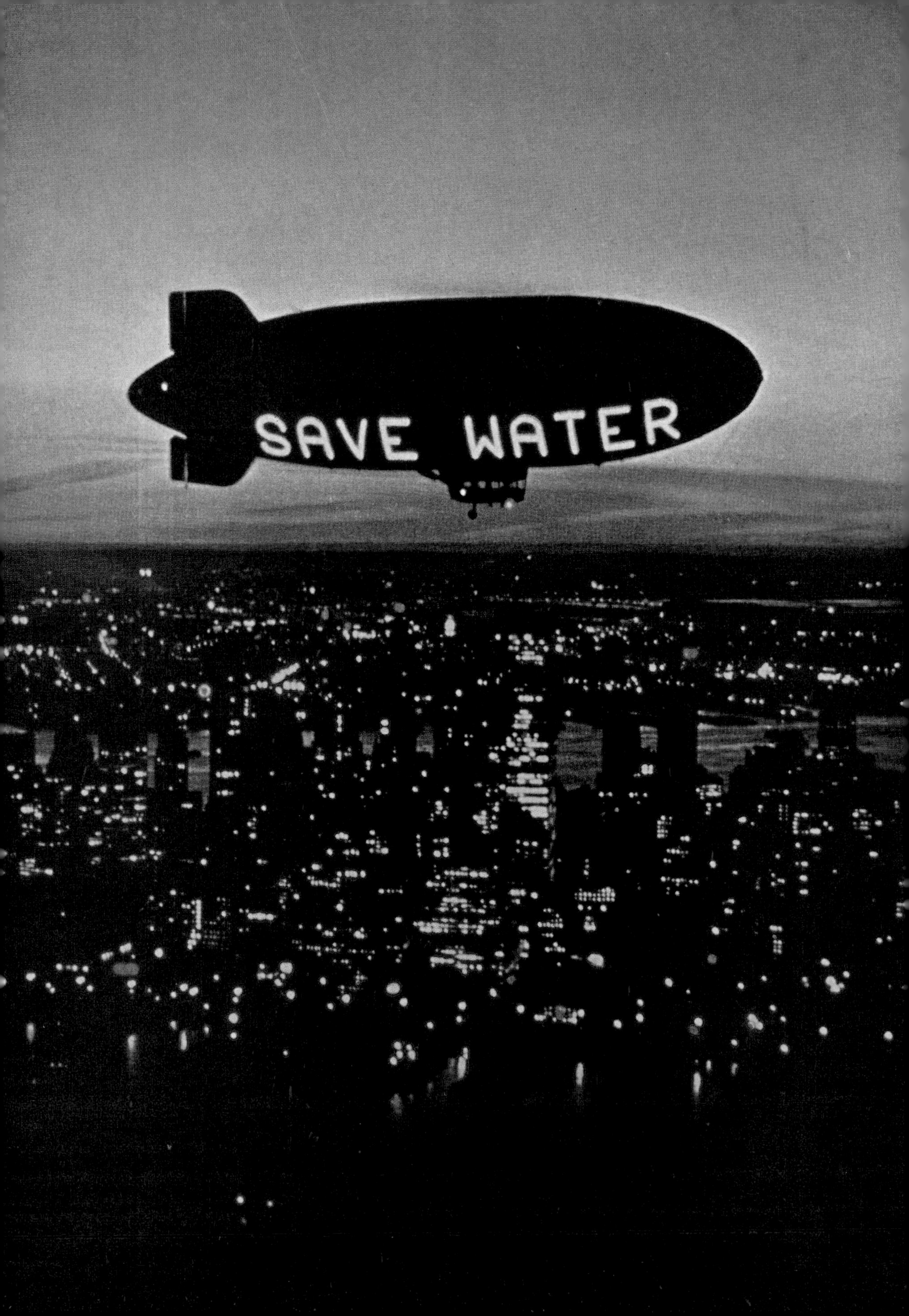
SAVE WATER

WATER
For a
Thirsty World

Though Most of the Earth Is Covered by Water, Much of Mankind Is Faced with a Shortage. Now Scientists Have Launched a World-Wide Investigation to Find Answers to One of Man's Most Basic Problems.

By Lorus and Margery Milne

When rain streaks the windows of our home in New Hampshire, we tend to take water for granted. Most people in the United States do. Yet the postman pulls a letter postmarked New York City from under his dripping raincoat, its stamp canceled with an urgent plea to "SAVE WATER."

We look through a spattered pane at storm clouds billowed and twisted by the wind from the west, realizing that only a few hundred miles south of us another west wind villainously pushes air laden with moisture out over the Atlantic Ocean. There, a heavy rainfall of fresh, pure water blends into the sea. But the parched watersheds and caking fringes of reservoirs serving New York City, Boston, and Philadelphia are left dry.

In 1965, one of the most densely populated areas on earth was in its fifth year of drought. The shrinking water reserves of New York City fell to the one-third of capacity mark. There were fears that the shortage might grow even worse. New York City's water commissioner, the mayor, the U.S. Secretary of the Interior, and even the President of the United States sought, but could not find, a quick way to satisfy the giant thirst of the city.

A blimp hovering over New York City in the summer of 1965 conveys a clear and urgent message. Unless new water sources are found, this message will be repeated in other urban areas.

Ben Martin for Time Inc.
from Pictorial Parade

183

Each day, New York City consumes more than a billion gallons of fresh water. Even a heavy downpour replenishes its reservoirs for only a day or two. What the long-range solution to the New York water crisis will be no one can say, but this much is certain: the future of New York and of all our great cities—in fact of humanity itself— depends upon the wise use of water. For the earth's water supply is fixed; we cannot increase it. We can only find where it is, transport it to where we need it, and decontaminate it of salt and other impurities so that it is suitable for continued use and reuse.

Fortunately, the business of learning how we can best do these things has already begun. On Jan. 1, 1965, the United Nations Educational, Scientific, and Cultural Organization (UNESCO) inaugurated the International Hydrological Decade, a multinational scientific study of the world's water supply. Among the intriguing riddles to be studied is our planet's water cycle.

Some of the water pelting our windows in New Hampshire has traveled 3,000 miles. It was evaporated out of the Pacific Ocean by the sun, and for more than a week has been held as invisible water vapor in a great mass of air spinning eastward across the continent. Chilled over New Hampshire's highlands, it appeared as heavy clouds in which turbulence dashed small droplets together, making large drops heavy enough to fall. We watch in fascination as the drops slant downward, and disappear into the soft earth.

The authors:
The husband-and-wife team of Drs. Lorus and Margery Milne has worked together since college days. They are now professors at the University of New Hampshire. The Milne's travels have taken them over 500,000 miles through four continents. The latest of their 17 books is "Water and Life."

When the rain stops, much of the moisture will evaporate again, giving the gentle breeze its pleasant softness. Some of the rain will run into streams, making them gurgle. From there, the water will gush into a nearby river, its slow current emptying into a different sea—the Atlantic Ocean.

This cycle—liberation of fresh water from the sea and its return to the sea—occurs rapidly wherever a small island rises out of a tropical ocean. We discovered this on a visit to St. Lucia in the West Indies.

The dawning sun dispels the night's chill and warms the island. The air is heated, and rises. Humid air from offshore moves in to replace the dry air. As this column of moist air ascends, it expands and cools until it can no longer hold its load of water. A big white cloud forms, spreads, and thickens. By early afternoon, it grows black and heavy with vapor. Down comes the rain, drenching and cooling the island. The sun then breaks through again and evaporates most of the water from the dripping foliage and wet rocks. This evaporation cools the island, and the air column above it ceases to rise. Any remnant of cloud drifts away. The water sinks into the soil or is carried by streams to the sea. The water cycle is completed, almost like clockwork.

Fully one-fourth of the solar energy that penetrates the earth's atmosphere is used to power the cycle by lifting fresh water from the seas. This prodigious amount is over 7,000 times the energy man uses in all his machines combined. As the rotating earth brings one ocean after another into the sunshine, so much water vapor rises into the atmosphere that, if none were returned for a full year, ocean levels

Albert Fenn

This contrast between the parched desert and the vast but salty ocean symbolizes the uneven distribution of the world's water. Ironically, even if the oceans were fresh water, our water problems would not be solved. To solve them and meet the needs of the future, mankind must learn how to purify and shift more water from areas of plenty to areas of thirst.

would fall by nearly four feet. Actually, of course, most of the evaporated moisture falls back into the oceans. Only about 9 per cent falls onto the land, where it is readily useful to man. And much of this moisture, too, eventually returns to the seas.

Although Leonardo da Vinci and many others since have grasped the essentials of the water cycle, its details remain a mystery. No one really knows how much fresh water lies deep in the soil, or the complex routes it takes between a soaking rain and its return to the seas. Also, the water cycle is affected by changes in weather, such as the series of dry years that appear to follow a succession of wet years about three times each century. These changes have no known basis that

What They Cost in Water

40,000 gallons are needed to make the steel in one car.

50 gallons a day are taken from the soil by an average tree.

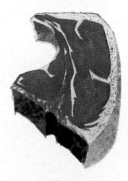

3,000 gallons in food and water are used to produce a pound of beef.

YEAR BOOK Art

might permit either accurate prediction or attempts to control them.

If drinking water were our only requirement, there would be plenty for everybody. Each person needs only about three quarts daily in beverages and wet foods. But that is just the beginning. Fresh water is also needed to bathe, to wash clothing and dishes, to dispose of waste, to water lawns, to fight fires. How much water does all this take? The average city dweller in the United States uses about 158 gallons of fresh water daily from his community's water system.

People in highly developed countries such as the United States put additional demands on water. They want an automobile or two in the garage. They want lettuce from Arizona in the middle of winter, and corn and strawberries from California in off-seasons. They want a newspaper every day and one or two thick ones on Sunday, plus magazines and books. They want electric power so cheap that they can use it freely to open and close the garage door, to carve a turkey, to vibrate a toothbrush, or to provide music throughout the house. Every one of these has a high price in water.

Our civilization depends, for example, upon equipment made of steel. The manufacture of a ton of steel requires 65,000 gallons of water of moderate purity. When we stroll home with a thick Sunday newspaper under an arm, we are carrying the result of 180 gallons (six bathtubfuls) of fresh water used in the paper mill, plus water to grow the spruce trees to pulpwood size, plus water for the manufacture and operation of logging machinery, printing presses, and distribution equipment. About 300 gallons of fresh water are needed for the few wheat stalks that provide grain for a day's bread for one person—if bread alone is eaten. Adding up all our needs, 16,000 gallons of fresh water are actually required every day to support the accepted standard of living for each person in the United States.

Wherever we travel, we meet people striving to raise their standard of living. On a return visit to Nairobi, Kenya, after an absence of four years, we noticed that bicycles, which contain only a small amount of steel, were now outnumbered by heavy automobiles. Certainly no perspiring bicyclist consumes as much water as a refinery uses in making the gasoline to propel an automobile the same number of miles. Even the change from tribal to Western dress reflected an increase in water use, for mechanization of a clothing industry requires an added supply of water.

Industrial growth and an expanding world population seem inevitable. The Statistical Office of the United Nations expects the world population to reach 7,000,000,000 by 1999. This is double today's population—just a generation from now. If everyone then is to use 16,000 gallons of fresh water each day, from where will it come? How can disastrous water shortages be prevented?

Perhaps the desalination of sea water will be one answer. Presently several methods are being tested. One involves distillation in which salt water is boiled, and the pure water that escapes as steam is condensed and collected. Another involves freezing. Ice crystals formed from salt water are themselves pure, but they are coated with salt. This is rinsed off, and the crystals are then melted into fresh water. Still other methods make use of thin plastic semipermeable membranes through which pure water can be obtained from salt water, either by mechanical or electric power.

There are about 50 major saline water conversion plants in operation or under construction in various parts of the world, and more are being planned. For the most part, these installations supply fresh water for islands, extremely arid or desert regions, or other special locations. While the methods for producing artificially desalinated water are not now economically feasible for use on a widespread basis, they do hold some promise for regions with supplies of salt water.

But as Roger Revelle, former director of the Scripps Institution of Oceanography at the University of California at La Jolla, points out, even if all of the oceans were fresh water, our water problems would not be solved because sea water is at such a low elevation. It would cost untold sums to pump billions of gallons of sea water far inland, or to places higher than a few hundred feet above sea level. Thus, while large coastal cities may resort more and more to sea water for municipal uses, inland areas will have to learn to use their normal water resources more efficiently.

We asked Raymond L. Nace, a leading hydrologist in the U.S. Geological Survey, about the whole problem of water supply. "Thinking on a continental scale is now necessary," he responded, "involving projects that may require 10 years to plan and 20 to 40 years to build. Such planning is essential to assure rational use of our finite water supply to meet a potentially limitless water demand."

Of the 16,000 gallons per person per day used for modern civilized living, most evaporates into the air; less than half returns to rivers or sinks into the ground. This supply of used water is precious, for it can be purified and reused. Even now, the same water is used nearly four times during certain periods of the year as it passes from Pittsburgh, Pa., to Cairo, Ill., along the Ohio River. Yet, there are too many instances in which communities show little regard for water.

If arid regions are to prosper, huge amounts of water must be brought in. Already, 790 gallons of water per person per day are used for irrigation in the United States. No other single use of fresh water demands so great a volume. In this area, too, we must practice economy in the use of water, and find new means of obtaining and reusing it.

Just as communities have grown, so have local water problems. Effective action now depends upon broader views, more expensive undertakings, and a higher level of cooperative action. Feats of "continental engineering" are needed to correct the natural inequities in the distribution of fresh water. But success is possible only if people are willing to cooperate, forgetting age-old rivalries. Emotional obstacles still loom large in Southeast Asia and in the Middle East, where the fresh waters of the great Mekong River and of the River Jordan provide a major basis for a higher standard of living.

Where Precipitation Goes

RETURNED TO ATMOSPHERE BY EVAPORATION, 71%

USED BY CITIES, 0.6%
USED BY INDUSTRY, 3.4%
USED FOR IRRIGATION, 3.4%

RETURNED TO OCEAN UNUSED, 21.6%

YEAR BOOK Chart

Of all the moisture that falls on the U.S., less than 8 per cent is directed by man for his special uses. Most precipitation returns naturally to the atmosphere or the oceans.

Nature's Hidden Reservoir

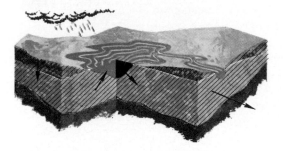

There is 20 times as much water under the land's surface as in all lakes and rivers combined. This ground water continually interchanges with water on the surface. Like surface water, it is constantly in motion.

If there were no ground water, a river would be reduced to a trickle in a few rainless weeks. In actuality, water that is absorbed into the ground in rainy periods (left), empties into the river during dry periods to sustain its flow (right).

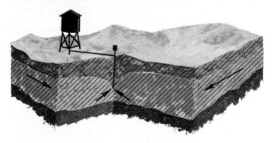

When ground water is pumped to the surface of the earth, the water table sinks near the well. If too much water is pumped from the ground, all but the deepest wells will temporarily go dry.

 SURFACE WATER

 NONPOROUS ROCK

POROUS ROCK AND SOIL

NONSATURATED

⌐WATER TABLE

SATURATED

YEAR BOOK Diagrams

Unfortunately, even within a country, the diversion of valuable fresh water from one region to another is likely to cause disputes. Arguments over water rights in the U.S. Southwest, for example, began during the 1930s, when a pipeline was installed to carry 1,000,000,000 gallons of Colorado River water to Los Angeles and San Diego daily. As California's cities grew, more aqueducts were added, and conflicts multiplied. In June, 1963, the Supreme Court of the United States reapportioned the water of the great river that runs through seven states and Mexico. California's share was limited to less than 3,900,000,000 gallons a day, not the 4,500,000,000 gallons actually being taken. Fortunately, Californians were by then busy laying new intrastate pipelines from the Feather River, north of Sacramento, to areas in the south.

A Los Angeles engineering firm, the Ralph M. Parsons Company, has calculated the costs and gains from diverting large amounts of water from such sources as the Fraser River and the upper reaches of the Columbia River in western Canada to dry areas in North America. This plan certainly qualifies as "continental engineering." The primary purpose of this ambitious 30-year project is to pipe water about 1,200 miles from the vast Canadian watershed. By investing $80,000,000,000 to $100,000,000,000—almost the entire U.S. federal budget for one year—in the vast project, arid states might receive daily 129,000,000,000 gallons of irrigation water, 32,000,000,000 gallons of industrial water, and, as a by-product, 100,000,000 kilowatts of hydroelectric power.

When Parsons engineers explained the details of this North American Water and Power Alliance plan to 300 officials and businessmen from both countries, many of the Canadians asked how much of the estimated income of $4,000,000,000 a year from the sale of the water would be paid to Canada. It is becoming increasingly clear that this rather common liquid, which most everyone takes for granted, has become a valuable commodity.

Baldwin-Lima-Hamilton Corp.

In the shadow of the legendary King Solomon's Mines, at Elath, Israel, a new plant desalts a precious 1,000,000 gallons of water from the Red Sea each day. Though still an expensive source of fresh water, desalination pays its way in parched areas where it is virtually the only source.

Lloyd A. Royal, a Canadian who directs the International Pacific Salmon Fisheries Commission, foresees a serious side effect. "Most certainly, the Parsons plan as projected would destroy a vast salmon-producing empire," he said. Others ask whether a decrease in the flow from these two great rivers might not alter the whole circulation pattern of the Pacific Ocean from Oregon to Alaska.

Often the drawbacks of a giant engineering project cannot be predicted. In proposing the Unified Water Plan for the development of

Bradford Washburn

At any time, over 75 per cent of the earth's fresh water is frozen in icecaps and glaciers. This volume is equal to the flow of all the earth's rivers for 1,000 years. Possible effects on climate and ocean level, however, give scientists pause when schemes to melt glacial ice are proposed.

the River Jordan basin, engineers appointed by the United Nations allotted Israel 232,000,000 gallons a day. But when the Israelis began pumping water at a rate of 186,000,000 gallons a day to their croplands in the northern Negev Desert, the level of Lake Tiberias (the Sea of Galilee) fell three feet in just a few months. Saline springs in the lake bottom increased their flow, rendering the water dangerously salty. To again get water of usable quality, the yield of fresh water from this ambitious and controversial project had to be cut back to about 125,000,000 gallons a day.

The much-publicized Aswan High Dam may do little more than enhance the political popularity of Egypt's president, Gamal Abdel Nasser. When completed, the dam will hold a reservoir nearly 200 miles long, harnessing the Nile River for the first time. Below the dam, all of the water will flow through irrigation canals, allowing continuous production of rice and other crops on 3,000 square miles of now useless desert. The food produced is expected to nourish Egypt's growing population and provide commodities for export. Electric power from the great turbines is to help industrialize the country.

Some engineers wonder, however, if the dam might not produce as many problems as it solves. They are willing to accept the loss of the Nile as a navigable corridor for commerce, but they worry about the amount of water the dry air will evaporate from the huge reservoir and from the man-made ditches through which the irrigation water will travel, in boiling heat, for 1,000 miles to the Mediterranean Sea. Not only will water be lost by evaporation, but the shrinking remainder will become increasingly concentrated with salts. When it reaches Lower Egypt, where crops irrigated by the Nile are now raised, it may be too salty for use.

In addition, the health of Egyptians on the upper side of the dam is almost sure to deteriorate rapidly as soon as irrigation water flows from Aswan on a year-round basis. In any hot country that has poor sanitation, blood flukes and other agents of chronic disease penetrate the skin of people who wade in and drink irrigation water. When irrigation was introduced in Lower Egypt, the proportion of people with debilitating blood-fluke infections rose from 5 per cent to 80 per cent. Because of this, the Egyptian army finds that its rejection rate for men of the Lower Nile is now seven times as high as that of men from nonirrigated Upper Egypt. Much of the country's heavy labor force is supplied from Upper Egypt, where there is a very low incidence of blood flukes. Infections caused by this parasite are presently incurable, and even now have markedly lowered the productivity of Egypt.

President Nasser and his government are relying on the chance that a way will be found to control blood flukes and other diseases associated with continued irrigation in a warm climate. However, doctors who work in the tropics regard the Aswan High Dam

A CONTINENTAL WATER PLAN

One example of continental engineering is the Ralph M. Parsons Company plan for distributing water throughout wide areas of North America. Under this plan, rainfall in Alaska and Canada that now drains, unused, into the Pacific and Arctic oceans would be diverted to water-poor sections of the continent. This project, however, would require excavation of reservoirs and canals equivalent to more than 100 Panama Canals. And before work could begin, hydrologists would have to check for potentially harmful side effects.

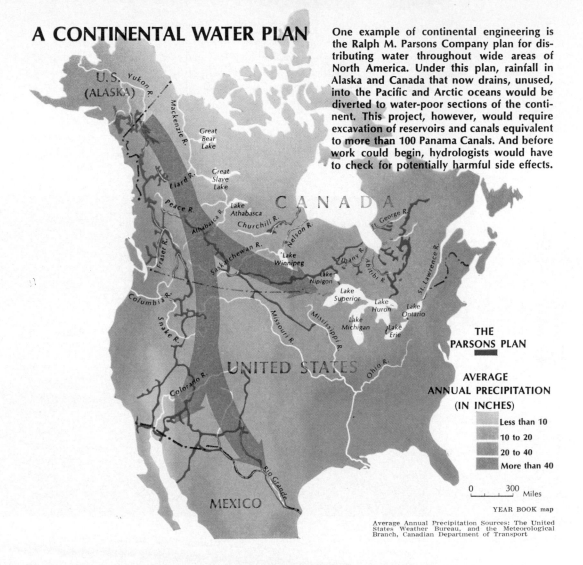

THE PARSONS PLAN

AVERAGE
ANNUAL PRECIPITATION
(IN INCHES)

Less than 10
10 to 20
20 to 40
More than 40

0   300   Miles

YEAR BOOK map

Average Annual Precipitation Sources: The United States Weather Bureau, and the Meteorological Branch, Canadian Department of Transport

as a desperate gamble, likely to cause far more harm than good.

Whatever the outcome of the Aswan High Dam project and other large-scale plans elsewhere, mankind must find ways of increasing the world's fresh water supply. To answer some of the most important questions raised by increasing water shortages in the United States, the Federal Council for Science and Technology, in June, 1960, invited Walter B. Langbein of the U.S. Geological Survey to head a Panel on Hydrology. Other top scientists on the panel represented the National Science Foundation, the U.S. Army Corps of Engineers, the Weather Bureau, the U.S. Public Health Service, and the Agricultural Research Service.

Because of the scope of the problem, international cooperation seemed essential. Langbein asked his colleague, Raymond L. Nace, for suggestions. Nace and Langbein produced the most far-reaching part of the panel's 37-page report, which called for a world-wide study of fresh water. Because weather dominates the water cycle and varies so much from year to year, coordinated, systematic observations for a period of at least 10 years seemed necessary.

Key officials in the U.S. Department of State were keenly interested, and encouraged the project. After much further work on the plan, UNESCO formally endorsed it in November, 1964. The organization proclaimed the International Hydrological Decade (IHD), to last from Jan. 1, 1965, through Dec. 31, 1974. Financial support was voted, and a 21-member Coordinating Council was authorized to administer it.

Most activities within the program of the IHD will relate to the

United Press Int.

Scarce surface water will be hoarded behind the Aswan High Dam when it is completed in 1969. The Egyptian government is hoping its people will reap great benefits from the dam, but scientists fear possible side effects.

collection and exchange of facts and ideas. For rarely has the distinction between basic scientific knowledge and its engineering applications been so great. The hard facts are that no one really knows yet exactly where the rain goes after it sinks into the soil, or what channels the meltwater from snow follows, determining whether rivers will flood disastrously this year or not. Guesses are not good enough: new and reliable sources of information must be found. Scarcely less important to hydrologists will be the education of world leaders, whose decisions influence the supply and quality of fresh water.

During the Decade, international efforts will focus on three fronts. One group of scientists will help establish an interlocking network of observation stations on all the continents and major islands of the world. With cooperation from local governments and individual scientists, the group will strive for standardization in methods of measurement of precipitation, stream flow, sediment transport, ground water, evaporation, snow, and ice. Reliable information is now deficient or lacking for two-thirds of the land areas of the world.

The second group will assist specialists in all of the participating countries to gather their existing records into the form of "national inventories" of fresh water. From these, a reliable picture of the water balance over the entire globe will be constructed for the first time. Almost surely it will indicate the location and size of uncharted rivers and reservoirs deep in the earth. Recent discoveries prove this to be no dream. Long-abandoned wells dug by the Romans in Tunisia contain an abundance of usable water. Porous rocks beneath the Sahara are full of fresh water—perhaps the largest untapped supply in the world.

The third group will strive to assist fundamental research. Its concern will be the many factors affecting precipitation, evaporation and transpiration, and surface runoff. It will study the dynamics of reservoirs and natural lakes and rivers, the transport and deposition of sediments, movements of soil moisture, interaction between fresh water and ocean water in estuaries, river deltas, and along coasts. It will examine meltwater from snowfields, glaciers, and icecaps, and the quality and chemistry of fresh water. Perhaps most important, it will study the complex influence of man upon many of these factors.

Deliberately excluded, though, are most of the short-range problems that seem so pressing in various parts of the world: water for New York and other cities; for industry, irrigation, water power, and navigation. These, like waste disposal and pollution, await the determination of the people who must raise and spend the money necessary to solve them.

The IHD has already begun to bear fruit in some of the more advanced countries. The British government has established a Water Resources Planning Board to spur action by communities and industries to conserve water. The Congress of the United States has passed the Water Resources Research Act of 1964 which provides grants for universities and scientific foundations to tackle critical water problems. It has also passed the Water Resources Planning Act of 1965 which provides for the establishment of a water resources council and river basin commissions and encourages state participation in resolving water problems. Early in 1965, the first allotments of research funds were made to establish water research institutes in fourteen states.

The IHD is the largest international scientific program yet begun. Coming at a time when a water crisis threatens most of mankind, every one of us will gain from it. Dr. E. L. Hendricks, chief of the Surface Water Branch in the U.S. Geological Survey, repeats the point that "a science may be gauged by its ability to predict." Hydrologists want the forward strides made during the International Hydrological Decade to permit predictions that will guarantee success in providing fresh water for an increasingly thirsty world. To us, the message is clear: to manage fresh water wisely is to conserve life itself.

See also Section Two, *Polluted America;* Section Three, NEW YORK CITY; WATER AND FLOOD CONTROL.

THE NEW

*An Old Region Rallies
Its Resources and People
To Enter a New Age of
Skill and Science*

By Robert A. Irwin

NEW ENGLAND

Standing in front of Boston's historic Faneuil Hall, I looked up at a bronze statue of Samuel Adams. If the statue's metallic eyes had suddenly widened in wonder, I would have been only slightly surprised. Sam Adams, garbed in a tarnished frock coat, was gazing majestically across 60 acres of rubble—and renewal. A sign nearby proclaimed this to be Boston's ambitious Government Center project.

Gone were all traces of honky-tonk Scollay Square and those steep, alleylike streets, Cornhill and Brattle, with their musty, second-hand bookstores. They had been leveled by bulldozers.

Their demise symbolized one of the greatest changes in Boston in the 162 years since Sam Adams had died. Amid the rubble, skyscrapers were going up. Gigantic cranes hovered among the rising structures. It was an impressive sight; particularly to a native who had left New England 30 years before, as I had.

The New England I had known could be characterized by one word: "old." Its factories, its institutions, its customs, its public buildings—even the attitudes of its people—were old. This gave the region a certain antique charm, but also placed it outside the mainstream of American development. Now something new, radically new, was happening. Throughout a 1,500-mile tour of the six New England states, I noticed many sights and sounds that signified change—and progress.

In Vermont, long noted for its pastoral quiet and the fact that it had more cows than people, scientists passed farmers on the way to work in a research laboratory that had, quite naturally, sprung up in a pasture. In Rhode Island, Providence had rescued its main shopping thoroughfare from the noise, fumes, and peril of auto traffic by converting Westminster Street into an attractive mall. In Connecticut, there was Hartford's Constitution Plaza; a dazzling testimonial to progress. In Maine, 75 miles north of Portland, a silvery, balloonlike radome lay in a bowl of low-lying hills; its huge horn antenna relaying television signals from the Early Bird communications satellite. In New Hampshire, in the once-depressed textile city of Keene, business leaders were busily recruiting workers from outside the community to keep pace with the demands of the city's now booming, diversified industries.

Nor was this all. Most important, New England's educational institutions were assuming a new, vital role. They were no longer regarded as cultural luxuries, but as necessities for the economic survival of the region. And they were attracting increasing numbers of dedicated researchers and teachers, as well as inquisitive students.

Quite evidently, New England had developed a new faith in the future. It seemed to be recapturing the spirit of an earlier age. From the 17th through the 19th centuries, New England and its people had played a dominant role in national life. Its swift clipper ships dominated world trade. Its shrewd Yankee traders amassed fortunes that furnished the means to build a growing nation's railroads, canals, and new industries. Its skilled craftsmen produced clocks, tools, instruments, and machines. Its fishermen harvested cod and haddock for the markets of the East. Its mills and factories clothed and shod the nation.

New England produced the literary giants of the day—Ralph Waldo Emerson, Nathaniel Hawthorne, Henry James, Henry David Thoreau, and others. New England also gave the nation its first successful ironworks, its first newspaper, its first permanent symphony orchestra.

As a result of the rapid development of the United States, it was perhaps inevitable that New England's influence would decline. Few, however, expected the decline to become as pronounced as it did. New England's share of U.S. personal income and number of factory jobs fell by more than 40 per cent from 1900 to the early 1950s. Its

YEAR BOOK photos on pages 194-195 and above by Ted Polumbaum

Foreign-born Population

■ New England
■ United States

For decades, New England's percentage of foreign born has been about twice that of the United States.

In the exclusive Boston Athenaeum, Boston's Irish mayor, John F. Collins, right, and Brahmin Charles A. Coolidge get down to work on the new Boston's problems.

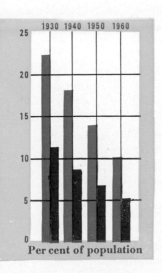

Per cent of population

share of *value added by manufacture* (the difference between the price of a finished product and the cost of the materials that go into it), declined from about 16 per cent of the U.S. total in 1900 to a little more than 7 per cent in 1958.

But resource-poor New England had suffered other periodic setbacks in its long past. There had been one when its forests were depleted; another when the clipper ships and whalers outlived their glory. New England had experienced an economic defeat when the building of the Erie Canal and the railroads shifted the center of trade and finance to New York. Yet, Yankee ingenuity had somehow overcome those crises. The decline in the 20th century, however, involved problems seemingly even more grave than those of the past.

One was the exodus of manpower, which had begun in the 19th century but which did not become serious until the 1920s. As I stood beside the statue of Sam Adams, I thought back to the time in 1935, when I, too, had joined the exodus. In the decade 1930–1940, 43,000

197

Yankee ingenuity and water power laid the foundations of old New England's industries, such as this first successful U.S. mill for cotton spinning built by Samuel Slater in Pawtucket, R.I.

more people left New England than moved in. It was not until 1950–1960 that the net outward flow was stanched, particularly in the last five of those years. To the thousands of us who had fled in 1935, New England seemed a forgotten, dusty old corner of a country on the move. Relations among the region's various ethnic groups were far from harmonious. Politically, economically, and socially, the Irish fought the Yankees and the Italians fought the Irish. The New England I had left had an atmosphere drained of vitality.

By 1965, however, New England had experienced a dramatic turnabout in its attitudes, discarding many of the prejudices of the past and experiencing a revitalization of its inner self. In Connecticut, Rhode Island, and Massachusetts, politicians were being elected and defeated, not on the basis of their ethnic backgrounds, but because of their ability, or lack of it. Maine, New Hampshire, and Vermont, long one-party strongholds, had become two-party states.

But, of all the changes, the most striking had occurred in the area's economic development. From 1947 to the end of 1962, for example, while jobs in the textile industry were shrinking from 279,000 to 110,300, employment in the transportation equipment and electrical machinery industries rose from 167,300 to 270,000. This transition occurred without fanfare. George H. Ellis, president of the Federal Reserve Bank of Boston, told of a survey of U.S. businessmen's attitudes toward New England. The great majority, he said, were "at least a generation out of date. The great transition to science-based and skilled-service industries here had not dawned on them." They still thought of this area as "that place where all the textiles left."

How is the individual New Englander faring today? Probably the best measure of his economic health is per capita income. New

YEAR BOOK photo by Ethel M. Irwin

Typical of the new New England are these laboratories of the Scientific Engineering Institute overlooking Massachusetts Route 128 in the Waltham Research and Development Park.

England's 1950–1963 increase in absolute terms was greater than that for the nation as a whole or for any other region in the United States. Here are the figures for New England, its two leading regional contenders, and the United States:

	1950	*1963*	*Increase*
New England	$1,629	$2,766	$1,137
Pacific	1,786	2,871	1,085
Middle Atlantic	1,757	2,810	1,053
United States	1,491	2,449	958

New England obviously has shaken itself out of its slump. But how?

My quest for the answers to that question began in Greater Boston. Tom Winship, editor of the *Boston Globe*, pointed out that the first turnabout came in the early 1950s with the building of a road in the countryside surrounding Boston. "This," said Winship with typical New England understatement, "was one piece of luck; the construction of the Circumferential Highway, Route 128." (Only in Boston would a belt highway be called a circumferential road!) Eventually, "hungry" professors at Massachusetts Institute of Technology (M.I.T.) and Harvard University set up businesses along Route 128 based on some of their scientific discoveries. "Thus," said Winship, "a marriage was consummated between the academic and economic communities."

When Sputnik I was launched in 1957, the growth was intensified. As Winship put it: "The shock of the emerging Space Age caused people to take stock. They knew things had to be done—right away."

Coupled with the movement of professors into industry was an influx of new faces into politics. The election of John F. Kennedy to the presidency gave New Englanders new confidence and pride. It also helped them to overcome their long-standing distrust of the federal government.

Boston's new mayor, John F. Collins, was "another stroke of luck." His upset election in 1959 gave him a mandate for change. One of his first steps was to bring in Edward J. Logue from New Haven, Conn., to head Boston's ambitious urban renewal program. In May, 1965, the city's banking community demonstrated its faith in Collins' new Boston. The First National Bank of Boston agreed, for the first time in six years, to head a syndicate to bid on the city's bonds, which had lost their A rating on the Moody scale of municipal financial standings.

The "Circumferential Highway" Winship mentioned and the new turnpikes and other interstate highways have given New England a fresh, liberating mobility. The old, hilly, twisting, horse-and-buggy roads between thickly populated towns had discouraged meaningful communication. As a result, cities as close to one another as Providence, R.I., and Fall River, Mass. (16 miles apart), had gone their separate ways. Even an untrained ear could detect the differences in accents between the people of the two cities.

"We have been close together, but far apart," was the apt observation of Geoffrey Glendinning, vice-president of Arlington Trust Company in Lawrence, Mass. "Now the auto and the expressways have converted our congestion into an advantage. Lawrence can tap a labor pool for miles around, and our people can commute to Boston, Manchester, N.H., Route 128 plants, or wherever."

This new ease of getting from one location to another is making an interconnected urban complex of all New England, with the exception

Roads That Mean Mobility

New, liberating lines of communications, such as the interstate highways, are ending the region's crippling congestion.

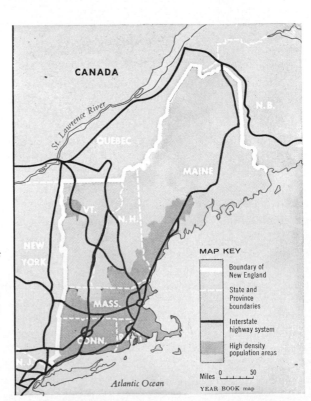

200

of its most out-of-the-way corners. It has widened job opportunities, choice of residence and friends, as well as the scope of recreational and cultural options. It has quickened the tempo and enriched the life of the New Englander. Bostonians think nothing of making an evening out of a Tanglewood concert in the Berkshires 125 miles away.

Even New England's remote "last stand of the Yankee" areas are coming under the influence of the interstate highways. The Dartmouth College region is one. It also epitomizes many other changes that are reshaping New England. This area's three chief towns—Hanover and Lebanon, N.H., and White River Junction, Vt.—are in a breathtaking period of transformation.

"We're sitting right in the middle of a historic crossroads in the making. We will be athwart the new interstates, one from Boston to Montreal, and the other from New York City up the Connecticut Valley and eventually to Quebec City. Industry and business know it and are buying property around here like mad," said Walter Paine, the vigorous, young publisher of the *Valley News* in West Lebanon. He pointed across the road from his neat, little publishing plant to a small, scrubby field and continued: "Eight years ago I could have bought that acre for $600. This spring I paid $6,000 for it."

Paine himself is typical of the new breed of Yankee I met. Since he

Intricate interchange of Route 128, running from upper left to lower right, with the Massachusetts Turnpike gives easy access to scores of nearby science-based industries and businesses.

201

took over the then four-year-old daily newspaper in 1956, circulation has risen 44 per cent. Paine emigrated to this area from suburban Boston "because it's an attractive, relaxing, yet exciting, place to work and live. The old disadvantages of remoteness have disappeared. The superhighway and the airplane are taking care of that."

This new mobility has not only infused fresh blood into this old Yankee area, but has also sparked some revolutionary changes in attitudes. The outlook of the people has, for one thing, become regional, rather than local. Support for the bi-state area's airport is a case in point. Funds for the Lebanon Regional Airport Authority are voted by taxpayers in both New Hampshire and Vermont.

"Those people," Paine told me, "don't care if one town is going to use the airport more than another. It's what it will do for the entire area."

This regional spirit has spread. The towns of Norwich, Vt., and Hanover, N.H., after three years of effort, an act of Congress, and the approval of the two state legislatures, set up the nation's first bi-state, regional high school district, called the Dresden School District. The Hanover high school opened to regional students in 1964.

In the same period, the area achieved another first. Its Upper Valley Development Council, founded in 1962, was the first regular interstate multicommunity, economic development council in the United States. Its director, Paul H. Guilderson, a former industrial salesman, told me how Lebanon's aldermen drafted a redevelopment plan under the Federal Housing Act only three weeks after the disastrous fire of June 19, 1964, had leveled half the city's business district. "This amounted to a revolution up here—business and city officials working on a program partly financed by federal funds," Guilderson said.

Dartmouth College has been conducting a quiet social and educational revolution right on its ivied campus in Hanover, N.H. Project ABC—"A Better Chance"—enrolled 81 bright but poor teen-age boys, mostly Negroes, in the summer of 1965. The boys who pass the intensive eight-week course are offered scholarships to one of New England's once-exclusive private preparatory schools.

George Cabot Lodge, a former U.S. Assistant Secretary of Labor and son of U.S. Ambassador Henry Cabot Lodge, is an enthusiastic supporter of ABC for his "prep" school, Groton. He commented: "The prep schools, along with New England's colleges and universities, have broadened their bases geographically, economically, and socially. It is an upgrading of education to attract the best qualified students, no matter where they come from."

Lodge and others like him are speeding a social revolution that is liberating New England even more than its expressways. Another old-line Yankee who has helped bring about this new social mobility is Boston lawyer Charles A. Coolidge. He is the son of architect Charles Coolidge and a distant relative of President Calvin Coolidge. Lawyer Coolidge was instrumental in helping to bring an end to more than a century of bitter feuding between Boston's Yankee community and its Irish population.

Historic Faneuil Hall keeps a lonely vigil as Boston builds its new Government Center.

YEAR BOOK photo by Ethel M. Irwin

Constitution Plaza has revitalized a former slum area of downtown Hartford, Conn. One of its striking showpieces is the Phoenix Mutual Life Insurance Company building, center.

I met Coolidge, a vigorous, alert 70, in his comfortable, homey office on the top floor of a substantial old stone building in Boston's financial district. He settled himself in a well-worn wooden chair behind a polished desk, which had been his grandfather's, and began: "It started six or seven years ago when a small group sat down together at Boston College. That, as you know, is the Catholic university here. The group recognized the tremendous cost to the community of the continuing lack of communication between the people who "owned" Boston (the Yankee Brahmins) and the people who "ran" it (the Irish and others). A continuing series of representative seminars was organized under Father W. Seavey Joyce, the college's dean of business. These have made a major contribution to revitalizing Boston."

That represented a revolutionary social change from the New England of deep distrust and suspicion that I had grown up in. Only after I left the region, did I realize that we old New Englanders had really been a minority. We had lived in the most foreign of all U.S. regions. As late as 1940, New Englanders who were either born abroad or had at least one foreign-born parent made up 51.5 per cent of the region's white population. The national figure was 17.8 per cent.

Despite waves of immigrants, the old stock held onto its power for decades. The late mayor James M. Curley could with truth refer to "that downtrodden majority, Boston's Irish!" In the early 1950s, a transplanted California educator remarked to Sevellon Brown, associate editor of the *Providence Journal*, that that city was "the only community I have ever lived in where the majority felt like the minority, and the minority acted as if it were the majority."

203

New England's greatest asset, brain power, is nurtured on its college campuses, such as that of the Massachusetts Institute of Technology (M.I.T.).

M.I.T., as other New England colleges, attracts talented students from many parts of the world.

Dartmouth's new Center for Mathematics rises beside the college's old Church of Christ.

YEAR BOOK photo by Ted Polumbaum

*Not only at M.I.T., but also at Harvard's new Engineering Sciences
Laboratory, students are extending scientific frontiers.*

YEAR BOOK photo by
Ethel M. Irwin

I went back to Boston University to see if a former professor of mine,
sociologist Albert Morris, could explain why New England's melting
pot had been so slow to heat up. "What has to be remembered," he
began, "is that New England was a stable, homogeneous society for
more than 200 years. Then newcomers, fleeing the Irish potato famine,
arrived during the 1840s. They had been living in sod huts, suffering
starvation and terrible deprivation. They were of a different religion,
Roman Catholic, and many were illiterate. The old, established New
Englanders reacted strongly; they weren't about to be pushed aside."

In the pioneer society of the Middle West and West, on the other
hand, Morris explained, both the overseas immigrants and the U.S.
natives were settlers working side by side in the building of new cities
and the opening of new farmlands.

What it meant to be an immigrant in New England is told by
Donald Cole in his *Immigrant City*, a historical study of Lawrence, Mass.
He describes how a fire in 1875 "laid bare the shabbiness of the immigrants' living conditions. In a shack, measuring 100 x 20 feet and
divided in the middle, lived a family, 77 boarders and two girl cooks.
The fire started at 1:30 A.M. in a cubicle usually occupied by the two
cooks but empty at the moment because they were sleeping on the floor
of the main room to escape bedbugs."

Now, 90 years later, banker Geoffrey Glendinning, himself a de-
scendant of a Yorkshire weaver, told me how far the children and
grandchildren of Lawrence's immigrants had traveled. He read at random some of the names of chief executives from the city's industrial

*George Cabot Lodge
typifies the continuing
educational concern of
old Yankee families.*

205

YEAR BOOK photo by Ollie Atkins

Presque Isle, Me., refused to give up when its huge air base closed in 1961. It hired James K. Keefe, a Maine-educated Bay Stater, to head its Industrial Council. He and the council induced businesses to move into the former hangars and missile sheds, creating more than 1,000 new jobs—almost four times as many as had been lost when the base shut down.

YEAR BOOK photo by Ted Polumbaum

Sheldon Dietz, Harvard (1941) and a resident of Martha's Vineyard, Mass., has brought about a revolutionary change in one of New England's oldest industries—fisheries. He has adapted the long-line method of fishing to catching swordfish, which were found to frequent New England waters at varying depths all year, not just in the summer. His two specially designed vessels carry miles of hooked and buoyed nylon rope.

directory—Batal, Forma, Giragosian, Grieco, Privitera, Rappaport, Valeska, and Vinciguerra. "Certainly," Glendinning added, "second- and third-generation Americans are as great participants in Lawrence's leadership today as the descendants of the original Yankee stock."

Wendell D. Macdonald, regional director of the U.S. Bureau of Labor Statistics in Boston, had pointed to the same general trend: "Most New Englanders are losing their old prejudices. There is a new spirit of cooperation that is making the social climate much more pleasant."

He then went into the human side of the story of New England's successful shift from textiles. New England's inventors such as Samuel Slater and Eli Whitney had simplified textile manufacturing. It was unskilled, low-paid work, and the immigrants did it. Eventually, however, as their sons and daughters became better educated, they were ready for higher paid, more skilled jobs.

As New England textile wages inched higher, the mills began to shut down and move South, where wage levels were lower. "Most of the men over 50 never got another job," Macdonald said. "The younger people found work in offices and in our growing industries. We've still got some depressed areas, and there's some suffering, but all in all the textile shut-downs have worked out to be a healthy thing for the economy of New England."

Education had helped to break down the old social barriers and get rid of the textile drag on the economy. Later it was to play a major part in leading the region into a Space Age economy. Lawyer Coolidge had

YEAR BOOK photo by Ted Polumbaum

Edward W. Brooke typifies the new politics of New England. Brooke, a Republican and a Negro, defied the Democratic tide in 1964 and was re-elected attorney general of Massachusetts.

Polaroid Corporation

Scientist Edwin H. Land, the inventor-president of Polaroid Corporation, is an example of a successful science-industry marriage.

YEAR BOOK photo by
Ted Polumbaum

José Luis Sert, the world-famed Spanish architect, has been a New Englander and dean of Harvard's graduate school of design since 1953. He is standing in front of a Harvard dormitory that he designed.

noted that by the turn of the century New Englanders had become less adventurous than their enterprising forefathers. "The doldrums had set in. The people attracted to such institutions as Harvard and M.I.T. and the ideas that were generated there," he said, "tended to pull us out." George Lodge vigorously seconded Coolidge's appraisal, stressing the "extraordinary importance of Harvard and M.I.T." in the transformation of New England's economy.

Up at the University of New Hampshire, I asked economist John Hogan if this Harvard-M.I.T. influence was being felt there. He replied: "Of course it is. Its influence is permeating all of New England. Here in Durham, the federal government is putting a lot of money into scientific research. This wouldn't be going on if it weren't for the spark that came from the Harvard-M.I.T. knowledge explosion. We have some of the top people in missiles and space work right here."

The Boston-Cambridge complex—34 colleges and universities within a radius of 50 miles from downtown Boston—is perhaps New England's greatest asset. For, as Myron Tribus, Dartmouth's dean of engineering, pointed out, "Business and industry have entered a new era in which knowledge has become a prime resource. Sometime in the 1950s management began to realize this. Management also became aware that there was an actual dollar value in being close to educational facilities." This has produced some dramatic results.

Science-based industries and the educational complex that helped spawn them have served as a magnet to draw new people into the region. Thus, New England, in addition to upgrading its home-grown human resources, is recruiting outside talent.

Coolidge had observed: "In my 30 years as a Harvard fellow (five fellows, along with the president and treasurer *ex officio*, manage the university), Harvard has drawn heavily from across the nation for its

207

deans, faculty, and most of its graduate students. Talent and brains no longer are being drained away from New England. In fact, the reverse is true."

The proportion of non-New England freshmen entering M.I.T. climbed from 62 per cent in 1949 to 85 per cent in 1963. Many of them chose to make their futures in New England. A recent survey of the graduates of the 11 science and engineering colleges and universities in the Boston area disclosed that more than half remained in the region.

In a speech several years ago, M.I.T. chairman James R. Killian, Jr., cited another survey of 41,000 U.S. scientists, 14 per cent of whom had received their Ph.D. degrees in New England. He went on to say: "Because of the environment they find here, many of these outstanding men and women who came here to study elect to remain. The excellence of the region in the scientific personnel it attracts and retains is shown in its share of the total members of the nation's top scientific societies. Over 20 per cent of the members of the National Academy of Sciences work in New England."

Gerald W. Blakely, Jr., the young president of one of Boston's oldest real estate firms, Cabot, Cabot and Forbes (CCF), documented this "brain magnetism." He quickly ran down a list of seven outstanding Boston business institutions: New England Mutual Life Insurance Company, John Hancock Mutual Life Insurance Company, the Gillette Company, New England Merchants National Bank of Boston, State Street Bank and Trust Company, Polaroid Corporation, and Raytheon Company. Only the last was headed by a Bostonian, Charles F. Adams. All the others were "foreigners."

A native New Englander himself, Blakely is an "outsider" in a sense. He is the first non-Harvard man ever to head CCF. But more important, it was his vision that led to the industrial development of "the Road"—Route 128—and to providing the kind of environment Killian alluded to. Its industrial parks, Blakely said, have "proved physically attractive to research people who were already sold on the area's educational, cultural, and recreational advantages, as well as its generally relaxed atmosphere. What we are seeing in New England," he concluded, "is a solid and steady growth, a growth in quality—quality of product, skills, and way of life."

The author:

Robert A. Irwin, a World Book Year Book *senior editor, attended Newton (Mass.) public schools before he emigrated to the Middle West. He has written two other Special Reports for past* Year Books: Breakthrough in the Breadbasket (*1963*) *and* Call to the Wilderness (*1965*).

Too many years in the doldrums, New England is now showing that an old, urbanized region need not blindly resist change; that with brain and will, it can adapt to it instead. New England is once more making the most of its assets: its new mobility, both physical and social; the brains, mechanical ingenuity, and skills of all its people. Of overriding significance is the dramatic surge of its educational system. The vitality of its schools and colleges, with the ever-growing dependence of business and industry upon them, has given the whole region, in Tom Winship's phrase, a Space Age "leg up" on many other areas of the nation. Clearly, the old New England I left a generation ago has become a *new* New England.

See also Section One, Focus, Lawrence A. Cremin on Education.

CONTENTS OF SECTION THREE

YEAR BOOK contributors report on the major developments of 1965 in their respective fields.

THE YEAR ON FILE, 1965

Articles in this section are arranged alphabetically by subject matter. Titles refer directly to articles in THE WORLD BOOK ENCYCLOPEDIA.

ADEN. See SOUTH ARABIA, FEDERATION OF.

ADVERTISING in the United States and around the world exhibited strong signs of growth in 1965. Total U.S. dollar volume increased nearly 5 per cent to more than $14,500,000,000. Television led the way. Magazine advertising continued a healthy comeback (up 6 per cent). Procter & Gamble was again the top U.S. advertiser, with an advertising budget of $225,000,000.

In Canada, ad agencies billed $320,000,000, a gain of more than $23,000,000 for the year. The story was the same around the globe. As living standards increased, advertising assumed a greater importance. In terms of money spent, the major advertising countries, after the United States, were, in order, Britain, West Germany, Japan, France, Italy, and Australia.

Major U.S. developments included:
- The warning by the National Better Business Bureau that the government might crack down unless advertisers reversed the trend toward naming rivals' products and returned to the more polite practice of referring to "Brand X."
- Grey Advertising, Inc., became the fourth big agency to sell stock to the public.
- The federal Highway Beautification Act, with its restrictions on billboard advertising, became law (see ROADS AND HIGHWAYS). EDWIN W. DARBY

See also PUBLISHING; RETAILING; TELEVISION.

AFGHANISTAN proceeded haltingly in 1965 toward its goal of a democratically based constitutional monarchy. In September, the nation elected the 216 members of the lower house and 28 of the 84 members in the upper house. Of the 56 other members in the upper house, 28 were to be named by the king; 28 elected by provincial councils.

The new government was short-lived, however. On October 24, after King Mohammed Zahir Shah asked former Prime Minister Mohammed Yousof to form a cabinet, student riots broke out. As a result, Yousof resigned, and Mohammed Hashim Maiwandwal, a former ambassador to the United States, was appointed prime minister.

Meanwhile, the East and West continued to aid Afghanistan. The Soviet Union completed an agricultural survey of thousands of acres in northern Afghanistan. The International Bank for Reconstruction and Development loaned Afghanistan $350,000 for an irrigation survey of Kundūz Valley. A consortium of U.S. universities was formed to help develop engineering education at the University of Kabul.

Population: 16,070,000. **Government:** King Mohammed Zahir Shah; Prime Minister Mohammed Hashim Maiwandwal. **Monetary Unit:** afghani (50 afghanis equal U.S. $1). **Foreign Trade:** exports, $69,000,000; imports, $126,000,000. **Principal Exports:** caracul, carpets, wool. WILLIAM SPENCER

See also MIDDLE EAST.

AFRICA

GUINEA

Political crisis and change again characterized the African continent during 1965. Nigeria opened the year deep in the throes of its worst political crisis since independence. In the aftermath of its general elections which were held on Dec. 30, 1964, Nigeria suffered three days of political strife that was unmatched in the country's short history of independence.

Burundi, too, began the year in a sudden burst of political turmoil. Its new prime minister, Pierre Ngendandumwe, who had been asked on January 7 to form a government, was assassinated one week later. In the political maneuvering that followed, King Mwambutsa IV acted to consolidate his power. By July, he had taken personal charge

AFRICAN ANGER over Rhodesia's self-declared independence explodes as Ghana's Kwame Nkrumah, left, demands that British troops be used to prevent the move.
Wide World

GHANA

of the army, the gendarmerie, and key positions in the cabinet.

Dahomey was the scene of a political upheaval late in November when its government was ousted in a military coup. Shortly thereafter, Congo (Léopoldville) followed suit: Congolese Major General Joseph Mobutu deposed President Joseph Kasavubu and proclaimed himself head of the state. Malawi, a former member of the defunct Federation of Rhodesia and Nyasaland, and Togo, too, were embroiled in political plots and counterplots during the year. So were Angola and Mozambique, where African guerrillas continued their struggle for independence.

Turmoil in Rhodesia. It was Rhodesia, however, that managed to capture the world spotlight for 1965. On November 11, after the breakdown of a long series of dramatic exchanges with British leaders, the white minority government of Rhodesia's Prime Minister Ian Smith unilaterally declared itself independent from Britain. The British had refused to grant the country independence unless the minority government, firmly controlled by about 220,000 whites, took steps to assure eventual majority rule by Rhodesia's 4,000,000 Africans.

British Reaction. The British government denounced the Smith declaration as rebellion and treason. It expelled Rhodesia from the pound sterling monetary area and suspended its preferential tariff treatment. Controls on trade and currency were imposed, and a ban was placed on the purchase of Rhodesia's main crops, sugar and tobacco, an action that would cost Rhodesia an estimated $50,000,000 annually.

Britain's Prime Minister Harold Wilson rejected the use of British troops to bring about a change but reserved the right to send troops to maintain law and order. Legislation was immediately introduced in London to give Wilson and his cabinet far-reaching powers to legislate for Rhodesia by decree, to amend the existing Rhodesian constitution, and to wipe out any actions of Prime Minister Smith's rebellious regime. Underlying the legislation was the theme central to Britain's case, that Rhodesia remains British territory and that Smith and his government have no lawful title.

UN Condemnation. Prior to Rhodesia's unilateral seizure of independence, the United Nations (UN) General Assembly had called on Britain on October 12 to use all possible means to avert such a declaration. Following the Smith government's action, the UN Security Council condemned Rhodesia's move. The United States announced it would place a comprehensive embargo on shipments of military equipment to Rhodesia.

The Organization of African Unity (OAU) unanimously adopted a resolution threatening military intervention in Rhodesia and the breaking of diplomatic relations with Britain unless the British took decisive steps to crush Rhodesia's white minority government by December 15.

Political Life in the African nations, however, was not all ferment and upheaval. During 1965, a number of countries remained on a relatively even keel and conducted "politics as usual" through less spectacular and more conventional channels. In Cameroon, President Ahmadou Ahidjo was re-elected in peaceful balloting procedures. The Malagasy Republic likewise re-elected its President Philibert Tsiranana without political incidents. Ghana, Kenya, Senegal, and Uganda all remained relatively calm during 1965.

Inter-African Cooperation continued during the year on a number of different levels. The OAU, through its various commissions, continued to function successfully as a supranational body. Its Liberation Committee, its Social and Economic Commission, and its Educational and Cultural Commission were active throughout the year in a number of vital political and social areas.

The African Development Bank continued to serve pan-Africanism through its policy of giving special priority to projects which, by their nature or scope, concerned several members or made the economies of its members increasingly complementary. In February, the Organization for Afro-Malagasy Economic Cooperation (AMCE) was transformed into a new organization known as the Afro-Malagasy Common Organization. Operating within the context of

"Our host has been detained."

the OAU, it would seek to reinforce cooperation and solidarity between Afro-Malagasy states, as well as to speed their economic and cultural development.

In other efforts at inter-African cooperation, ministers of Guinea, Ivory Coast, Liberia, and Sierra Leone met in May to advance plans for a free trade area embracing all four countries. Representatives of nine West African states met in August and agreed in principle to establish an iron and steel authority to develop West African metallurgy.

Economic Development. Financial problems and setbacks dominated the economic climate in a number of African countries. The financial situation in Congo (Léopoldville) was reportedly worse, due in part to the cost of its continuing military operations against rebel forces. By August, however, a number of French experts were in Congo with promises of additional technical assistance. Promises of economic aid were obtained from West Germany. An agreement was also reached with Belgium under which the Congolese government's capital holdings and voting rights in the Union Miniére du Haut-Katanga were greatly increased. See BELGIUM.

Economic problems were reported in the Malagasy Republic, due largely to poor banana, rice, and sugar harvests. Malawi, whose growing budget deficit was attributable largely to the falling price of tea, was promised development aid in money or services from Australia, Denmark, Great Britain, New Zealand, Nigeria, and the United States. Ghana's economy was overshadowed by a sizable budgetary deficit, as well as a deficit in its balance of payments position abroad. Nevertheless, a variety of measures were undertaken to strengthen the country's economic position.

The Ivory Coast secured a sizable European Development Fund Loan with which to establish an 80,000-acre palm plantation and construct seven palm oil processing plants.

Other Expansion Programs. Mozambique laid plans for the construction of its first sugar refinery. It also completed and put into service a 187-mile oil pipeline. In Gabon, hopes for a deepwater port at Owende grew with receipt of a European Economic Community (EEC, or Common Market) loan of $263,000 for technical studies. In Kenya, construction began on the $103,600,000 Seven Forks hydroelectric project on the Tana River. In Nigeria, plans were made to establish a steel industry.

Liberia laid plans for the construction of an oil refinery and an iron ore washing and pelletizing plant. Cameroon, with the aid of an EEC loan negotiated late in 1964, acted to develop its second five-year development plan aimed at improving its coffee, cotton, and peanut crops.   BENJAMIN E. THOMAS

See also the various African countries.

TROUBLE SPOTS IN AFRICA IN 1965

① ALGERIA
Army ousts President Ahmed Ben Bella.

② CONGO
(Léopoldville)
General Joseph Mobutu seizes power.

③ DAHOMEY
Government toppled in bloodless coup.

④ MALAWI
Crushes army rebellion.

⑤ MOROCCO
Racked by antigovernment riots.

⑥ MOZAMBIQUE
Harassed by anti-Portuguese rebels.

⑦ RHODESIA
Defies Great Britain, declares independence.

⑧ SUDAN
Rent by violence in southern provinces.

0   500   1,000 Miles

YEAR BOOK map

AGRICULTURE. Most nations of the world, including those under communist rule, continued to marvel at the accomplishments of U.S. farmers. But U.S. agriculture—which had long played a dominant political and economic role in American life—found itself assuming a "minority" position. That change was dramatized in the 89th Congress by the tough battles over farm subsidies and by the defeat of the so-called "bread tax"—largely at the hands of city and suburban Congressmen. At the same time the farmers' political voice was being steadily diminished in the state legislatures, as well as in Congress, by the aftereffects of the 1964 U.S. Supreme Court "one man, one vote" decisions. Thus, U.S. agriculture was accepting the change, and, in the process, it matured a bit in 1965.

Agricultural production was the most pressing communist problem. Russia again lost face as it went into world markets to trade valuable rubles for food. Shortages in Communist China were reported. Poland, with its noncollectivized agriculture embarrassed other communist-bloc agricultural planners with its continued high production.

U.S. Farmers did well in 1965. Their incomes were the highest since 1952—$14,000,000,000, up more than $1,000,000,000, or $400 per farm, over 1964. Government payments rose to about $2,400,000,000. A strong economy resulted in good demand for agricultural produce. Farm exports reached record levels.

Production expenses rose $1,000,000,000, but were more than offset by increased receipts. Feeder livestock costs went up sharply. Prices of fertilizer, repairs, taxes, interest, and depreciation also rose.

Weather was good. Spring drought in the Southwest was mostly gone by summer. The drought in the extreme Northeast cut production, but not enough to offset the fine year elsewhere. The 1965 all-crops production estimate by the U.S. Department of Agriculture (USDA) rose to a record 117 per cent of the 1957-1959 average, sharply ahead of 1964's figure of 109.

The record 161,000,000-ton production of feed grains (barley, corn, grain sorghums, and oats) was 23,000,000 tons larger than the 1964 output. It increased total supply to 217,000,000 tons. The four grains' spectacular 18 per cent increase in average yield per acre—on a 1 per cent smaller amount of land—accounted for the year's output gain. All but 5,000,000 tons of the 1965 crop was used, increasing carry-over into 1966-1967 to 60,-000,000 tons—about 25,000,000 tons below the record 1961-1962 carry-over.

Wheat *disappearance* (total use) exceeded production for the fifth consecutive year, reducing surplus stores. The cotton crop held about level with 1964 and disappearance was up slightly. But carry-over on Aug. 1, 1966, is expected to reach a new high of 16,200,000 bales. Citrus fruit production was moderately up. Fall potato output set a new high.

With larger harvests, farmers' all-crop prices in October declined an average of $5\frac{1}{2}$ per cent from the 1964 month. On specific crops the percentage

Output of Major U.S. Crops
(millions of bushels)

Crop	1965*	1964	1959-1963‡
Corn	4,171	3,584	3,817
Sorghums	666	492	550
Oats	959	882	1,044
Wheat	1,327	1,291	1,190
Soybeans	844	702	627
Rice (a)	760	731	597
Potatoes (c)	289	239	267
Sugar (b)	5,450	5,587	4,486
Cotton (d)	151	151	147
Tobacco (e)	1,913	2,227	2,092

*Preliminary; ‡average
(a) 100,000 cwt. (b) 1,000 tons; (c) 1,000,000 cwt; (d) 100,000 bales‡ (e) 1,000,000 pounds

declines were: soybeans, 10; cotton, 5; corn, 4; potatoes, 22; and orange and grapefruit, 45 per cent.

Livestock and Animal Products accounted for most of the thrust in 1965's rising farm income. With per capita red meat supplies 4 per cent lower than in 1964, prices for hogs, cattle, and lambs rose 15 per cent in the year. Retail prices were up sharply. As a result, red meat consumption per person was

U.S. Production of Animal Products
(millions of pounds)

	1965*	1964	1957-1959†
Beef	18,620	18,448	13,704
Veal	1,020	1,011	1,240
Lamb and mutton	650	715	711
Pork	11,470	12,531	10,957
Eggs (a)	5,350	5,379	5,475
Chicken	6,655	6,252	4,880
Turkey	1,520	1,433	1,065
Total milk (b)	1,255	1,266	1,233
Cheese	1,755	1,726	1,396
Ice cream	3,600	3,531	3,212
Butter	1,415	1,468	1,477

*Preliminary; †average
(a) 1,000,000 dozens; (b) 100,000,000 pounds

seven pounds less than the 175 pounds in 1964. Most of the decline was in pork, with lamb and mutton down slightly and beef up slightly. Poultry consumption, however, increased two pounds, to $40\frac{1}{2}$ pounds per person.

The number of cattle on farms declined by more than 1,000,000 head, the first decrease since 1958. Cattle and calf slaughter at 40,500,000 head, rose 4 per cent from 1964. Fed-cattle prices averaged higher. Hog slaughter dropped 9 per cent, and the June-November 1965 pig crop fell about 7 per cent in the year. Hogs and pigs on farms in September numbered 12 per cent fewer than 12 months earlier. As a result, hog prices rose sharply to an $11\frac{1}{2}$-year high of $30 a hundredweight in December, from $16.50 a year earlier. While slaughter of sheep fell 10 per cent, prices rose to the highest level in years.

Farm Finances. U.S. farmers' total assets rose $15,000,000,000 in the year to an estimated value of $253,200,000,000. The rise in total land value alone accounted for more than $10,000,000,000 of the asset gain. Farm debts, however, rose about $3,600,000,000, chiefly for enlargement and improvement of farms.

The Market Place. Food in 1965 was a good buy. Slightly less than 1964's record low of $18\frac{1}{2}$ per cent of consumer income went for food. Per capita food consumption declined slightly, mainly in livestock products. Historically, such a decline has come only with very high prices, indicating that the well-fed, meat-consuming American will not take easily to less palatable foods (see FOOD).

Food expenditures, less alcoholic beverages, rose 6 per cent to $83,500,000,000 and furnished a living for over 5,000,000 people on farms and twice that many in marketing. Agriculture's interrelatedness with marketing was made evident by the more than 1,200 commodity trade associations, which spent $100,000,000 to promote food in 1965. One,

the farm-supported American Dairy Association, spent $8,200,000 to help sell dairy products.

Technology, which is constantly rewriting agricultural history, came up with many new production ideas in 1965. Among them were:
- Radio signals that operated solenoid air valves controlling irrigation water levels.
- Rolled feed grains resembling breakfast cereals to improve livestock feeding efficiency.
- Nonsouring milk that needs no refrigeration and will keep for several months, after a brief heating to 280°F. It was marketed by a British dairy early in 1965.
- Use of chemicals to accelerate defoliation and simplify harvesting of cotton, flowers, and fruits.
- Artificial insemination of quail to aid poultry genetics.

U.S. Farm Legislation. The Food and Agriculture Act of 1965 contained a number of surprises. First of all, the passage of such an important act in an off-election year may have signaled a trend away from politics in farm legislation. And for the first time since 1938, Congress enacted a farm program for a four-year period, extending into 1969.

The act was an amalgamation of general price support programs of recent years and a new set of tailored commodity plans. Direct subsidy payments to agriculture are not new, but the degree of

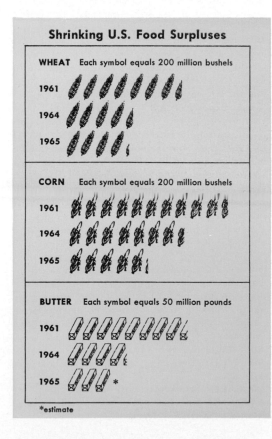

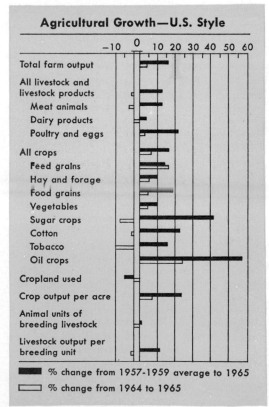

Source: U. S. Department of Agriculture Economic Research Service

emphasis in the 1965 act was new. It supported prices not only of wheat and feed grains, but also of cotton at market levels. Under this scheme, consumers pay lower prices, so, of course, the farmers receive lower prices, which are supplemented by direct payments from the U.S. Treasury. The aim was to increase both consumption at home and sales overseas. Only peanuts, rice, and tobacco remained under the old, rigid system of high price supports.

In the words of Secretary of Agriculture Orville L. Freeman, this new legislation represented "a shift in policy away from price supports for the major commodities at levels above world market prices to a policy of using the market, both domestic and foreign, to the maximum by setting price supports as close to market levels as possible."

The main thrust of the legislation was to bring rural America into the Great Society. Secretary Freeman even suggested calling his department the Department of Food, Agriculture, and Rural Affairs.

Aside from acreage controls for specified crops, the act provided a four-year Cropland Adjustment Program to take 40,000,000 acres out of agricultural production and place it in a "scenic soil bank." The idled cropland will provide open space for recreation, wildlife protection, and other "natural beauty" purposes. Five-to-10-year land retirement contracts with individual farmers were authorized.

A Turnabout in Agriculture. Between the continued policy of crop curtailment and rising consumption, U.S. food surpluses have dwindled. By 1970, the government's surplus stocks of grain will be gone, President Lyndon B. Johnson said on signing the farm bill on November 5. The new law recognized this change. It authorized the government to go into the market and purchase food to meet needs for food assistance programs regardless of price support stock, or market prices. The Food for Peace program was shifted to the U.S. Department of State from the USDA on November 1.

A Price-Support Program for major crops through 1969 was written into the act. The major innovation was in cotton. "One-price cotton" for domestic and export sales was maintained—but at lower support levels, 21 cents a pound in 1966 versus 27.1 cents in 1965. Support would be no more than 90 per cent of the world market price after 1966. Cash subsidies of at least 9 cents a pound or more—depending on the size of and reduction in his acreage allotments— will go to the grower. The major aim was to reduce the record glut by making U.S. cotton competitive at home and in overseas markets.

The 1965 act covered revised support and subsidy programs for feed grains, rice, wheat, and wool. All entailed acreage or production curtailments, with more flexibility in cash payments. The act offered dairy farmers in milk-marketing areas a chance to vote on production quotas for fluid milk at an established premium price. Sales of milk for cheese or butter would be at lower prices.

World Agriculture. Despite adverse weather conditions in some areas, notably Australia, Communist China, and the Soviet Union, world production of most crops was at record or near-record levels. Wheat production was down slightly at 9,108,000,000 bushels from the record 1964 crop, but 14 per cent above 1955-1959. Bumper crops in Africa, Europe, and North America were offset by decreased harvests in the Soviet Union and Communist China. Both nations had to make heavy purchases (see CANADA). World corn output was also high.

WORLD CROP PRODUCTION (000,000 omitted)				
Crop	1955–59	1964	1965 (est.)	% U.S.
Barley (bu.)	3,255	4,260	4,080	10
Corn (bu.)	6,480	7,780	8,150	50
Oats (bu.)	4,085	2,920	3,075	32
Wheat (bu.)	7,969	9,300	9,180	15
Rice*	132.8	168.8	164.1	2
Sugar (tons)	49.6	72.0	70.0	8
Coffee (bags†)	58.4	51.8	76 8	0
Cotton (bales)	43.8	52.0	52.0	29

*Metric tons: excluding communist Asia. †132.276 lb.
Source: U.S. Department of Agriculture, Foreign Agricultural Service.

U.S. agriculture continued to demonstrate superiority over the Soviet system. Although the Soviet Union utilizes 75 per cent more cropland and seven times more farmworkers, it produces only half as much cotton, 10 per cent as much corn, and 5 per cent as many soybeans. It lags far behind in all meats, as well as in milk, eggs, and lard. Only butter, potato, wheat, and wool totals are above U.S. levels. See EUROPE; INTERNATIONAL TRADE AND FINANCE; RUSSIA; Section Two, INSIDE RURAL INDIA and INSIDE RURAL CHINA; and the various country articles.

U.S. Exports of agricultural goods, which have risen yearly since 1959, continued to be the largest of any nation. At a record $6,300,000,000 for all of 1964, they were double the 1955 total. One-half of all sales of U.S. rice, soybeans, and wheat were overseas. Exports accounted for $1 out of every $6 of U.S. farmers' sales. Imports of farm products slipped to $3,998,000,000. Only Great Britain's agricultural imports were higher than the U.S. total. The total volume of world trade came to about $31,000,000,000 in 1964.

The hope was real in 1965 that someday the entire world would be adequately fed. Toward this end, surplus food continued to be exported to developing nations. Over $1,500,000,000, or one-fourth of U.S. farm exports, went to the developing nations of the world under the Food for Peace program   CHARLES E. FRENCH

AIR FORCE, U.S. See NATIONAL DEFENSE.

AIR POLLUTION. See Section Two, POLLUTED AMERICA.

AIR RACES. See AVIATION.

AIRPLANE. See ARMED FORCES OF THE WORLD; AVIATION; NATIONAL DEFENSE.

ALBANIA remained a stronghold of Stalinism and a Western outlet for Communist China's views. It continued to denounce the United States as the "head of the imperialist camp." The Soviet Union, however, ran a close second for Albania's wrath, with Premier Aleksei N. Kosygin and Communist Party Secretary Leonid I. Brezhnev under attack as "the greatest splitters of the world communist movement." Both were condemned for refusing to help Pakistan in its war with India, and for appeasing the United States in Vietnam.

No significant changes occurred in domestic politics. Communist Party First Secretary Enver Hoxha remained in firm control. However, an increase of interest in the West among Albania's youth seemed to worry the regime.

Although facts about the self-isolated nation remained elusive, it was known that the regime expected to inaugurate approximately 100 industrial projects financed through $125,000,000 in credits from Communist China.

Population: 1,919,000. **Government:** Communist Party First Secretary Enver Hoxha; Premier Mehmet Shehu. **Monetary Unit:** lek (5 = U.S. $1). **Foreign Trade:** exports, $48,000,000; imports, $71,000,000. **Principal Exports:** chrome ore, foodstuffs, minerals, tobacco.   TOM AND HARLE DAMMANN

See also EUROPE.

ALBERTA. See CANADA.

ALGERIA. The three-year rule of President Ahmed Ben Bella came to an abrupt end in the predawn hours of June 19, 1965. With tanks clanking in the background, Colonel Houari Boumedienne, Ben Bella's defense minister, seized power in a bloodless coup d'état.

Until then, Ben Bella had seemed to be growing in power. Moussa Hassani, the last guerrilla leader of the Socialist Forces Front (FFS), had surrendered to army troops. Hocine Aït Ahmed, the FFS commander captured in October, 1964, had been tried in secret and sentenced to death for high treason. But, in a move to reconcile all factions, Ben Bella pardoned Aït Ahmed. He also released several opposition leaders from house arrest.

Crackdown on Communists. Boumedienne's coup brought a set of new faces into the government. Most were military men or former officers. In assuming the presidency of a 26-member National Revolutionary Council, Boumedienne delegated authority to a 20-member cabinet, including 10 holdovers from the Ben Bella regime. He called for cooperation with all nations, social and economic development, and the rebuilding of the National Liberation Front (FLN) as a dynamic force in the nation. The new regime won quick recognition internationally, but was criticized by Albania and China as being "revisionist" (see CHINA).

Under Ben Bella, Algeria had a declared policy of "socialism" and was drifting toward closer relations

Pictorial Parade

TWO OLD FRIENDS, shown in 1963 photo, parted company in 1965. President Ahmed Ben Bella, left, was overthrown by Colonel Houari Boumedienne, right, in Algerian coup d'état.

with Communist China. With Boumedienne in control, Algeria began to edge toward friendlier relations with the West. In fact, the new government cracked down on communist elements.

Economic Agreements. After 20 months of hard bargaining, significant agreements were reached with France in July on oil and gas production in the Sahara. The Saharan fields will be developed jointly by France and Algeria, with additional concessions for non-French oil companies. Companies would be guaranteed against nationalization for 15 years. A revised royalty and tax schedule, based on a higher "agreed price" per barrel than any existing elsewhere in the Middle East, would boost Algerian oil revenues from $80,000,000 in 1965 to $240,000,000 in 1970. France also agreed to provide $400,000,000 for the purchase of French industrial equipment.

Another Franco-Algerian accord placed the 225,000 Algerian workers in France under the French pension and social security system. A technical cooperation pact was signed with the Soviet Union, and Communist China furnished a 13,000-ton merchant ship, doubling Algeria's merchant marine.

Population: 12,790,000. **Government:** President Houari Boumedienne. **Monetary Unit:** dinar (4.937 dinars = U.S. $1). **Foreign Trade:** exports, $625,-000,000; imports, $695,000,000. **Principal Exports:** citrus fruits, crude oil, wines.   WILLIAM SPENCER

See also AFRICA; MIDDLE EAST.

AMERICAN LEGION. See VETERANS.

AMERICAN LIBRARY ASSOCIATION (ALA).

Congressional awareness of growing library needs was reflected in the passage of legislation providing for more than $155,000,000 for training and research and for grants to public, elementary, and secondary school and college libraries.

Though this legislation, supported by the ALA, eased library needs, delegates to the 84th annual ALA conference at Detroit, Mich., in July were told that an additional $3,700,000,000 was necessary to bring libraries in the United States up to minimum national standards.

Noting that established library standards were already becoming outmoded, one ALA division, the Public Library Association, started a revision program with a $17,855 fund from the J. Morris Jones-World Book Encyclopedia-ALA Goals Award. The balance of the $25,000 fund to ALA is to be used for support of the International Relations Office of the association.

The delegates to the annual conference also considered ways of providing library service to the culturally deprived and the functionally illiterate. William T. Knox, chairman of the government's Committee on Scientific and Technical Information and a member of the President's Committee on Science and Technology, outlined a tentative plan for a network of information systems with national libraries as the heart of the complex.

Intellectual Freedom. A conference on intellectual freedom was held in Washington, D.C., during the midwinter meeting of the ALA. It brought together 65 representatives of national labor, religious, educational, civil rights, and service organizations, publishers groups, learned societies, and education associations. A legislative workshop was also held to give librarians a working knowledge of the legislative process. Both projects were supported by grants from the 1964 J. Morris Jones-World Book Encyclopedia-ALA Goals Award. An ALA conference on "Education and the Nation's Libraries" was held at Airlie House in Warrenton, Va., in the spring. The meeting attracted representatives of 54 national organizations.

Grants. ALA received a grant of $75,000 from the H. W. Wilson Foundation, Inc., to be paid over a six-year period, for the establishment of an ALA office for recruitment, education, and utilization of librarians. Grants from a number of sources were also used to initiate or continue 38 projects, of which eight were in operation overseas.

Film Award. The motion picture ". . . And Something More," prepared by the Knapp School Libraries Project, won the American Film Festival and CINE Golden Eagle awards.

The project, which is supported by the Knapp Foundation, made grants in 1965 to Farrer Junior High School in Provo, Utah; Oak Park and River Forest High School in Oak Park, Ill.; and Roosevelt High School in Portland, Ore. They will receive sufficient funds over a three-year period to bring their school libraries up to the minimum standards required by the ALA.

New Officers. Robert Vosper, librarian of the University of California Research Library (Los Angeles), was installed as president of ALA. Mary V. Gaver, professor of library service at Rutgers University, was installed as vice-president and president-elect.

Other Awards in 1965 included:

Melvil Dewey Medal for creative professional achievement, to Bertha Margaret Frick, former associate professor, Columbia University School of Library Service.

E. P. Dutton-John Macrae Award, of $1,000 for advanced study, to Mrs. Joan Allene Parmeter Nolan, librarian, Shady Grove Junior High School, Ambler, Pa.

Grolier Award of $1,000, to Sarah Lewis Jones, chief library consultant, Georgia State Department of Education, for her outstanding contributions to the reading needs of young people.

Lippincott Award of $1,000 for distinguished service to librarianship, to Mrs. Frances Clarke Sayers, former senior lecturer, School of Library Service, University of California, Los Angeles.

Melcher Scholarship of $1,500 for study in children's librarianship, to Mrs. Mary Ann Stevenson, television storytelling specialist.   CHARLES R. CARNER

See also CANADIAN LIBRARY ASSOCIATION; CANADIAN LITERATURE; EDUCATION; LIBRARY; LITERATURE FOR CHILDREN (Awards).

ANGOLA.

Holden Roberto, president of the revolutionary government-in-exile of Angola, saw his influence decline in 1965. The Organization of African Unity (OAU) withdrew financial aid from Roberto's movement for independence from Portugal and offered support to the Popular Movement for the Liberation of Angola (MPLA).

Within his government-in-exile, Roberto was challenged by Armaments Minister Alexandre Taty and his supporters, who wrecked the organization's headquarters in Léopoldville, Congo. An invitation by André Martins Soma-Kassinda, leader of the newly formed Council of Angolan People, for all nationalist movements to unite and to meet with the Portuguese government was snubbed by both Roberto and the MPLA.

To counter the rebellious factions, the Portuguese government maintained an army of 48,000 in Angola. Portuguese sources claimed that rebel African forces, which once controlled 15 per cent of Angola, now had almost no territorial footholds.

Population: 4,939,000. **Government:** Governor-General Silveiro Marques. **Monetary Unit:** escudo (28.75 escudos = U.S. $1). **Foreign Trade:** exports, $148,000,000; imports, $136,000,000. **Principal Exports:** coffee, petroleum, sugar.   BENJAMIN E. THOMAS

See also AFRICA; PORTUGAL.

ANIMAL.

See AGRICULTURE; LIVESTOCK; LIVESTOCK SHOW; PET; WILDLIFE; ZOOLOGY.

ANTARCTICA.

See EXPLORATION.

ANTHROPOLOGY. Evidence of new types of men on the family tree gave anthropologists more areas of disagreement in 1965. The latest proposal concerning the structure of its branches came from Professor Phillip V. Tobias of the University of Witwatersrand in Johannesburg, South Africa. His suggestion is in accord with that of Louis S. B. Leakey that the branch including modern man should begin with the 2,000,000-year-old *Homo habilis* (see 1965 YEAR BOOK, MAN'S BEGINNINGS).

Tobias, however, would put Java-Peking man on the same branch rather than on a side branch, as does Leakey. Tobias puts the near-man creature *Zinjanthropus*, a skull of which Leakey discovered at the Olduvai Gorge in 1959, and *Australopithecus* from South Africa on two separate branches of the family tree, whereas Leakey considers them to be enough alike that they can be placed on the same branch.

The proposals of both Tobias and Leakey are disputed by those who agree with Professor John T. Robinson of the University of Wisconsin, who holds that the branch leading to man begins with *Australopithecus* and includes Java-Peking man. Robinson considers *Homo habilis* but a small Australopithecine.

The debate was brought into sharp conflict at a symposium on the origin of man held at the University of Chicago in April, 1965, and addressed by both Leakey and Robinson. At this symposium, Leakey announced that Mrs. Leakey had completed the restoration of a new *Homo habilis* skull. This skull from the Olduvai Gorge was found in hundreds of pieces, some smaller than the head of a match. Mrs. Leakey's painstaking reassembly of the find was praised as a monumental accomplishment.

Neanderthal Types. Dr. D. M. Badoux of the Institute of Veterinary Anatomy, Utrecht, The Netherlands, completed a study of skulls of Neanderthal men, some of whom lived during cold glacial times and others who lived during warmer (and earlier) interglacial times. He has found the skulls of those from the glacial period different in a number of ways from those of the interglacial period. Badoux suggested that these differences are due to the fact that the populations were adapted to different environments. This finding strengthened the suggestion of F. Clark Howell of the University of Chicago that the robustly built Neanderthals, with thick brow ridges, were a strictly Western European kind of man, cut off from other Neanderthal populations by the great ice sheets.

Lake Chad Man. Professor Yves Coppens, a French prehistorian and paleontologist, has assigned the name *Tchadanthropus uxori* (my wife's Chadman) to a skull fragment he found in 1961 near Lake Chad in north-central Africa. The find is of significance since it resembles the well-known Java-Peking men, but is of a much earlier period. LESLIE G. FREEMAN, JR.

ANTI-POVERTY. See POVERTY.

ARABIA. See SAUDI ARABIA.

ARCHAEOLOGY. Edward Lanning of Columbia University, who established in 1961 that men lived in Peru as early as 8500 B.C., showed in 1965 that five successive groups of hunting and gathering people occupied camps along the Peruvian coast over a period of 6,000 years. Although the region north of Lima is one of the most rainless deserts in the world, early men were able to eke out an existence there. Along the fog-nourished *loma* (broad-topped hill) meadows of the coast, they fished, gathered seeds and milled them into flour, collected snails, and hunted deer and guanaco.

Lanning has named the five successive cultures Arenal (8500-6000 B.C.), Luz (6000-5000 B.C.), Canario (5000-4200 B.C.), Corbina (4200-3600 B.C.), and Encanto (3600-2500 B.C.). Agriculture existed, he points out, at least as early as Encanto times, when cotton was cultivated. Fishermen-farmers established the first permanent villages by 2500 B.C. About this time, a large ceremonial center (one of the largest known in that area) was constructed at Chuquitanta.

In the Peruvian central highlands, another archaeologist, Rogger Ravines, discovered a workshop site where stone tools similar to those of the Canario period were made. The site, called Ambo, is thus an important link between the cultures of the coastal and highland regions.

Neanderthal Life. Though archaeologists have uncovered many Neanderthal skeletons and stone tools, only lately have they been able to piece together aspects of prehistoric man's daily life. Remains recently discovered in the Soviet Union may be of key importance. At the site of Molodova I on the banks of the Dnestr River, archaeologists found the remains of an oval hut, 23 x 33 feet in size. The remains, well over 40,000 years old, consist of many huge fragments of mammoth bone, and enclose numerous small fireplaces. Whether the structure was a dwelling, a storage area, or a ceremonial building is still unknown.

In southeastern France, Eugéne Bonifay discovered that the Neanderthal inhabitants of the Regordou Cave built numerous mounds of bones, rock, and earth. He suggested that some of the structures might have had importance in religious ceremonials.

Holy Land. Excavations by Kathleen Kenyon, director of the British School of Archaeology in Jerusalem, established the fact that the Church of the Holy Sepulchre may, indeed, stand atop Calvary and the tomb of Jesus, as tradition states. At least, the excavations establish that the church—as did Calvary—stands outside of what were the walls of Jerusalem in Herod's time. The church was built in the 4th century A.D. by the Empress Helena, who was guided by the pious tradition concerning the site of Calvary.

An early Christian manuscript, written on parchment, was found in an abandoned monastery in the

FACE-LIFTING. The 3,200-year-old great stone head of Ramses II, weighing 30 tons, was sliced from the face of the Temple of Abu Simbel and moved to higher ground to be reassembled.

Nubian Valley of Egypt. It contains a "Hymn to the Cross" and other elements of the oral tradition of early Christianity. See PROTESTANT.

Abu Simbel. After 3,200 years, the mighty Egyptian monument to Pharaoh Ramses II, Abu Simbel, standing at the edge of the Upper Nile River, was being moved by an international team of engineers. The $36,000,000 salvage operation is sponsored by the United Nations Educational, Scientific, and Cultural Organization (UNESCO). The moving process involves sawing the sandstone temple, and a smaller adjoining temple to Ramses' Queen Nefertari, into blocks weighing up to 30 tons, and then transporting them to higher ground, where they can be reassembled.

While work is going on, a lake is backing up behind the new Aswan High Dam, 175 miles downstream. By August, 1966, the rising waters are expected to spill over the temporary dam that has been built to protect the temples. The project is considered a major engineering feat.

One of the world's wonders, the temple of Abu Simbel was hewn from a sandstone cliff. Four colossal and identical stone images of the god-king, Ramses II, were carved across the 108-foot-high façade of the great temple. Each image is 67 feet high. But the statues are not the sole wonders of the temple. Abu Simbel has high-ceilinged rooms and columned halls with beautiful friezes cut 200 feet into the heart of the cliff.　LESLIE G. FREEMAN, JR.

WHITE TILED DOME near Jerusalem,
designed by U.S. architects
Frederick Kiesler and Armand Bartos,
is a shrine for Dead Sea Scrolls.

ARCHITECTURE. One of the truly great architects of the 20th century, Charles Édouard Jeanneret, known as Le Corbusier, died on Aug. 27, 1965. His landmark works, such as the Villa Savoye in Poissy, France; the Swiss Pavilion at the Cité Universitaire, Paris; Chandigarh, the capital of the Indian state of East Punjab; and the Cathedral of Notre Dame du Haut at Ronchamp, France, were an evident influence on the notable works produced by other architects in 1965. Of the cathedral at Ronchamp Le Corbusier said, "Light is the key," and he died in the bright sun of a Mediterranean morning while swimming at the age of 77.

Unlike his architectural works, his city plans—such as the ribbon of expressways surmounting long terraces of houses and shops proposed for Algiers in 1931—remain mainly unexecuted. But they, too, were prophecies in 1965, when the scale and scope of architecture reached out toward total city design.

Campus Microcity. In Chicago, the University of Illinois opened its circle campus on the southwestern edge of the Loop in September. Designed by Walter Netsch, Jr., of Skidmore, Owings & Merrill (designer of the Air Force Academy), the campus spreads out from a central court of exterior assembly spaces on a grid of esplanades that are raised over the campus ground.

Skyscrapers. Without benefit of such substantial ground organization, Skidmore, Owings & Merrill prepared foundations in 1965 for a tapered steel

100-STORY TALL John Hancock
Center in Chicago will be the second
tallest building in the world and a
combination office-apartment tower.

221

shaft 100 stories high in Chicago for the John Hancock Mutual Life Insurance Company. In New York City, two structures, each 110 stories high, were slated for construction by the Port of New York Authority on a relatively small site in lower Manhattan. Designed by architect Minoru Yamasaki, the twin towers of the authority's World Trade Center will be the tallest buildings in the world, 1,350 feet high. See BUILDING AND CONSTRUCTION.

The Arch. Ascension of the 630-foot high catenary arch in St. Louis (an early design of the late Eero Saarinen) promised to be a treat for visitors to that city in 1966. When the visitors reach the keystone of the arch, placed in 1965, they will see a city rebuilding mightily, but on the familiar 18th century grid pattern. St. Louis was following other cities, where giant buildings were imposed on single-level city plans, unlike the plans of Le Corbusier.

Culture Complexes. With the completion of the Vivian Beaumont Theater in October, New York's Lincoln Center for the Performing Arts got its best building to date. And with the foundation laid for the Juilliard School of Music there, the lines of the granddaddy of U.S. cultural complexes could at last be perceived. Culture, indeed, took up architecture in thirsty gulps in 1965. The huge John F. Kennedy Center for the Performing Arts, designed by Edward Durell Stone, was begun on the banks of the Potomac in Washington, D.C. The Los Angeles County Museum of Art, by architect William Pereira, was a glittering opening success. And cities and colleges from Houston, Tex., to Smith College in Northampton, Mass., opened or began theater construction projects. See THEATER (Picture).

Civic Pride. Toronto completed its city hall. The two boomerang-shaped skyscraper office slabs, nestling a domed council chamber, were conceived as civic symbols by architect Viljo Revell of Finland. The result, like so much architecture in 1965, was grandiose, but, some thought, empty.

It was evident in a review of 1965, when many notable works of architecture were completed and more were on the drawing boards, that architecture considered by itself was not enough. In only a few places—and quite unnoticed—was architecture considered in the larger context of man and his massive problems. In Harlem, several imaginative playgrounds were opened within public housing projects. New, private planned communities developed apace in Columbia, Md.; Reston, Va.; and other areas beyond the suburban sprawl. And in Cambridge, Mass., architects Sert, Jackson & Gourley completed a married students' colony for Harvard graduate students. It was lively, economical, and contained. It demonstrated a commitment to life and indicated a model for cities in direct descent from Le Corbusier's own city plans.　　RICHARD MILLER

See also CANADA; CITY PLANNING; DEATHS OF NOTABLE PERSONS; LOS ANGELES; PAINTING AND SCULPTURE; Section Two, THE NEW NEW ENGLAND.

ARGENTINA. The government of President Arturo Umberto Illia faced mounting criticism from civilian and military quarters. After two years in office, it had not been able to obtain any substantial foreign loans for the country's development. It had also failed to totally settle an oil dispute involving major foreign companies, and it was having little luck in keeping prices down.

The government's relationship with military leaders had cooled considerably during the two-year period. There was widespread disenchantment, too, with President Illia's economic and political policies. Many private banks were reluctant to renew loans to the government. The national pension fund was almost bankrupt due to the government's policy of using these funds for other purposes.

The Popular Union Party, whose members were followers of exiled dictator Juan D. Perón, was allowed to participate in congressional elections held on March 14. The party emerged as the second strongest in congress, winning better than 36 per cent of the popular vote. Observers felt, however, that the vote was not one of confidence in Perón but rather in protest of the inflationary pinch.

With foreign reserves and the trade surplus falling, Argentina's 1965 balance of payments was expected to show an unfavorable deficit of about $300,000,000, if not more. The federal budget was expected to show a $1,200,000,000 deficit. The republic had to debase its peso four times in 1965. On April 19, the peso was devaluated by 15 per cent from 149 to 173 per U.S. $1; by December 6, it had fallen to 178 per U.S. $1. These actions, however, did not help the meat and wool exporters to any notable degree, especially since the retention quotas remained in force.

Living Costs, meanwhile, rose an estimated 30 per cent. Predictions that the country was heading for a new recession proved false, however. Employment remained satisfactory. Industry generally maintained a high level of activity—an exception being the export meat packers, with several thousand workers idle. There was abundant spending power, especially in the interior, due to good harvests and high cattle prices. Industrial production was expected to rise an average 15.4 per cent; the Gross National Product by 7.5 per cent.

On June 25, Argentina formally concluded debt negotiations with 11 European nations, Japan, and the United States, for an easing of the republic's foreign indebtedness. At the close of 1964, Argentina's total public and private foreign obligations amounted to $3,355,800,000.

Population: 23,035,000. **Government:** President Arturo Umberto Illia. **Monetary Unit:** peso (178 = U.S. $1). **Gross National Product:** 1,114,-900,000,000 pesos. **Foreign Trade:** exports, $1,410,-000,000; imports, $1,077,000,000. **Principal Exports:** maize, meat, petroleum, wheat.　　MARY C. WEBSTER

See also LATIN AMERICA.

ARMED FORCES OF THE WORLD. Both the United States and Russia shifted more strongly to missiles during 1965 in maintaining the nuclear balance of terror. And both had more than enough in their intercontinental ballistics missile (ICBM) force to eradicate each other. To break the grim deadlock each raced to be first to produce an anti-ICBM missile.

There was a stand-off, also, in conventional arms. The communists' greater military manpower was at least balanced by U.S. firepower, mobility, and flexibility, plus the experience gained in actual combat in Vietnam.

Missiles. The United States' ICBM lead over Russia, which was 4-to-1 in 1964, dropped to 3-to-1 during 1965, because the United States scrapped 95 Atlas and 54 Titan missiles as obsolete, and because the U.S. missile program shifted its emphasis from production to updating, improving, and refining target and guidance systems. In 1965, 800 Minuteman and 54 Titan rockets were in place in dispersed underground silos. An additional 200 Minuteman IIs, considered eight times more effective than Minuteman Is, will be deployed in 1966.

Meanwhile, the Soviets were also improving their own deadly missile system. Their ICBM force increased from 200 to 270, some in hardened silos. According to qualified observers, there were two principal advances in this field. These were the development of a solid-fueled ICBM similar to Minuteman, and a Polaris-type weapon. Formerly Russia relied upon the much bulkier liquid-fueled ICBMs. However, the Soviet Polaris-type weapon is believed to be far inferior to the new U.S. Polaris, which has a 2,500-mile range. In November, the Russians claimed to have a nuclear rocket which could be fired from a satellite in earth orbit.

The number of Soviet intermediate-range missiles remained at about 800. Most of them were fixed and zeroed in on European targets, but some were on submarines or otherwise mobile. The U.S. counterforce of 528 Polaris missiles will increase to 656 aboard 41 submarines by the end of 1966.

Air Power. The United States disclosed it will cut its strategic bomber fleet of 600 B-52s to 255 late-model B-52s by 1971. It will drop all its 80 B-58 bombers during the same period. Additionally, about 100 U.S. Navy fighter-bombers assigned strategic targets were being relieved of that responsibility. But Defense Secretary Robert McNamara hinted that a new aircraft, a variation of the F-111, the tactical fighter-bomber under development for both the navy and air force, would be introduced.

The Soviets retained their fleet of 270 bombers capable of a round-trip flight to the U.S. mainland and 1,300 medium and light jet bombers which could make it only one way.

Manpower. U.S. forces grew to support a commitment of 180,000 men in Vietnam. Meanwhile, the North Atlantic Treaty Organization (NATO) and its communist counterpoise, the nations of the Warsaw Pact, each still had about 4,500,000 men under arms.

NATO deployed 26 divisions in Europe—12 West German, five U.S., three British, two French, two Belgian, and two Dutch—plus one Canadian brigade. The Warsaw Pact nations had 212 divisions —150 Soviet and 62 eastern European—but they

COMPARATIVE MILITARY MANPOWER

	United States	Russia	Communist China
Army	1,017,000	2,000,000	2,600,000
Navy	909,000*	400,000	60,000
Air Force	834,000	900,000†	175,000
Totals	2,760,000	3,300,000	2,835,000

*Includes 204,000 marines
†Includes 230,000 Strategic Rocket Forces

were considerably under strength and only about half were combat-ready. The 150 Soviet divisions included 20 in East Germany, two in Poland, four in Hungary, and 40 in western Russia.

Communist China exploded its second nuclear device. Its continuing use of uranium-235 indicated that its goal is a hydrogen bomb. The Communist Chinese fighting force was woefully short of modern equipment. Cut off by its ideological split with the Soviet Union, the Peking regime was reported to be starting to make its own tanks, fighter aircraft, and even submarines. — WARREN ROGERS

See also NATIONAL DEFENSE.

ARRUPE, PEDRO (1907-   ), a 27-year veteran of Jesuit service in Japan, was elected Father General of the Society of Jesus at a secret conclave in Rome on May 22, 1965. He serves for life, succeeding the late Father Jean Baptiste Janssens of Belgium. The new Father General came to office at a time of great change, when the Ecumenical Council and the pope were redefining the basic doctrines of the Roman Catholic Church. Father Arrupe is the 28th head of the international order for Roman Catholic men. It has given the church teachers and scholars for the past 430 years.

One of the first rescue teams in Hiroshima after the United States dropped its atomic bomb there in August, 1945, was led by Father Arrupe. He lived just outside the city at the time, and helped care for the bomb victims. Japan was made an independent Jesuit province in 1958, and Father Arrupe was elevated to Provincial, or head, of the area.

Pedro Arrupe was born at Bilbao in the Basque region of Spain. His father founded the influential Roman Catholic newspaper *La Gaceta del Norte*. Young Arrupe studied medicine at the University of Madrid before entering the Jesuit order in 1927. Four years later, after the Spanish Republic was established, Jesuits were banned in Spain. Arrupe continued his studies and training in various other European countries and in the United States. He was ordained in 1936, and sent to Japan in 1938.

ART. See PAINTING AND SCULPTURE.

ASIA

With its teeming millions, Asia remained the focus of a global struggle. It was primarily a three-way struggle for power and influence involving the anticommunist West led by the United States, the communism of the Soviet Union, and the vigorous expansionism of the Chinese communists. But a secondary struggle, no less desperate, was also being waged to achieve somehow an economic breakthrough that would enable the vast area to feed its millions. Finally, there was the struggle for political stability, with such major issues as subversion, open warfare, inefficiency, and even corruption confounding the governments of the countries in Asia.

The conflicts between the communists and anticommunists became more widespread and more intense during the year. The most active of these conflicts obviously was centered in Vietnam. The gradual disruption of the South Vietnamese government forced the administration of U.S. President Lyndon B. Johnson to make a fundamental policy decision.

Change in U.S. Policy. In April, after due consideration, President Johnson announced that the United States would do everything in its power to ensure that South Vietnam remained free of the communists.

U.S. troops poured into South Vietnam; by the end of the year, a U.S. force estimated at 200,000 men was actively engaged in the war. "Search and destroy" missions began to flush out Viet Cong regulars, as well as guerrillas, in substantial numbers. U.S. forces, consolidating their seacoast positions and bases, actively pursued the enemy into the highland areas along the Laotian and Cambodian borders. See VIETNAM.

The Escalation of the War by the United States was greeted with both relief and alarm. The Chinese communists warned that such actions would be subject to retaliation, but as 1965 ended, they had yet to make such an open move. France, too, greeted the escalation with alarm.

Australia, Britain, and New Zealand, however, backed the United States and its policies, faced as they were with Indonesia's threats and its occasional moves against Malaysia (see INDONESIA; MALAYSIA, FEDERATION OF).

Conflict over Kashmir. The war in Vietnam was only one aspect of the larger struggle. For years, India and Pakistan had engaged in a hot dispute over Kashmir. Repeated efforts by the United Nations (UN) had averted open fighting, and an uneasy truce had prevailed. But the increasing friendliness between Pakistan and Communist China, and the desire of a group of young Pakistanis to develop a more pro-Peking stance, led to an outbreak of hostilities on August 5. India charged that the

PICTURES OF THE YEAR/ W. E. Garrett © National Geographic Society

BRUTAL WAR in Asia embroils the young and the innocent as well as the combatants. These two children were orphaned by guerrilla warfare in South Vietnam.

move began with armed infiltrators disguised as passengers slipping over the Kashmir border and into Indian territory. These elements were soon followed by more obvious military units. The Indian army quickly retaliated.

Repeated efforts by the UN and the Western nations finally convinced both combatants of the need for a cease-fire. This was arranged after several weeks of intense fighting. But the issue of Kashmir remained unresolved. See INDIA; PAKISTAN.

On Other Fronts. Open violence in the power struggles of Asia was not limited to Vietnam and Kashmir. Malaysia, faced with Indonesia's "confrontation" policy, prepared its defenses for a showdown. Some Indonesian raids took place in Sarawak, where the guerrillas killed key villagers in certain areas. Similarly, Indonesian irregulars moved into Malaya proper from bases near Singapore. These were quickly disposed of, however, by Malayan troops. Again, Communist China's support for Indonesia's "crush Malaysia" policy was clearly evident, especially since some of the irregulars in Sarawak proved to be Chinese infiltrators coming directly from China via Indonesia. As if the Indonesian threats were not enough, Malaya faced a revival of communist guerrilla bands along its border with Thailand. The Federation of Malaysia, itself, lost one of its member states.

There were significant signs, however, that the Chinese use of subversion and insurgency was being effectively countered. Laos, benefiting from U.S. aid and U.S. actions in Vietnam, began to mop up Pathet Lao insurgents. Indonesia, which was closely aligning itself with Communist China, found its campaign against Malaysia sputtering. There was also a growing disaffection with the Chinese alignment on the part of Indonesia's army, which forestalled a coup by the air force and the Indonesian Communist party (PKI) late in the year.

The growing disaffection for the Chinese communists could be seen also in Thailand where resistance to the communists was stiffened along its Chinese and Laotian borders. Burma not only tightened its border restrictions against the Chinese, but it also began eliminating alien Chinese elements within the country (see BURMA).

Waning Communist Influence. The Philippines continued to be wary of Communist Chinese demands that they be permitted to work with the Chinese minority in The Philippines. Formosa maintained a strong military garrison, whose attentions were riveted on the Chinese mainland. Even Japan, while remaining meticulously neutral toward the conflicts in Asia, began to tighten up its restrictions on trade with Communist China. The Republic of Korea, ignoring the obvious communist threat from

TROUBLE SPOTS IN ASIA IN 1965

① BURMA
Racked by year-long guerrilla warfare.

② CAMBODIA
Clashes with Thailand over border dispute.

③ CHINA
Masses troops on India's borders.

④ INDIA
Battles Pakistan over Rann of Kutch.

⑤ INDONESIA
Army foils plot to overthrow Sukarno.

⑥ KASHMIR
Sparks war between India and Pakistan.

⑦ MALAYSIA
Harassed by Indonesian and Chinese guerrillas.

⑧ VIETNAM
United States escalates war against Viet Cong.

YEAR BOOK map

North Korea, sent several battalions of crack troops to fight the Viet Cong in Vietnam. In effect, these moves all indicated that the threat of Communist China was being more clearly recognized by the Asian governments.

In addition, this growing sophistication was being matched by an increasing political awareness of the international dangers of the Chinese communist threat. This was most clearly seen in the splintering of the Indian Communist party. The pro-Soviet Union faction within the Indian party hotly denounced China's role in the dispute with Pakistan. By year's end, it appeared well on its way to taking over control of the Communist party in India.

Similarly, Russia's studied aloofness and disapproval was having a marked effect on leftists in Southeast Asia. A major election held in Ceylon marked the end of the procommunist government of Prime Minister Sirimavo Bandaranaike. The triumph of the middle-of-the-road conservatives over the leftist government was considered a major breakthrough in the fight against communism. These, then, were political pluses from the West's point of view.

Signs of Stability. While instability still marked many of the governments of Asia, this was not the total picture. Both Japan and the Republic of Korea managed to maintain stable governments. Korea was even able to conclude a reparations and fishing agreement with Japan despite militant student opposition. The Philippines held a national election with relatively minor bloodshed, unseating President Diosdado Macapagal and electing Ferdinand E. Marcos as its next president (see MARCOS, FERDINAND E.; PHILIPPINES, THE). Thailand survived the passing of Field Marshal Sarit Thanarat and managed to make the transition to a new prime minister very smoothly (see THAILAND).

Perhaps most important, in a general sense, was the demonstrated capacity of certain Southeast Asian governments to come together on mutual problems on economic development. This was best illustrated by the signing of an agreement in Vientiane, Laos, in August, covering the UN-sponsored Mekong River project. Cambodia, Laos, South Vietnam, and Thailand, the four countries immediately concerned, signed the agreement to harness the Mekong River system despite their pronounced differences in foreign policies and their attitudes toward Communist China.

The General Economic Picture of Asia had some bright spots but in the overall sense the picture was not encouraging. While Formosa, Japan, The Philippines, the Republic of Korea, and Thailand had relatively prosperous economies, the same was not true of other areas. India, Malaysia, and Pakistan, faced with dire threats of war, had to divert their meager surpluses to military build-ups. In some nations, such as Indonesia, the preoccupation with military adventuring threw the economies into tailspins and sent standards of living plummeting.

"I'd hide, if I knew which side of the tree is safe."

The key to much of the economic picture of Asia was, of course, Communist China. There were indications that the Chinese were relaxing some of their theoretical rigidity and allowing a small amount of private enterprise to exist in order to step-up production. Despite this, Communist China continued to depend on the international market for foodstuffs, and its promises of aid to the Asian and African countries it was wooing were meager, indeed.

Struggle for Power. Asia, then, remained an arena in which the large powers jockeyed for position. The United States, pursuing a hard-core policy against the communists, appeared to have seized the initiative in Southeast Asia for the first time. Britain, its strongest ally, provided unwavering backing via its resources in Malaysia. France alone of the Western nations appeared desirous of taking what it believed to be an accommodating position toward the Chinese. See FRANCE.

The Soviet Union, anxious over Chinese communist expansionism, continued its ideological dispute with Peking (see COMMUNISM; RUSSIA). The neutral position of India no longer held the international attraction it once had under the leadership of its late prime minister, Jawaharlal Nehru. Japan remained a question mark in Asia. Its great organizational capacities had yet to be declared on either side in any meaningful way.   JOHN N. STALKER

See also Section Two, INSIDE RURAL INDIA and INSIDE RURAL CHINA.

ASTRONAUTS

ASTRONAUTS. Twelve men spent a total of 1,392 weightless man-hours in space in 1965, with U.S. astronauts accounting for all but 52 man-hours. In total time aloft, the United States now had a whopping-big lead over the Russians, 1,354 to 507. And the excellent physical condition of Navy Commander James A. Lovell, Jr., and his flying companion, Air Force Lieutenant Colonel Frank Borman, after almost 14 days in space aboard Gemini VII in December was proof that man could survive lack of exercise, radiation, time disorientation, and weightlessness long enough to visit the moon and return. Another first for the United States occurred on December 16, when Navy Captain Walter M. Schirra, Jr., and Air Force Major Thomas P. Stafford were shot into space to keep a rendezvous with Lovell and Borman. See SPACE TRAVEL.

In June, the National Aeronautics and Space Administration (NASA) for the first time chose six scientists and medical doctors for astronaut training (see photos). One of the six, Duane E. Graveline, M.D., 34, resigned from the program on August 18 for personal reasons.

As of Jan. 1, 1966, NASA had 28 pilot-astronauts and five scientist-astronauts in its manned space flight program. More pilots and 10 to 20 scientists will be selected in 1966 for Project Apollo and other advanced space missions.

Wide World

NO BEATNIKS. Astronauts Charles Conrad, Jr., left, and Leroy Gordon Cooper, Jr., compare beards after their splashdown from their eight-day orbit in August.

THE NEW ASTRONAUTS

The fourth and most highly educated group of astronauts was chosen by NASA on June 29. Within the next five years or so, at least one of them might stand on the moon. These Project Apollo trainees, unlike most of the previously selected astronauts, are not experienced test pilots.

Owen K. Garriott, Ph.D., 35, was a professor of electrical engineering at Stanford University, where he specialized in ionospheric physics. He has a private pilot's license. Garriott, from Enid, Okla., is married and has three sons.

Edward G. Gibson, Ph.D., 29, was born in Buffalo, N.Y. An engineering-physicist, Gibson specialized in jet propulsion and atmospheric physics while working for his doctorate. He is married and has a son and a daughter.

Joseph P. Kerwin, M.D., 33, was a flight surgeon before becoming a qualified jet pilot in the U.S. Navy. Kerwin was born in Oak Park, Ill., and has been in the navy since 1958. Kerwin is married and has a daughter.

F. Curtis Michel, Ph.D., 31, was assistant professor of space science at Rice University, Houston. He has done research in nuclear physics and the effects of solar wind on the moon's atmosphere. He is married and has a son.

Harrison H. Schmitt, Ph.D., 30, was with the astrogeology branch of the U.S. Geological Survey at Flagstaff, Ariz. He developed lunar exploration techniques for NASA, and has trained astronauts in geology. Schmitt is unmarried.

World Book Science Service, Inc.

Gemini Crews were named for future missions. They are: *Gemini VIII* (scheduled for February or March, 1966): command pilot, Neil A. Armstrong; copilot, David R. Scott. *Gemini IX* (after July 1, 1966): command pilot, Elliot M. See, Jr.; copilot, Charles A. Bassett II.

Both Scott and Bassett are to attempt walks in space for one full orbit. Also, both Gemini craft will try to dock with an orbiting Agena rocket. This skillful "flying" by the astronauts was originally scheduled for the first Gemini VI shot.

Air Force in Orbit. Eight military pilots began training for the U.S. Air Force Manned Orbital Laboratory (MOL) project announced by President Lyndon B. Johnson on August 25. They are at the Aerospace Research Pilot School at Edwards Air Force Base in California. All the pilots have college degrees in engineering or physical science. They are:

Major Michael J. Adams, USAF, 35, Sacramento, Calif.; Major Albert H. Crews, USAF, 36, Alexandria, Va.; Lieutenant John L. Finley, USN, 29, Memphis, Tenn.; Captain Richard E. Lawyer, USAF, 33, Inglewood, Calif.; Captain Lachlan Macleay, USAF, 34, Redlands, Calif.; Captain F. Gregory Neubeck, USAF, 33, Washington, D.C.; Captain James M. Taylor, USAF, 34, Lewisville, Ark.; and Lieutenant Richard H. Truly, USN, 28, Meridian, Miss. Twelve more MOL astronauts will be picked in 1966 (see SPACE TRAVEL). WADE TILLEUX

ASTRONOMY. On July 14, 1965, the Mariner IV spacecraft passed at about 5,600 miles of Mars, snapped 22 pictures, and then began beaming the first "close-up" photos of another planet back across 134,000,000 miles of space to an anxious audience on earth. The principal revelation of the photos was that the planet believed to be most like earth appears to be as barren as the moon.

The historic photos, which brought Mars 30 times closer than the best earthbound telescopes, showed a surface heavily pock-marked with craters formed by the impact of asteroids and meteoroids. About 70 craters were visible in pictures 5 through 15, indicating a probable total of more than 10,000 for the entire surface of Mars.

Some of the craters are quite deep and have sharp rims. The large number of craters also indicates that there has been little erosion of the planet's surface. Nowhere in the photographs was there any sign of water. Nor was there a sign of the "canals" some astronomers have claimed to have seen through their telescopes. Mars appears to be a very cold, dry, and lifeless planet.

Yet, the photos do not finally resolve whether there is life on Mars. Many scientists, among them Stanley L. Miller, associate professor of chemistry at the University of California, San Diego, feel there might be microenvironments on Mars able to sustain living organisms. Miller and others are working on life detecting systems that could be landed on

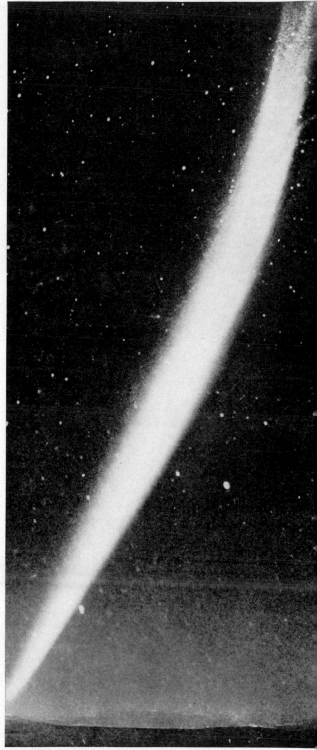

Wide World

VISITOR FROM DEEP SPACE. Comet Ikeya-Seki, with its 75,000,000-mile tail, was easily seen as it passed near the earth on its voyage around the sun.

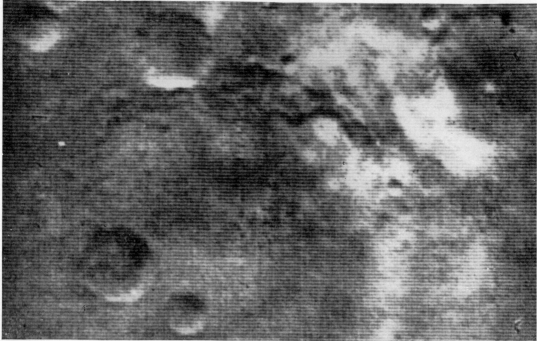

Jet Propulsion Laboratory, California Institute of Technology

MARS CLOSE-UP. To everyone's surprise the first photographs of Mars, taken from a spacecraft, showed that the planet's surface is cratered much like the moon.

Mars by spacecraft in the Voyager series, the first of which may be launched in 1971.

Mariner IV's sensing devices were unable to detect a magnetic field around Mars. Therefore, if one exists, it is probably extremely weak and does not protect the Martian surface from high energy radiation from space as does the earth's atmosphere.

The radio signals transmitted by the spacecraft indicated that the atmospheric pressure on Mars is only about $\frac{1}{2000}$ of the earth's sea level pressure. The signals also confirmed that nitrogen is the most abundant element in the Martian atmosphere, though they also indicated that carbon dioxide is plentiful. The electron density at various levels in the atmosphere was found to be lower than theoretically predicted, and indicated that the planet's surface temperatures are probably between $-135°$ F. and $-150°$ F.

On its flight to Mars, Mariner IV collected data on particles, magnetic fields, and micrometeoroids. Additional information has been gathered since the spacecraft passed by the planet. Scientists are hopeful that the interplanetary probe will provide still more information when its looping orbit around the sun returns it to the vicinity of the earth.

Moon. Lunar experts continued their analysis and interpretation of the thousands of photographs of the moon obtained by Ranger VII, VIII, and IX spacecraft on July 31, 1964; February 20, 1965; and March 24, 1965. Even with these remarkable photos,

some showing craters only $2\frac{1}{2}$ feet across, scientists could not agree about the depth or firmness of the dust covering the moon's surface. They did agree, however, that most of the craters on the moon were formed by the impact of meteoroids. Some small craters, they also theorized, were created by the collapse of the lunar surface.

Photos of the far side of the moon, taken by the Soviet spacecraft Zond III, confirmed that it differs markedly from the side always facing the earth. The photographs taken on July 20 from a distance of about 6,000 miles, revealed a greater number of craters per square mile, and few large plainlike areas.

Solar Eclipse. The total solar eclipse of May 30 was particularly significant because of its longer than average duration—5 minutes 15.9 seconds—and because it occurred at a time of minimum sunspot activity.

As the moon passed between the earth and the sun, its shadow swept along an 8,000-mile path from New Zealand, across the Pacific, to Peru. Observations were made from a few small islands in the Cook and Society groups, and from ships, balloons, rockets, and several jet aircraft flying along the path of the eclipse.

Rotation of the Planets. Radio astronomers observing the nearby planets found that Mercury does not always show the same face to the sun. For 80 years it had been believed that the planet's period of rotation was the same as its orbital period—88 days. By bouncing radio waves off Mercury, astronomers at Cornell University's Arecibo Ionospheric Observatory in Puerto Rico established its rotation period as 59 days, plus or minus five days. The scientists also found that the planet has no detectable atmosphere and that its surface is probably similar to that of the moon.

More accurate radio observations by the Arecibo astronomers pinpointed Venus' westward rotation period at 247 days, plus or minus five days. Radio astronomers also gathered evidence that Jupiter's solid core changed its rate of rotation in 1960. Measurement of the planet's radio emission indicated that its rotational period increased by 1.2 seconds.

Comets. At Mount Wilson and Palomar Observatories, Jesse L. Greenstein and Antoni Stawikowski of the Nicolaus Copernicus University in Poland found evidence of the rare isotope carbon 13 in Comet Ikeya. Carbon 13, they found, exists in the same ratio to carbon 12 in the comet as it does on the earth. The researchers concluded that comets must have been formed in the same region of the solar system as the earth. If they had been born far from the earth, their chemical composition would probably be different from that of the earth or sun. The astronomers suggested that after the comets came into existence near the sun and earth, they were forced into very elongated, elliptical orbits by the particles and radiation released by the sun during the earliest period of the solar system.

Two Japanese amateur astronomers, K. Ikeya and T. Seki, discovered the brightest comet of the 20th century on September 18. Following its discovery, Comet Ikeya-Seki was observed by astronomers around the world. Its brightness allowed valuable observations even during daylight. After the comet passed within 300,000 miles of the sun, on October 21, its nucleus broke into several fragments.

Stars. Astronomers using the 62-inch infrared telescope at Mount Wilson Observatory found two red stars with the lowest surface temperatures known. Though both stars have about the normal 25,000,000° F. interior temperature, one star's surface temperature is only about 1200° F., and the surface temperature of the other is as low as 800° F.

Quasars and Blue Galaxies. Maarten Schmidt, working at Mount Wilson and Palomar, continued to discover more remote, fast moving quasi-stellar radio sources, or quasars. In 1965, he found five such sources farther from the earth than any other known objects. The most distant of the five, 3C-9, is many billions of light-years distant and moving away at about 149,000 miles a second, or 80 per cent of the velocity of light (186,300 miles per second).

Astronomers generally believe that a quasi-stellar source has a mass at least 100,000,000 times that of our sun, and that its energy is produced in a core that is surrounded by two layers of clouds. The innermost layer is of visible luminous gas, while the outer, invisible layer is made up of rapidly moving electrons that give off energy as radio signals as they spiral in the magnetic field surrounding the object. See 1965 YEAR BOOK, *Special Report*, THE UNFOLDING UNIVERSE.

In June, the Mount Wilson and Palomar Observatories announced that Allan Sandage had discovered an unexpected type of distant extragalactic object. According to Sandage, the nearest of the new objects is approximately 20,000,000 light-years from the earth. He named this group of objects "quasi-stellar blue galaxies." Sandage said that galaxies seem related to the quasi-stellar radio sources, but do not emit detectable radio energy even though they produce as much as 100 times more radiation than an ordinary galaxy.

One of the quasi-stellar blue galaxies, designated BSO-1, is receding at a rate of 125,000 miles per second. This speed, which also indicates its distance, makes it the second most distant object known (second to 3C-9).

The new type of quasi-stellar objects is approximately 500 times more numerous than the quasi-stellar radio sources, and at such great distances that observations of them may enable astronomers to determine the geometry of remote space and perhaps learn which of the several theories of the origin of the universe is valid.   ROBERT I. JOHNSON

See also SPACE TRAVEL.

ATLANTA. The mighty construction boom in this metropolis of the Southeast was stifled for a time by a 67-day ironworkers strike that started Sept. 1, 1965. The biggest project halted was the 41-story First National Bank, tallest and most spacious skyscraper in the Southeast. In June, the Peachtree Center Building, a 30-story office tower opened in the hub of downtown. Also under construction in the center was the 800-room Regency Hotel. The Butler Street renewal project gave strong impetus to the economy with offices, motels, and apartments under construction.

The city's new $18,000,000 Atlanta Stadium opened in April. It fulfilled local hopes when it captured major league football (Atlanta Falcons) and baseball (Atlanta Braves) franchises.

With a population doubled in 15 years and mounting traffic congestion, the metropolitan area moved ahead with plans for a 66-mile transit system. Growth also posed human problems. To fight one of the nation's highest metropolitan crime rates, 38 local law enforcement agencies created Metropol, a six-county, crime-fighting agency, in the summer of 1965.

With 40 per cent of the residents in corporate Atlanta Negroes, the city added to its stature as a stronghold of racial moderation in 1965. Mayor Ivan Allen, Jr., who testified in Washington, D.C., for the civil rights bill of 1964, was re-elected to a second term with minor opposition.   DONALD W. LIEF

231

ATOMIC ENERGY. For the first time since the start of the atomic age, annual federal expenditures for peaceful uses of the atom bomb began to edge up on military nuclear outlays. During the 20 years since the first man-made nuclear explosion seared the desert at Trinity Site, near Alamogordo, N.Mex., on July 16, 1945, the Atomic Energy Commission (AEC) had budgeted over $28,000,000,000 for military atomic development against $6,000,000,000 for nonmilitary uses. The AEC in 1965, however, shut down three plutonium reactors at Hanford, Wash., leaving only 10 still in operation to produce fissionable material for bombs.

Though military requirements were largely satisfied for the time being, civilian utilization of the atom became a growing field. Sigvard Eklund, director general of the International Atomic Energy Agency, predicted that the total world nuclear power generating capacity would increase almost fivefold by 1970, an increase from the present 5,000,000 kilowatts to between 20,000,000 and 25,000,000 kilowatts. By September, 1965, U.S. firms alone had contracts for 2,500,000 kilowatts of new nuclear power capacity—equal to half the present world operating total.

Major U.S. public utility companies announced plans to expand their nuclear power plants in Illinois and New York, while the Public Service Company of Colorado ordered the West's first nuclear power station to be built 33 miles north of Denver. In Sweden, planners announced that 30 per cent of that country's power will be supplied by nuclear energy in 1980.

Reactor Development. The AEC shifted its emphasis in reactor research and development from the long-established boiling water and pressurized water reactors to advanced converters and near-breeder reactors. A converter is a reactor that uses one kind of fuel and produces another. A breeder is a converter that produces more fissionable atoms than it consumes.

A reactor pilot plant of the breeder type was placed in operation in 1965 at Oak Ridge National Laboratory in Tennessee. This reactor uses uranium dissolved in molten salt—a fuel concept which the laboratory scientists believe has potential economic advantages for electric power production. The reactor eventually will be used to test a breeder concept by transmutation of thorium to uranium.

The highest flux level ever obtained in a reactor was achieved on March 4 at the AEC Savannah River plant. A record four and two-tenths quadrillion neutrons per square centimeter per second was achieved in the production of curium 244.

Useful Explosions. Preliminary studies by two government agencies and an industrial firm indicate that nuclear blasts may unlock vast underground stores of natural gas. The El Paso Natural Gas Company in Texas has proposed a joint experiment with the AEC and the U.S. Bureau of Mines to test the technique. If accepted, it will be the first government-industry use of nuclear explosions for industrial purposes. The nuclear explosions would be used to fracture gas-bearing rock. Geologists believe that the method could recover up to seven times as much gas as is now available in the Rocky Mountain area.

The use of nuclear explosions for large-scale excavation was also studied. Among the projects considered was a new, sea-level Panama Canal. Researchers at the Lawrence Radiation Laboratory at the University of California suggested that the arid surface of the moon may be mined for water by dehydrating water-bearing deposits with nuclear explosives. They said that the method would be feasible for supplying water for lunar base operations and for direct consumption after decontamination.

Desalination of the earth's sea water by atomic power is economically feasible only for plants operating on a large scale, according to a report presented in October at the First International Desalination Symposium at Washington, D.C. Gordon F. Leitner of Aqua-Chem, Inc., Waukesha, Wis., reported that a 50,000,000 watt atomic power capability would be required to compete with fossil fuel desalination plants, even in areas where fossil fuels are relatively costly. Glenn T. Seaborg, chairman of the AEC, predicted that dual-purpose reactors designed both for desalination and the generation of electricity will be commercially available in five to 10 years. See WATER AND FLOOD CONTROL.

Neutron Trap. Scientists of the Los Alamos Scientific Laboratory have devised a method of trapping neutrons from underground atomic blasts to yield data that might require centuries to gather through the use of conventional laboratory neutron sources. The neutron trap consists of a 600-foot long vacuum pipe which channels high-energy neutrons to the ground surface and snaps shut before bomb debris or radioactive gases can escape. A wealth of data on neutron interactions is recorded in approximately 5,000th of a second. The technique also makes possible investigations of materials which are so radioactive that their own natural radiation would obliterate the effects produced by laboratory neutron sources. The new device was described to the American Physical Society, meeting in Washington, D.C., by Dr. A. W. Hemmendinger of Los Alamos.

Atomic Wood. Gamma irradiation of specially treated wood resulted in a new wood-plastic combination that is stronger and more water resistant than natural wood. The new product also resists marring, yet retains its natural wood beauty. The AEC selected 78 wood products companies in 1965 for participation in a program to develop the new material. The process, developed at West Virginia University under an AEC contract, involves impregnating wood with a liquid plastic and bombarding it with ionizing radiation. SERGEI LENORMAND

See also ELECTRIC POWER; NUCLEAR PHYSICS.

AUSTRALIA, although visibly prosperous, was worried about its high imports and its falling international reserves. There were also misgivings in mid-summer over a budget providing for expenditures that would exceed annual revenue by $286,728,000. Despite this, the government of Prime Minister Sir Robert Gordon Menzies firmly rejected industry demands for import restrictions.

A 10-year limited free-trade agreement between Australia and New Zealand was signed on August 31 (see NEW ZEALAND). The new pact was to become effective in 1966. Earlier in the year, Australia announced that its currency system would be converted to dollar-and-cent units in February, 1966.

Defense spending increased heavily in 1965 with Australia placing orders for U.S. military equipment totaling $350,000,000. Australia continued to give military aid to South Vietnam and Malaysia.

Viscount De L'Isle retired as Governor-General in May. He was succeeded by Lord Richard Gardiner Casey (see CASEY, LORD RICHARD GARDINER).

Population: 11,450,000. **Government:** Governor-General Lord Richard Gardiner Casey; Prime Minister Robert Gordon Menzies. **Monetary Unit:** Australian pound (1 = U.S. $2.23). **Gross National Product:** £7,732,000,000. **Foreign Trade:** exports, $3,038,000,000; imports, $3,313,000,000. **Principal Exports:** meat, wheat, wool.   ALASTAIR BURNET

See also ASIA; GREAT BRITAIN; VIETNAM.

AUSTRIA. The coalition government that had ruled Austria since the end of World War II was dissolved in 1965. The two-party cabinet, headed by Chancellor Josef Klaus, resigned on October 22. It had been unable to resolve differences over a forthcoming budget within the time limit set by the constitution. This meant a temporary end of the conservative People's party-Socialist party coalition which most Austrians felt had given them their best years.

President Franz Jonas reappointed the cabinet in a caretaker status until new elections could be held in the spring of 1966. Jonas had succeeded President Adolf Schaerf who had died on February 28 (see JONAS, FRANZ). Generally, it was agreed that a new coalition would be formed.

Spirit of Neutrality. During the year, the nation observed the 600th anniversary of the University of Vienna, the 150th anniversary of the Congress of Vienna, and the 150th anniversary of the founding of the Vienna Institute of Technology (see CELEBRATIONS). Also celebrated in 1965 was the 10th anniversary of the signing of the Austrian State Treaty with France, Great Britain, the United States, and the Union of Soviet Socialist Republics. The treaty had ended Allied occupation after World War II and had restored Austrian freedom on a basis of strict neutrality.

Vienna continued to serve as a meeting place for the East and the West. It facilitated cultural and business exchanges, and initiated a number of tele-

vision panel shows that employed top-flight personalities from the East and the West. Austria's relations with the East had improved with the final settlement of all war claims (except with Czechoslovakia). Terrorist outbreaks continued, however, in Italian Tyrol (see ITALY).

National Economy. For the first time in years, the nation showed a $2,000,000 deficit in its balance of trade payments, as opposed to a surplus of $41,000,000 in 1964. The reason given was that Austria no longer depended on foreign loans to bolster the economy.

Bad weather, which included damaging floods and a summer drought, cut into the highly profitable tourist trade. It also affected agriculture and construction. A labor shortage still persisted.

Austria's gold reserves and foreign credits were still among the world's highest. Meanwhile, Austria's application for membership in the European Economic Community (EEC, or Common Market) continued to hang fire.

Population: 7,166,000. **Government:** President Franz Jonas; Chancellor Josef Klaus. **Monetary Unit:** schilling (25.87 schillings = U.S. $1). **Gross National Product:** 186,600,000,000 schillings. **Foreign Trade:** exports, $1,446,000,000; imports, $1,863,000,000. **Principal Exports:** iron, lumber, machinery, steel.   TOM AND HARLE DAMMANN

See also EUROPE.

AUTOMATION was viewed with considerably more optimism along the labor front in 1965 than in previous years. Continued technological advances contributed to significant increases in productivity. But, as opposed to the 1957-1962 period, unemployment decreased instead of rising.

The auto industry continued to automate assembly operations. Typically—as in the automation of the assembly of Pontiac differential gears—some operator functions were maintained, but output was increased and the volume of rejects lowered.

A new fiberglass boat factory incorporating automation ideas from the auto industry was opened by the Stanray Company in Danville, Ill. Company officials said that this one plant with its 500 workers could match the entire industry's 1964 output of small aluminum and fiberglass boats.

Numerical Control of machine tools made gains, pointing to wider use in the coming years. Only about 1,200 such units had been installed between 1954 and the end of 1961. But by 1967 there is expected to be 10 times as many such units in use. This would represent a conversion of approximately 1 per cent of the standard machine tools to automated tape controls. Unit labor cost savings from the use of numerical controls ran from 25 to 80 per cent in examples reported in a U.S. Department of Labor study.

Computers were performing more and more office tasks. In private industry, one wide survey of personnel officers showed that the most common areas automated were accounting, material handling, payroll, record keeping, and sales analysis. Two-thirds of the firms reported no employment decreases despite the introduction of automation. Automation in the office seemed to be slowing down employment increases rather than causing a substantial net loss of jobs.

Government experience with computers confirmed this appraisal. Adoption of computers helped hold federal civilian employment at the 2,500,000 mark despite substantial increases in programs and operations. Computers, for example, were turning out GI insurance dividend checks at $\frac{1}{50}$ of the cost of doing it manually.

Reasons for Adopting Automation were studied by the Department of Labor. One report noted: "Cost reduction, primarily through the effect of automation on labor productivity, appears to be a major objective in decisions to automate." The case studies in the report showed substantial reduction in unit labor requirements and fewer jobs in the affected departments, but that no one was "laid off." This was accomplished by *attrition* (quitting, retirement, or death) and by transfers to expanding operations in other departments or plants.

Productivity increases reflected the widespread introduction of automation and new technology, along with the continued operation of the economy at an efficient level. A Federal Reserve Board study late in the year reported: "Output per man-hour in manufacturing has grown at a rate of about 4 per cent a year since 1960. This is a higher rate than for the postwar period as a whole or for any of the preceding cyclical upswings." Preliminary data in 1965 suggested that the trend was continuing.

Unit labor costs in manufacturing, which had been increasing in the early post-World War II period, remained almost completely stable in the previous five years. That stability stemmed from the greater-than-average productivity gains and smaller-than-average increases in employee compensation. Compensation (wages and fringe benefits) rose at an annual rate of 3.5 per cent in 1959-1964, compared with 6 per cent per year in the previous 12-year period.

Recommendations for dealing with automation problems were expected in the forthcoming reports from the National Commission on Technology, Automation, and Economic Progress and from state commissions. However, the sense of urgency had diminished as the economy continued to expand at a rate that provided jobs for all but a small percentage of the labor force.

Unemployment in September fell below 3,000,000 for the first time since October, 1957, while manufacturing employment rose more in the 12 months ended in August, 1965, than in the previous four years combined. See LABOR.   JAMES L. STERN

See also COMPUTER; MANUFACTURING.

AUTOMOBILE

The U.S. auto industry had its biggest year in 1965, with production, sales, employment, and profits soaring to all-time highs. An estimated 9,000,000 cars rolled off U.S. assembly lines during the year. This easily shattered the old industry record of 7,941,538, set in 1955. These, plus 550,000 foreign imports, ran sales a whopping million units ahead of 1964's 8,065,150 (including 486,000 imports).

There was general belief among U.S. auto industry executives that a 9,000,000 sales figure would be reached again in 1966 with an annual sale of 10,000,000 new cars likely within three years.

To pay for "wheels" in 1965, U.S. new-car buyers spent about $36,000,000,000, about $4,000,000,000 more than last year. This drove auto industry profits beyond the $3,000,000,000 mark. General Motors (GM), the industry heavyweight, broke its own record for the highest profits of any company in history.

FRONT-WHEEL DRIVE of Oldsmobile's Toronado is the most dramatic innovation of the 1966 model year. The six-passenger car has a specially modified V-8 engine.
Oldsmobile Div., G.M.C.

Porsche of America

Rolls-Royce, Inc.

Mercedes-Benz

NEW STYLING marked three prestigious imports. The 911 model, top, gave Porsche its first new look in 16 years, while the Rolls-Royce Silver Shadow, center, had a low, sleek monocoque design, and Mercedes-Benz's luxury sedan, bottom, featured a flat roofline.

Another all-time high was reached in 1965: traffic deaths edged above 1964's record 47,800 (see SAFETY). U.S. Secretary of Commerce John T. Conner called the death toll "intolerable." Style-conscious Detroit was forced by government action to pay more attention to the good health of the people—both inside and outside the cars it sells.

Air Pollution. All U.S.-built new cars sold in smog-sensitive California were equipped, for the first time, with a $45 device that reduced carbon monoxide and certain other gases emitted by internal combustion engines. See Section Two, POLLUTED AMERICA.

On the national scene, a U.S. Senate subcommittee on air and water pollution, headed by Senator Edmund S. Muskie (D., Me.) met to determine whether a nationwide requirement of exhaust control devices would be in the public interest. Automobile makers showed some reluctance about nationwide application of the devices, which, they insisted, were not necessary in lightly populated areas. The automakers said, however, that they could comply with whatever conditions the Senate set up, provided they had a minimum of two years to prepare for any program adopted.

President Lyndon B. Johnson signed the Clean Air Act, containing many of the committee's proposals, on October 20. The act authorizes the Department of Health, Education, and Welfare to draw up national standards to cut down on automobile air pollution by 1968.

Crash Protection. The U.S. General Services Administration announced the 17 safety features it would demand on each of the 40,000 or so 1967 model cars it will buy. These included an exhaust-fume control device, a collapsible steering wheel, and a dual braking system.

In July, Senator Abraham Ribicoff (D., Conn.) led the Government Operations Subcommittee on Executive Reorganization to question industry leaders in a study of the government's role in highway safety. They found it difficult to get an admission from the industry that car design played a significant role in auto deaths. But they did obtain a few token concessions, and committee pressure did force some promises of future safety features.

For its 1966 cars, the industry made up a "safety package," including backup lights, multiple windshield wipers, padded dashboard, padded sun visors, rear seat belts, and windshield washers. The price of the items averaged about $50. Since the package was "standard" on all 1966 U.S. cars, the cost was passed along to the buyer.

This additional cost offset a reduction, from 10 to 7 per cent, in the federal excise tax, which went into effect May 15, 1965. An additional 1 per cent cut will occur Jan. 1, 1966, with further cuts scheduled for the future.

The combination of the tax cut and the added cost of the safety package complicated efforts to determine whether 1966 car prices were up or down in 1965. The trade publication *Automotive News* said: "When equipment changes are considered, the prices showed little change from the after tax-cut figures. GM and American Motors are down slightly, Ford held the line, and Chrysler is up."

What's New. For the U.S. industry as a whole, there were few major styling and engineering changes in the 1966 models. The four major U.S. auto companies—General Motors, Ford, Chrysler, and American Motors—offered a postwar record of 364 body styles, up 18 from a year earlier. They emphasized optional equipment designed to lure additional dollars from the buyer by allowing him to "tailor" the car of his choice. Engine and transmission options were readily available. Before options, transportation, or financing charges were added, prices ranged from $2,004 for a Rambler American to $10,456 for a Cadillac limousine.

The most unusual U.S. car among the 1966 models was Oldsmobile's Toronado. It was the first U.S. front-wheel-drive car since 1937, when the famed Cord was discontinued. The Toronado was available only as a six-passenger coupé. In simplest terms, the Toronado is pulled by its front wheels rather than by being pushed by its rear wheels.

Among the innovations on 1966 models were the Ford Motor Company's station wagon dual-action tailgate, which opened either sideways or up and down; and a stereo tape player with four speakers. Also new were Pontiac's overhead-cam, six-cylinder engine, the first such unit offered by a U.S. manufacturer; Chrysler's unique safety door handles; and American Motors' self-adjusting clutch.

Expansion Programs. Both on the domestic front and overseas, U.S. automakers allocated more than $2,000,000,000 for new plants and additions in 1965. U.S. auto firms made especially big investments abroad as they realized that production and sales of new cars in other Free World countries, estimated at over 19,000,000 cars in 1965, exceeded those in the United States. Ford Motor Company, for example, now has 124 overseas plants.

On the personnel front, the major change in the year was at General Motors, where James M. Roche succeeded John F. Gordon as head of the world's biggest manufacturing concern. CHARLES C. CAIN III

AUTOMOBILE RACING. Jim Clark dominated the auto racing world as few men have. The 29-year-old farmer from Duns, Scotland, not only won the World Grand Prix Drivers' title for the second time, but also captured first in the Indianapolis 500.

Driving a Lotus, Clark won six of the 10 Grand Prix races, clinching the world title on August 1, the earliest in history. England's Graham Hill, 1962 champion and 1964 runner-up, was second. Newcomer Jacky Stewart, another Scot, was third. At Indianapolis, Clark's Lotus-Ford finished more than a lap ahead of Parnelli Jones of Torrance, Calif. Mario Andretti of Nazareth, Pa., was third.

Ned Jarrett of Camden, S.C., led the 1965 National Association for Stock Car Racing (NASCAR) standings. In sports car racing, two Chevrolet-powered Chaparrals, built by Jim Hall and Hap Sharp of Midland, Tex., won almost every race they entered.

Craig Breedlove of Los Angeles, Calif., and Art Arfons of Akron, Ohio, battled again for the world land speed record, driving jet-engine racers across the Bonneville Salt Flats in Utah. On November 3, Breedlove broke Arfons' one-year-old record with a 555 mph two-way average. Then Arfons, who survived a tire blowout, raised it four days later to almost 577 mph. Finally, on November 15, Breedlove made it 600.601 mph. JAMES O. DUNAWAY

Wide World

WITH A SALUTE TO THE CROWD, Jim Clark of Duns, Scotland, won the Indianapolis 500 on Memorial Day in his Lotus-Ford racer. He later won other important events.

AVIATION

For the first time in the history of aviation, United States domestic trunk airlines topped $3,000,000,000 in annual revenues. Profits also set a record, reaching an estimated $245,000,000, about $115,000,000 more than the 1964 mark. About 49,000,000,000 revenue passenger-miles were flown, up 8,000,000,000 from 1964. Based on the historic correlation of U.S. traffic with world traffic, International Civil Aviation Organization (ICAO) members flew 120,000,000,000 passenger-miles, with estimated 1965 revenues of $9,000,000,000.

British Overseas Airways Corp.

New short-haul jet aircraft were introduced during the year. The first twin-rear-engine DC-9 was delivered to Delta Air Lines. Mohawk Airlines put the similar-appearing British BAC-III into operation, and Lake Central Airlines introduced a French-built, high-wing turboprop, the Nord 262. Orders continued for new equipment, with most manufacturers offering new configurations of present models or announcing new models, as in the case of the Boeing 737 due in 1967.

Anticipating the end of the subsidy for helicopter lines on Dec. 31, 1965, a new era of cooperation began between the airlines and the helicopter and air taxi services to and from large metropolitan airports. Airlines also featured attractive arrangements with rent-a-car operators and credit card agencies to lure more passengers.

The U.S. supersonic transport program progressed slowly. The final competitors—two airframe companies, Boeing and Lockheed, and two engine manufacturers, General Electric and Pratt and Whitney—started building their mock-ups and test engines under Federal Aviation Agency (FAA) contracts. The contracts call for a decision by the FAA on the builders of the prototype early in 1967.

Government Activities. During the year, the FAA completed the consolidation of its air traffic control centers, reducing their number from 29 to 21. The centers control all aircraft operating under Instrument Flight Rules (IFR). The new system, made possible by new developments in long-range radar, not only aided safety but also proved to be more economical.

A government task force was established to study interurban air transportation. Of special interest was the development of Vertical/Short Take-Off and Landing (V/STOL) aircraft as part of the national transportation system.

As an aid to planning, the FAA issued its predictions for the next five years. It forecast that by 1970 the airline passenger-miles will increase to 74,000,000,000 from the 54,000,000,000 flown by all U.S. airlines in 1964. General aviation (flying other than the military or commercial airlines) was expected to increase to 19,500,000 hours from

BRITISH CHALLENGER. *Rear engines whining, a new BAC Super-VC-10 left London March 7 for first test flight to New York.*

LANDING BY COMPUTER: AUTOFLARE

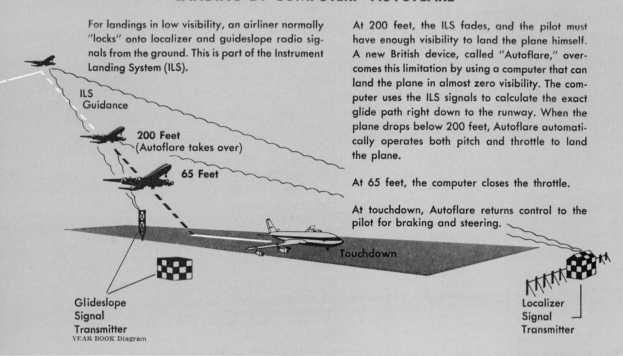

For landings in low visibility, an airliner normally "locks" onto localizer and guideslope radio signals from the ground. This is part of the Instrument Landing System (ILS).

ILS Guidance

200 Feet (Autoflare takes over)

65 Feet

At 200 feet, the ILS fades, and the pilot must have enough visibility to land the plane himself. A new British device, called "Autoflare," overcomes this limitation by using a computer that can land the plane in almost zero visibility. The computer uses the ILS signals to calculate the exact glide path right down to the runway. When the plane drops below 200 feet, Autoflare automatically operates both pitch and throttle to land the plane.

At 65 feet, the computer closes the throttle.

At touchdown, Autoflare returns control to the pilot for braking and steering.

Touchdown

Glideslope Signal Transmitter

Localizer Signal Transmitter

YEAR BOOK Diagram

15,500,000. The size of the air-carrier fleet was expected to remain constant at about 2,100 aircraft; of these, nearly 1,100 will be powered by jet engines. The general aviation fleet was expected to grow from about 85,000 to 105,000 aircraft. The bulk of these, the FAA predicted, will remain piston-engine powered.

Major changes in the requirements for flight engineers in transport-type aircraft were adopted by the FAA to bring the requirements in line with technical developments. Under the new regulations, the flight engineer must now be expertly qualified on a particular class of airplane rather than on aircraft in general.

Federal regulations specifically governing agricultural flying and related activities were announced by the FAA. They will be effective Jan. 1, 1966. The rules are designed to improve the safety of agricultural aviation and to protect persons and property on the ground. They established, for the first time, national standards for operator certificates, operating rules, aircraft airworthiness, pilot qualifications, and record keeping for more than 2,500 operators engaged in agricultural flying.

The first standardized-design airport tower was opened at Lawton, Okla. Each tower built under the new standards will have a functional design, tailored to air traffic control requirements, and will have a standardized working environment. They will be built entirely with FAA funds.

In a complete realignment of government agencies concerned with air transportation affairs, Charles S. Murphy became chairman of the Civil Aeronautics Board (CAB). Alan S. Boyd was appointed undersecretary of commerce for transportation, and William F. McKee FAA administrator.

Airports. In 1964, the FAA introduced a more extensive airport reporting service. This required airport operators to notify the agency before establishing or closing an airport. FAA reported 9,490 airports in operation at the beginning of 1965. This was an increase of 676 over the previous year, and compared favorably with the average annual increase of 623 over the past five years.

Texas, with 812 airports, led all other states. California, with 627 landing facilities, was second; and Alaska was third, with 549. Nearly two-thirds of the national total, 5,846, were privately owned. Lighted runways were provided at 2,773 airports, and paved runways at 2,630. At all but 29 of the nation's airports, the number of general aviation take-offs and landings exceeded those of the airlines. In 1965, the five busiest U.S. airports were Chicago-O'Hare International; Long Beach, Calif.; Van Nuys, Calif.; John F. Kennedy International (New York); and Los Angeles International.

The Spokane (Wash.) International Airport opened a new terminal building, and Dallas and Fort Worth, Tex., announced agreement on plans for a joint regional airport. See DALLAS.

Pictorial Parade

THE WORLD'S LARGEST AIRCRAFT, the Soviet AN-22, stole the show at the Paris International Air Exposition in June. It can carry 700 passengers.

International Transportation. Increased ranges of the latest aircraft enabled airlines to schedule nonstop flights between New York-Buenos Aires; Los Angeles-London; Tokyo-Seattle; and New York-Tel Aviv. Around-the-world service is now offered by at least six airlines. In July, Pan American World Airways began a weekly service of around-the-world cargo jet flights, uniting 17 of the world's major industrial centers.

The International Air Transport Association (IATA) reported a continuing rise in the number of passengers taking the North Atlantic route. During the first six months of 1965, traffic increased 18 per cent over 1964, with 1,477,850 passengers. Cargo increased 53 per cent, with 82,744 short tons. Lower passenger fares were projected for 1966, and numerous cargo fare reductions went into effect in September, 1965. Knut Hammarskjöld was named director general of IATA, effective April 1, 1966.

ICAO Assembly. The largest gathering of representatives of the 110 member states of the ICAO completed a month-long session in Montreal, Canada. The assembly, which last met in 1962, reviewed the organization's work and made decisions on future policies in the entire field of international civil aviation. The main work of the assembly was done by the executive committee and by the technical, economic, legal, and administrative commissions. These groups made recommendations on matters of general aviation, international

law, navigation equipment, regional planning, supersonic civil aircraft, and technical assistance and training.

General Aviation. The boom continued in general aviation, which includes all flying other than by the military and the airlines. General aviation aircraft output rose 20 per cent, totaling more than 12,000 aircraft. Manufacturers continued the trend toward providing a full selection of aircraft adapted to the various customer markets and announced plans to invest $20,000,000 in plant expansion. Most manufacturers were developing export businesses, and some were setting up assembly plants in foreign countries.

Noteworthy Flights. Mary Ann Noah, with her copilot, Mary Aikins, won the 19th Annual All-Women's Transcontinental Air Race (Powder Puff Derby) for the second year in a row. The race was from El Cajon, Calif., to Chattanooga, Tenn.

June Douglas, flying a Piper Cherokee 180, was the solo winner of the All-Women's International Air Race from Caldwell-Wright Airport, New Jersey, to Nassau, Bahamas.

Within a 25-hour period, Trans World Airways established three firsts in Boeing 707-320C jet aircraft. The longest of the three nonstop flights was from Oakland, Calif., to Tel Aviv, Israel, a distance of 7,998 statute miles, in 13 hours 30 minutes. The same aircraft had just returned from a flight of 5,460 miles in 10 hours 30 minutes. The third flight

241

was from Oakland, Calif., to Rio de Janeiro, Brazil, covering 6,908 miles in 13 hours 19 minutes.

The year was an active one for contests and record-breaking, with 28 international records and 40 U.S. records being established by U.S. citizens as of October 1. Of the total 722 Fédération Aéronautique Internationale aerospace recognized records, the United States holds 342 and the U.S.S.R., 135.

Aviation Trophy and Award winners in 1965:

American Institute of Astronautics and Aeronautics de Florez Training Award to Lloyd L. Kelly for his efforts in perfecting training simulators.

Barbour Air Safety Award to Arthur E. Jenks for his many contributions toward improving the techniques for flight-checking the accuracy of navigational aids.

Frank G. Brewer Trophy to Gill Robb Wilson for a lifetime of service to aviation education.

Robert J. Collier Trophy to General Curtis E. LeMay, USAF, in recognition of his accomplishments in 1964 as chief of staff of the U.S. Air Force.

Harmon International Aviation Trophies to Max Conrad for his 57-hour nonstop flight from Capetown, South Africa, to St. Petersburg, Fla., and to Joan Merriam Smith for her 27,000-mile solo flight around the world.

Wright Brothers Memorial Trophy to Jerome F. Lederer of the Flight Safety Foundation, Inc., for his contribution to aviation safety.   LESLIE A. BRYAN

See also ARMED FORCES OF THE WORLD; BALLOONS; DISASTERS; ENGINE AND ENERGY; INVENTION; NATIONAL DEFENSE; SPACE TRAVEL; TRAVEL.

AWARDS AND PRIZES presented in 1965 included the following:

General Awards

Academy of American Poets Awards. *Fellowship* to Marianne Moore, noted poet, critic, and translator. *Lamont Award* to Henri Coulette for his first book of poems *The War of the Secret Agent and Other Poems.*

American Academy of Arts and Letters and National Institute of Arts and Letters Awards. *Gold Medals* to Andrew Wyeth, painter, and Walter Lippmann, author and editor. *Marjorie Peabody Waite Award,* for "continuing integrity in his work, to Paul Burlin, painter. *Rosenthal Foundation Awards* to painter Marcia Marcus, and Thomas Berger for his novel *Little Big Man. William Dean Howells Medal,* awarded every five years for the most distinguished work of American fiction, to John Cheever for *The Wapshot Scandal. Arnold W. Bruner Award in Architecture* to Kevin Roche. *Awards in Literature* to poets Ben Belitt, Robert Bly, James V. Cunningham (also critic), and Denise Levertov; Joseph Mitchell, local historian; and novelists Pier M. Pasinetti, Henry Roth, and Harvey Swados. *Awards in Art* to graphic artists Sigmund Abeles and Joyce Reopel; painters Lee Gatch and Richard Mayhew; and sculptors David V. Hayes, Elliot Offner, and Thomas Stearns. *Awards in Music* to composers Mario Davidovsky, Gerald Humel, Earl Kim, and Harvey Sollberger. *Traveling Fellowship in Literature* to novelist Cormac McCarthy. *Award for Distinguished Service to the Arts* to Frances Steloff of The Gotham Book Mart in New York City and subject of *Wise Men Fish Here* (1965) by W. G. Rogers

American Academy of Arts and Sciences Emerson-Thoreau Medal, for distinguished achievement in literature, to Lewis Mumford for his work as a philosopher, critic, teacher, and writer.

American Institute of Architects Awards. *Honor Medal* to Hungarian-born Marcel Lajos Breuer, designer of the Whitney Museum of American Art in New York City and other notable buildings. *Allied Professions Medal* to Leonardo Zeevaert, University of Mexico professor and engineer. *Fine Arts Medal* to Mexican muralist and landscape designer Roberto Burle-Marx. *Industrial Arts Medal* to architect and industrial designer Eliot Noyes. *Edward C. Kemper Award,* for significant contributions to the institute and the architectural profession, to Joseph Watterson, editor of the journal published by the architectural institute.

American Sociological Association MacIver Award to William Goode of Columbia University for his book *World Revolution and Family Patterns* (1963).

Anisfield-Wolf Awards by the *Saturday Review,* for books that deal most creditably with race-relations problems, to Milton M. Gordon for *Assimilation in American Life;* James M. McPherson for *The Struggle for Equality: Abolitionists and the Negro in the Civil War and Reconstruction;* Abram L. Sacher for *A History of the American Jew;* and James A. Silver for *Mississippi: A Closed Society.*

Aspen Institute for Humanistic Studies Award to Martha Graham, creative dancer and choreographer, who formed her own company and established the Martha Graham School of Contemporary Dance.

Boston Medals for Distinguished Achievement, presented for the first time in 1965, to composer Richard Rodgers and Arthur Fiedler, Boston Pops Orchestra conductor for many years.

Brandeis University Creative Arts Awards to playwright Tennessee Williams, poet Stanley Kunitz, painter Mark Rothko, and composer Elliott Carter. *Notable Creative Achievement Award* to Alfred H. Barr, Jr., museum collections director at New York City's Museum of Modern Art. *Citation Awards,* for furtherance of their careers, to composer Salvatore Martirano, poet Anthony Hecht, painter Kenneth Noland, and drama critic Michael Smith.

British Royal Society of Arts Benjamin Franklin Medal to Paul Mellon, art collector and board chairman of the Mellon Institute of Industrial Research in Pittsburgh, Pa.

Columbia University Awards. *Alice M. Ditson Conductor's Award* to Jacob Avshalomov, Portland (Ore.) Junior Symphony Orchestra conductor. *Brevoort-Eickemayer Prize,* awarded every five years, to artist Edwin Dickinson, who was also honored with a retrospective exhibition at the Whitney Museum of American Art in 1965. *Frederic Bancroft Prizes,* for studies in American history, diplomacy, and international relations, to William B. Willcox, for *Portrait of a General: Sir Henry Clinton in the War of Independence;* Bradford Perkins for *Castlereagh and Adams: England and The United States, 1812–1823;* and Dorothy Borg for *The United States and the Far Eastern Crisis of 1933–1938.*

Denmark's Sonning Prize to Leonard Bernstein, composer, conductor, pianist, and New York Philharmonic musical director.

Four Freedoms Award, for service to the ideals of President Franklin D. Roosevelt, posthumously to President John F. Kennedy.

Freedom House Award to Harry S. Truman, former President of the United States (1945–1953), inscribed "Wise in policy, valiant in action, decisive in leadership, you gave a battered world new hope."

Freedoms Foundation George Washington Medal, the foundation's highest award, to Dewitt and Lila A. Wallace, editors and publishers of *Reader's Digest,* for "building under free enterprise a magazine invaluable in the continuing fight for freedom and dignity of every individual."

French Academy Novel Award to Jean Husson for *Le Cheval d'Herbeleau* (*Herbeleau's Horse*). The author was cited as "a young writer of a work of imagination and superior inspiration."

German Bookseller International Nonfiction Prize, awarded every three years, to *The New York Times* science editor Walter Sullivan for *We Are Not Alone.*

Goethe Institute Goethe Medal to Richard Wolf, German author and teacher, for teaching German abroad and acting as director of the Goethe Institute in Munich; Roy Pascal, University of Birmingham (England) German professor; and Elizabeth Wilkinson, University of London German professor and chairman of the British Goethe Society.

Goncourt Academy Award for Literature to Jacques Boral for his first novel, *L'Adoration.*

Hawthornden Prize, to a British writer under 41 years of age, was awarded to William Trevor, author of *The Old Boys.*

International Publishers Prizes, awarded to Americans for the first time. *Prix International de Littérature,* awarded to a living author of world stature for a work of fiction published within the last three years that will have the most significant influence on the literature of our time, to Saul Bellow for *Herzog* (see BELLOW, SAUL). *Prix Formentor* to Stephen Schneck, also an American, for *The Night Clerk,* his first novel, not published (at award time May, 1965).

Jan Sibelius Prizes; *Annual Music Prize* to British composer Benjamin Britten. *Centennial Prizes* to Finnish composers Erik Bergman, Usko Merilainen, and Eino-Juhani Rautavaara.

National Book Committee Awards. *National Book Awards: Fiction Award* to Saul Bellow for *Herzog* (see BELLOW, SAUL); *History and Biography Award* to Louis Fischer for *The Life of Lenin; Arts and Letters Award* to Eleanor Clark for *The Oysters of Locmariaquer; Poetry Award* to the late Theodore Roethke for *The Far Field,* a posthumous publication; *Science, Philosophy, and Religion Award* to the late Norbert Wiener for *God and Golem, Inc.,* a posthumous publication. *National Medal for Literature,* presented for the first time in 1965 at the first such White House ceremonies, to Thornton N. Wilder, novelist and playwright, for a lifetime of work.

Poetry Society of America Awards. *Alice Fay di Castagnola Award,* presented for the first time in 1965, to Paul Roche, English poet, for *Beyond All This Fiddle* (verse and prose); and Barbara Overmyer for her poetry collection and first book, not yet published. *Shelley Award* to Ruth Stone of Cambridge, Mass., as a promising poet. *Melville Cane Award* to Jean H. Hagstrum for *William Blake: Poet and Painter.*

Royal Institute of British Architects Gold Medal to Kenzo Tange, designer of the Peace Memorial Hall and Museum in Hiroshima and other buildings in Japan.

Society of American Historians Francis Parkman Prize to Willie Lee Rose for *Rehearsal for Reconstruction.*

University of Pisa International Italian History and Literature Prize to Hans Baron, University of Chicago professor and specialist on the cultural and political history and civilization of Italy.

Yale University Bollingen Prize, for American poetry, to Horace Gregory for his *Collected Poems.*

Science and Industry

Albert and Mary Lasker Foundation Awards. *Medical Journalism Awards: Newspaper Award* to Alton L. Blakeslee, The Associated Press science writer, and Jeremiah B. Stamler, Chicago Board of Health Heart Disease Control Program director, for their series "Your Heart Has Nine Lives." *Special Newspaper Citation* to Jack Nelson, *The Los Angeles Times* south-eastern bureau chief in Atlanta, for his series on the care of the mentally ill in Georgia in *The Atlanta Constitution. Magazine Award* to Matt Clark, *Newsweek* medicine editor, for his story "Birth Control: The Pill and the Church." *Television Award* to Fred W. Friendly and Jay McMullen for the Columbia Broadcasting System Reports program "The Business of Heroin." *Special Television Citation* to Edgar T. Bell, manager of station KWTV (Oklahoma City), for "The Twilight World," mental retardation program written and produced by Harlan Mendenhall. *Medical Research Awards* to Albert B. Sabin, University of Cincinnati College of Medicine Distinguished Service Professor, who developed a live oral poliomyelitis vaccine; and Robert W. Holley, Cornell University Professor of Biochemistry, who isolated and analyzed a 77-subunit strand of ribonucleic acid (RNA).

American Academy of Arts and Sciences Rumford Medal, awarded every two years, to Samuel C. Collins, Massachusetts Institute of Technology Professor Emeritus of Mechanical Engineering, who pioneered in low-temperature research and invented the Collins helium cryostat to produce liquid helium; and William D. McElroy, Johns Hopkins University Biology Department chairman and director of the McCollum-Pratt Institute there, for work on the molecular basis of bioluminescence (emission of light by plants and animals).

American Chemical Society Awards. *James T. Grady Award* to Isaac Asimov, Boston University biochemist and author of many science (fact and fiction) books. *Roger Adams Award* to Arthur Clay Cope, Massachusetts Institute of Technology Chemistry Department chairman, discoverer of the Cope Rearrangement (of allylic groups in three-carbon systems) and a useful barbiturate (Delvinal).

American Physical Society Irving Langmuir Award, presented for the first time in 1965, to John H. Van Vleck, Harvard University Professor of Physics, for his studies in chemical physics.

American Society of Industry Sir William Henry Perkin Medal to Carl Shipp Marvel, University of Arizona Professor of Chemistry, a pioneer in polymer research and recently engaged in the study of high-temperature polymers.

Case Institute of Technology Albert A. Michelson Award to Luis W. Alverez, University of California (Berkeley) Professor of Physics, for discovery of significant properties of cosmic rays, neutrons, isotopes, and nuclear transformation. He is also a leading developer of quantitative tools for nuclear physics, and a pioneer in radar and aircraft landing systems.

Dickinson College Joseph Priestley Memorial Award to Joel H. Hildebrand, University of California (Berkeley) Professor Emeritus of Chemistry, for research in solubility and the structure of liquids.

Formosa Chi-Tsin Culture Foundation Achievement in Science Award to Chien-shiung Wu, Columbia University professor, for her research in nuclear forces and structure, particularly in disproving the law of parity conservation.

Franklin Institute Awards. *Frank P. Brown Medal* to William J. Levitt, for development of large-volume, high-efficiency home construction. *John Price Wetherill Medals* to John Reynolds, University of California (Berkeley) Professor of Physics, for studies of xenon isotopes; and Frederick D. Rossini, University of Notre Dame College of Science dean, for contributions to petroleum hydrocarbon chemistry and engineering. *Stuart Ballantine Medal* to Alec Harley Reeves, English scientist, for his pulse code modulation system used by Mariner IV satellite to transmit television pictures from Mars to Earth.

AWARDS AND PRIZES

Institute of Electrical and Electronics Engineers Lamme Medal to A. Uno Lamm, Swedish scientist, for developing the high-power, high-voltage mercury-arc valve and a system of control and protection for its application as a rectifier and inverter in high-voltage DC power transmission.

Lewis and Rosa Strauss Memorial Fund Albert Einstein Medal to John Archibald Wheeler, Princeton University Professor of Physics and a specialist on Einstein's theory of relativity and nuclear physics.

National Academy of Sciences Awards. *Agassiz Medal* to Sir Edward Bullard, Cambridge University (England) Geophysics Professor, for original contribution in the science of oceanography. *Carty Medal* to Alfred Henry Sturtevant, California Institute of Technology Thomas Hunt Morgan Professor Emeritus of Biology, for his analysis of hereditary patterns in the common fruit fly *Drosophila melanogaster*. *Daniel G. Elliot Medal* to George Gaylord Simpson, Harvard University Museum of Comparative Zoology Alexander Agassiz Professor of Vertebrate Paleontology, for his book *Principles of Animal Taxonomy*. *Henry Draper Medal* to Martin Ryle, Cambridge University Mullard Radio Astronomy Observatory director, for original investigation in astronomical physics. *Kimber Genetics Medal* to Alfred Day Hershey, Carnegie Institution of Washington Genetics Research Unit director, as a leader in the discovery of DNA's (deoxyribonucleic acid) role in hereditary processes and for contributions to molecular genetics. *James Craig Watson Medal* to Paul Herget, University of Cincinnati Observatory director, for contributions to celestial mechanics, particularly his application of electronic computer techniques to calculations of comets, earth satellites, and asteroids orbits. *U.S. Steel Foundation Award in Molecular Biology* to Robert S. Edgar of California Institute of Technology for his development and application of the method of "conditional lethal mutants" to determine how genes (basic units of heredity) control virus development.

National Medal of Science, presented by President Johnson, to Roger Adams, distinguished organic chemist and University of Illinois Professor Emeritus of Chemistry; Othmar Hermann Ammann, bridge designer (see DEATHS OF NOTABLE PERSONS); Theodosius Dobzhansky, Rockefeller Institute professor, noted for fundamental studies of the genetic determinants of organic evolution; Charles Stark Draper, Massachusetts Institute of Technology Aeronautics and Astronautics Department head and a leader in missile guidance developments; Solomon Lefschetz, Princeton University Professor Emeritus of Mathematics and authority on algebraic topology; Neal Elgar Miller, Yale University James Rowland Angell Professor of Psychology, known for research on principles of learning and motivation; Harold Marston Morse, Institute for Advanced Study (Princeton, N.J.) mathematician and pioneer in differential topology; Marshall Warren Nirenberg, National Heart Institute Laboratory of Clinical Biochemistry Biochemical Genetics Section head, known for studies of the genetic control of protein synthesis; Julian Seymour Schwinger (see NOBEL PRIZES [Science]; SCHWINGER, JULIAN SEYMOUR); Harold Clayton Urey, Nobel chemistry laureate (1934) and University of California (San Diego), more recently acclaimed for work on the origin of the solar system and of life on earth; and Robert Burns Woodward, Harvard University Donner Professor of Science (see NOBEL PRIZES [Science]; WOODWARD, ROBERT BURNS).

Pacific Science Center Foundation Arches of Science Award, presented for the first time in 1965, to Warren Weaver, internationally known mathematician, educator, former research foundation executive, and author of *Lady Luck—The Theory of Probability; The Mathematical Theory of Communication; Science and Complexity; People, Energy and Food*, and other books and numerous articles. Weaver was cited "for his contributions toward public understanding of the meaning of science."

Royal Astronomical Society of London Awards. *Gold Medal* to Gerald Maurice Clemence, Yale University astronomy research associate, for his application of celestial mechanics to the motions in the solar system and for his "fundamental contributions to the study of time and the system of astronomical constants." *Eddington Medal* to Harvard Professor Robert V. Pound and Yale Assistant Professor Glen A. Rebka, Jr., for their experiments confirming Einstein's principle of equivalence (a basic assumption of the general relativity theory).

Royal Canadian Geographical Society Massey Medal to Hugh Samuel Bostock, for contributions to the Western Cordillera and the Yukon Territory. See BOSTOCK, HUGH SAMUEL.

Turin Academy of Medicine Saint-Vincent International Prize for Medical Science, awarded every four years by the Italian academy, to Michael Ellis DeBakey, Baylor University College of Medicine Surgery Department chairman, who pioneered in surgical procedures for heart and blood vessel diseases.

United Nations Educational, Scientific, and Cultural Organization Kalinga Prize, for popularization of science, to Warren Weaver, mathematician and author.

See also NOBEL PRIZES; PULITZER PRIZES; and Awards sections of articles such as ATOMIC ENERGY, AVIATION, and LITERATURE FOR CHILDREN.

BAHAMAS was temporarily stunned by a blow to its most lucrative source of trade. In June, the United States passed a law reducing American tourists' duty-free allowances for liquor and other goods purchased overseas. Bahamians feared this might discourage tourism and tourist purchases. The traffic held up, however, reaching a record 605,000 visitors.

American and other investors continued to recognize the Bahamas' value as a tax haven. Some U.S. Treasury officials hinted, however, that some funds flowing into the Western Hemisphere's "Little Switzerland" might be coming from American underworld sources.

Under the direction of Sir Stafford Sands, minister of finance and tourism, the United Bahamian party (UBP), which is dominated by Nassau merchants and professional men, helped maintain an economic boom. But growing opposition to the UBP by the Progressive Liberal party (PLP) indicated a political challenge was brewing among the islands' Negro majority.

Population: 122,000. **Government:** Governor Sir Ralph Grey. **Monetary Unit:** pound (1 = U.S. $2.80). **Foreign Trade:** imports, $79,141,820; exports, $2,687,292. **Principal Exports:** provisions, pulpwood, salt. ALASTAIR BURNET

See also GREAT BRITAIN.

BALLET. See DANCING.

BALLOONS. See ASTRONOMY; WEATHER.

BANKS AND BANKING enjoyed a prosperous year. Bank earnings increased. The time deposits of all U.S. commercial banks rose about 15 per cent in 1965. Nevertheless, their loan-to-deposit ratio climbed to a 30-year high of 65 per cent.

Banking institutions were increasingly strapped for funds. To attract deposits, many U.S. banks were paying interest at the legal limit: 4 per cent on savings and $4\frac{1}{2}$ per cent on certificates of deposit (CDs) with maturities of 90 days or longer. Some banks were selling savings bonds, or small-denomination CDs. Later in the year, CD limits were raised to $5\frac{1}{2}$ per cent (see MONEY).

Bank Rate Hike. The Federal Reserve Board on December 5 increased the *discount rate* from 4 per cent to $4\frac{1}{2}$ per cent. (Member banks must pay the discount rate on funds they borrow from the Federal Reserve banks.) The administration had been maintaining that increased lending rates were against public policy. Immediately after the rate boost, President Lyndon B. Johnson commented: "I particularly regret that this action was taken before January, when we will have before us the full facts on next year's budget, Vietnam costs . . . and other elements in the economic outlook." See ECONOMY, THE; PRESIDENT OF THE UNITED STATES.

During the year, banks generally were mindful that the few 1964 increases in prime rates were rescinded under presidential pressure. Some banks, accordingly, only gingerly raised rates to $4\frac{3}{4}$ per cent on loans to brokers and sales finance companies. But after the discount rate change, the prime rate was increased to 5 per cent.

Overseas Loan Curbs. Banks cooperated with the administration in a voluntary program to limit the size of overseas loans to no more than 5 per cent above 1964 levels. The balance in U.S. international payments weakened during the last half of 1965, however, and measures to strengthen the voluntary program were under investigation (see INTERNATIONAL TRADE AND FINANCE).

In Britain, the Labour government's first anti-inflationary pay freeze was applied to bank workers. And in June, it ordered the Bank of England's lending rate cut to 6 per cent. It had been at a 7 per cent "crisis" level since Nov. 23, 1964. In December, the Bank of Canada raised its discount rate to $4\frac{3}{4}$ per cent, from $4\frac{1}{4}$ per cent.

Savings and Loan Associations (SLAs). Early in the year, more than 100 SLAs with dividend rates above prevailing local levels were curbed from borrowing funds from Federal Home Loan Banks. Several California SLAs that had paid 5 per cent dividends cut back to 4.85 per cent. The Federal Home Loan Banks raised their rates on loans to SLAs to $4\frac{3}{4}$ per cent. And, in August, the Federal Home Loan Bank Board issued a stringent set of guidelines—later relaxed—on loans to SLAs.

Continued squabbles among bank regulatory agencies prompted the administration to set up a panel for regular interchanges among the Federal Reserve Board, Federal Deposit Insurance Corporation (FDIC), comptroller of the currency, and Federal Home Loan Bank Board. That bickering culminated in a plan to unify federal bank regulation. The American Bankers Association opposed it, arguing that it would destroy valuable checks and balances in the banking system.

A Major Bank Failure with overtones of scandal shook the banking community on Jan. 22, 1965, when the San Francisco National Bank was declared insolvent. It had been chartered less than three years. Large depositors—including the United Automobile Workers union ($3,000,000) and several West Coast SLAs—sued for recovery of their uninsured deposits. They charged that Comptroller of the Currency James J. Saxon covered up examination reports while he tried to shore up the shaky bank for a merger with a stronger one. The suits further alleged that Federal Reserve loans to the bank gave depositors a false impression of its solvency.

Banks Diversify. The First National Bank of New York won Security and Exchange Commission approval to set up a mutual fund—first such venture since most stock market operations of banks were outlawed by the 1934 Securities Exchange Act. New

Liquid Assets Held by the Public (billions of dollars)		
	1965	**Changes from Sept. 30, 1964**
Demand Deposits and Currency.	$160.7	$ 5.7	3.5%
Time Deposits:			
Commercial Banks.........	141.4	19.5	13.8%
Mutual Savings Banks......	51.6	3.7	7.2%
Postal Savings System........	.3	— .1	−33.3%
Savings and Loan Shares.....	107.7	8.6	8.0%
U.S. Government Savings Bonds	50.1	.7	1.4%
U.S. Government Securities Maturing Within One Year	49.7	2.3	4.6%
TOTAL*.................	561.6	40.6	7.2%

Note: Figures at end of September each year.
Sources: Council of Economic Advisers; *Economic Indicators*
*Detail may not add to total due to rounding.

rules governing disclosure of information to bank stockholders became effective April 30. Yet some accountants and security analysts remained critical of "misleading and inadequate" bank reports.

Merger Dispute. The nearly impossible task of breaking up already merged banks found in violation of antitrust laws led Congress to propose that six such mergers be legalized retroactively. (Two were already under court orders to unmerge.) The bill, which passed in the Senate, prohibited any lodging of antitrust charges later than 30 days after a merger. But Representative Wright Patman (D., Tex.), House Banking Committee chairman, was so opposed to the measure that he prevented a rebellious committee and the House from even considering it in 1965. WILLIAM G. DEWALD

See also Section One, SYLVIA PORTER ON THE ECONOMY.

BASEBALL

Sandy Koufax of the Los Angeles Dodgers made baseball history as he pitched outstanding games that won his team the National League pennant and the World Series. The 29-year-old left-hander, who has been called "a league unto himself," won 26 games in regular-season play and then pitched two shut-outs in the World Series.

The series matched teams that had come from sixth-place finishes in 1964 to win pennants in their respective leagues. The Minnesota Twins won the first two games of the series in Minnesota, and the Dodgers took the next three in Los Angeles. The Twins came back in the sixth game in Minnesota and then lost the clincher to Koufax, 2-0.

The National League. The Dodgers won the pennant with strong pitching, tight defense, and daring base-running (by Maury Wills, who stole an impressive 92 bases). The champions thus ended their regular season with a major league low of only 78 home runs. But they were credited with bringing a return to the old brand of baseball—tight defense and high-speed playing backed by strong pitching.

Five teams were in contention in the last month. The Dodgers then broke through with a 13-game winning streak in the last two weeks of the season, catching the San Francisco Giants, who were ahead up to the last week of play.

Koufax, whose career was threatened by an attack of bursitis in his pitching arm during the spring, came back to hurl more innings than any other pitcher. He pitched a perfect game, the fourth of his career, and he set a big league record of 382 strike-outs. Koufax, however, sat out the opening game of the World Series in observance of *Yom Kippur* (the Jewish Day of Atonement), and lost the second game before he pitched the two shutouts that won the series for the Dodgers.

Jim Maloney of Cincinnati pitched two no-hitters, one of which he lost to the New York Mets 1–0 in the 11th inning. The Mets finished last for the fourth time in as many years since joining the league. The defending champions, the St. Louis Cardinals, dropped to seventh place.

The American League. The New York Yankees finished sixth—their first time out of the first division since 1925. The first pennant came to the Twins in the fifth season of their shift to Minnesota from Washington, D.C.

The Twins' Tony Oliva repeated as batting champion of his league, as did Roberto Clemente of the Pittsburgh Pirates in the National League. Cleveland's Sam McDowell earned a reputation as the "Sandy Koufax of the American League" by striking out an impressive high of 325 batters during the season.

Satchel Paige, at 59, returned to organized baseball for the third time, and earned comeback-of-the-year mention by pitching three innings of a

Neil Leifer for *Sports Illustrated* © Time Inc.

SPORTSMANSHIP? San Francisco Giant's pitcher Juan Marichal clubbed Dodgers' catcher John Roseboro during a crucial game on August 22.

Business Week Magazine, Ted Rozumalski

HOUSTON'S NEW ASTRODOME, an air-conditioned sports and convention stadium, was packed by baseball fans opening day.

FINAL STANDINGS IN MAJOR LEAGUE BASEBALL

AMERICAN LEAGUE

	W.	L.	Pc.	GB.
Minnesota	102	60	.630	—
Chicago	95	67	.586	7
Baltimore	94	68	.580	8
Detroit	89	73	.549	13
Cleveland	87	75	.537	15
New York	77	85	.475	25
California	75	87	.463	27
Washington	70	92	.432	32
Boston	62	100	.383	40
Kansas City	59	103	.364	43

NATIONAL LEAGUE

	W.	L.	Pc.	GB.
Los Angeles	97	65	.599	—
San Francisco	95	67	.586	2
Pittsburgh	90	72	.556	7
Cincinnati	89	73	.549	8
Milwaukee	86	76	.531	11
Philadelphia	85	76	.528	11½
St. Louis	80	81	.497	16½
Chicago	72	90	.444	25
Houston	65	97	.401	32
New York	50	112	.309	47

Leading Batters

Batting Average—Tony Oliva, Minnesota	.321
Home Runs—Tony Conigliaro, Boston	32
Runs Batted In—Rocky Colavito, Cleveland	108
Hits—Tony Oliva, Minnesota	185
Runs—Tony Oliva, Minnesota	107

Leading Batters

Batting Average—Roberto Clemente, Pittsburgh	.329
Home Runs—Willie Mays, San Francisco	52
Runs Batted In—Deron Johnson, Cincinnati	130
Hits—Pete Rose, Cincinnati	209
Runs—Tommy Harper, Cincinnati	126

Leading Pitchers

Games Won—Jim Grant, Minnesota	21
Win Average—Jim Grant, Minnesota (21-7)	.750
Earned Run Average—Hoyt Wilhelm, Chicago	1.81
Strike-outs—Sam McDowell, Cleveland	325

Leading Pitchers

Games Won—Sandy Koufax, Los Angeles	26
Win Average—Sandy Koufax, Los Angeles (26-8)	.765
Earned Run Average—Frank Linzy, San Francisco	1.43
Strike-outs—Sandy Koufax, Los Angeles	382

one-hit, runless baseball game. The amazing veteran of almost 40 years of baseball was hired by the Kansas City Athletics late in the season, but only made this one appearance for the team.

Front Office. In a surprise move, the major league owners named William D. Eckert, retired U.S. Air Force lieutenant general, as the new commissioner of baseball to succeed Ford Frick (see ECKERT, WILLIAM D.). Earlier, the owners had established a five-man cabinet to assist the new commissioner. The National Broadcasting Company (NBC) was awarded a $30,600,000 contract to continue televising the World Series and All Star Games and to carry a "Game of the Week" for three years.

The dominance of the National League was reflected by its third straight World Series triumph; its 6-5 victory in the All Star Game; and its attendance of 13,576,521 for the season, a record for the major leagues.

The Braves, who moved from Boston in 1953, ended a 13-year stay in Milwaukee, with plans to move to Atlanta in 1966. The Los Angeles Angels paved the way during the year for their move to Anaheim, Calif., in 1966 by changing their name to the California Angels.

The controversial Leo Durocher, 59, returned to baseball after a short absence when he was named to manage the Chicago Cubs, succeeding Bob Kennedy. Durocher immediately announced he was the "manager" and not the "head coach," thereby ending the system of head coaches introduced by Cub owner Phil Wrigley.

Wes Westrum filled in for Casey Stengel after Casey broke his hip during the close of the 1965 season. He was named Mets manager for 1966. When Stengel retired, Don Heffner, a Mets coach, succeeded Dick Sisler as manager of the Reds. Sisler then took a job as coach with the St. Louis Cardinals, and Alvin Dark succeeded Heywood Sullivan as manager of the Kansas City Athletics.

Amateurs. Arizona State captured the National Collegiate Athletic Association (NCAA) title. The National Association of Intercollegiate Athletics (NAIA) crown went to Carson-Newman College of Tennessee. Windsor Locks, Conn., beat Stoney Creek, Ontario, Canada, for the Little League championship.

Award Winners in the major leagues were:
National League Most Valuable Player—Willie Mays of the San Francisco Giants.
American League Most Valuable Player—Zoilo Versalles of the Minnesota Twins.
Cy Young Award, to the "pitcher of the year"—Sandy Koufax of the Los Angeles Dodgers.
National League Rookie of the Year—Jim Lefebvre of the Los Angeles Dodgers.
American League Rookie of the Year—Curt Blefary of the Baltimore Orioles.
National League Manager of the Year—Walt Alston of the Los Angeles Dodgers.
American League Manager of the Year—Sam Mele of the Minnesota Twins. STANLEY ISAACS

BASKETBALL. An outstanding team—the University of California at Los Angeles (UCLA)—and an outstanding player—Bill Bradley—dominated college basketball in the 1964-1965 season.

UCLA, coached by John Wooden and led by All American Gail Goodrich, became the fifth team in the tournament's history to win successive National Collegiate Athletic Association (NCAA) championships. The UCLA team won the title by whipping through Brigham Young, San Francisco, and Wichita State, before beating Michigan, 91-80, in the final game at Portland, Ore.

Bradley carried a lightly regarded Princeton team from the Ivy League championship to a third-place finish at Portland, and scored a tournament record 58 points in the consolation game against Wichita,

1965 College All-American Team	
(Source: NCAA consensus All-American)	
Players	**School**
Gail Goodrich	UCLA
Bill Bradley	Princeton
Fred Hetzel	Davidson
Rick Barry	Miami
Cazzie Russell	Michigan

which Princeton won, 118-82. Regarded by some as the best college player of all time, Bradley forsook a handsome professional basketball offer from the New York Knickerbockers to become a Rhodes scholar at Oxford University in England.

St. John's University, Jamaica, N.Y., came through with a smashing victory for retiring coach Joe Lapchick in his final season by winning the National Invitation Tournament (NIT). Lapchick thus became the first coach to win four NIT titles. Evansville went undefeated in 29 games and won its second straight NCAA small-college title with an 85-82 victory over Southern Illinois.

The Armed Forces All-Stars won the men's Amateur Athletic Union (AAU) title, and Nashville Business College won the women's title for the fourth straight year.

Professional. The Boston Celtics continued as sport's greatest dynasty by winning their seventh straight National Basketball Association (NBA) championship. The Celtics survived a last-minute scare to beat the Wilt Chamberlain-led Philadelphia 76ers, 110-109, in the seventh game of the Eastern Division play-offs, and then scored a five-game triumph over the western champions, the Los Angeles Lakers.

Bill Russell of the Celtics won the league's most valuable player award for the fourth time in five years. Chamberlain, who was traded to Philadelphia from San Francisco in midseason, won his sixth straight scoring title, and Willis Reed of the New York Knickerbockers was awarded the rookie-of-the year honors. STANLEY ISAACS

BASUTOLAND

BASUTOLAND held its first general election on April 29, 1965, and became self-governing the following day. The country's new constitution, drawn up in London in May, 1964, provides for complete independence a year after the elections.

The general election gave the right-wing Basutoland National party 31 of the 60 contested seats in the national assembly. The Basutoland Congress party won 25 seats, and the remaining four went to the Marematlou Freedom party. Later in the year, however, two court decisions unseated several members of the National party and left it without a majority in the assembly. The National party chose Paramount Chief Sekhonyana Maseribane to serve as an interim prime minister following the defeat of its leader, Chief Leabua Jonathan, in the general election. In early July, Jonathan won a by-election and replaced Maseribane.

Chief Jonathan declared that Basutoland would continue to give refuge to political exiles from South Africa so long as they did not meddle in Basutoland's politics or use Basutoland as a base for their activities.

Population: 746,000. **Government:** Paramount Chief Motlotlehi Moshoeshoe II; Prime Minister Leabua Jonathan. **Monetary Unit:** Somali shilling (20 = U.S. $2.80). **Foreign Trade:** exports, $707,148; imports, $1,508,579. **Principal Exports:** maize, mohair, peas and beans, wool.   BENJAMIN E. THOMAS

See also AFRICA.

Wide World

CABINET CRISIS in Belgium ended in July when Pierre Harmel, who had been named prime minister, formed a coalition government.

BELGIUM changed leaders in 1965. In a general election held May 23, the coalition government of Prime Minister Théodore Lefèvre failed to capture a two-thirds majority of seats in the chamber of representatives. As a result, Lefèvre resigned and a new coalition cabinet, headed by Prime Minister Pierre Harmel, was sworn in on July 28 (see HARMEL, PIERRE). Foreign Minister Paul-Henri Spaak continued in his post. The defeat of the Lefèvre government was generally attributed to popular dissatisfaction with Belgium's linguistic law, passed in 1964, which made Flemish the official language in the northern part of the country and French the official language in the south.

Financial Differences between Belgium and its former colony, Congo (Léopoldville), were settled in talks held in Brussels early in February between Congolese Premier Moise Tshombe and Foreign Minister Spaak. Under terms of the agreement, Belgium turned over to Congo about $300,000,000 in securities that had been held by the Brussels government in private firms operating in Congo. Control of the huge Union Minière du Haut-Katanga and other mining assets was also turned over to Congo. See CONGO (LÉOPOLDVILLE).

Foreign Investments continued to play an important role in the nation's economy. In September, the U.S.-owned Caterpillar Tractor Company announced plans to build an $80,000,000 factory in southern Belgium. The General Motors Corporation went ahead with its plans to build a $100,000,000 plant near Antwerp.

Meanwhile, the Ford Motor Company announced plans for a $120,000,000 expansion program to increase its production facilities in northern Belgium. Altogether, according to an official survey, foreign holdings in Belgium totaled about $700,000,000 at the end of 1964.

With industrial output on the upswing, exports soared, particularly to the Federal Republic of Germany, where they were up 35 per cent over the first quarter of 1964. Rising retail prices and labor costs, however, neutralized the upswing.

Other Developments. The 150th anniversary of the Battle of Waterloo was the cause of some friction with neighboring France in June. French President Charles de Gaulle boycotted the celebrations, which were held near Brussels, because, it was said, he disliked being reminded of past defeats.

In November, Belgium mourned the death of dowager Queen Elisabeth. She was one of Europe's leading art patrons (see DEATHS OF NOTABLE PERSONS).

Population: 9,382,000. **Government:** King Baudouin I; Prime Minister Pierre Harmel. **Monetary Unit:** Belgian franc (49.65 = U.S. $1). **Gross National Product:** BF 672,000,000,000. **Foreign Trade:** exports, $5,590,000,000; imports, $5,901,000,000. **Principal Exports:** industrial machinery, iron and steel, textiles.   KENNETH BROWN

See also EUROPE.

BELLOW, SAUL (1915-   ), was awarded two distinguished literary prizes for his novel *Herzog*. He is, perhaps, the most outstanding American fiction writer of today. Bellow is the first American to receive the Prix International de Littérature, a $10,-000 annual prize awarded "to a living author of world stature." *Herzog* also won for its author the National Book fiction award in 1965. *The Adventures of Augie March* won the same award for him in 1954. See AWARDS AND PRIZES (General Awards).

Other fields in which Bellow is represented are short stories and essays. His play, *The Last Analysis*, about an aging comedian, had a 28-performance run at New York's Belasco Theater in 1964. *Seize the Day* (1956) is a collection of three short stories, a play, and a short novel. His first book, *Dangling Man* (1944), was followed by *The Victim* (1947). *Henderson, the Rain King* (1959), is a comic tale of a wealthy American on an African venture.

Saul Bellow comes from a Jewish family, which emigrated from Russia to Canada. He was born in Lachine, Quebec, July 10, 1915, and lived in Montreal until the family moved to Chicago in 1924. Bellow was graduated at Northwestern University (1937) with honors in anthropology and sociology. While establishing himself as a writer, Bellow taught at Pestalozzi-Froebel Teachers College, Minnesota and Princeton universities, and Bard College. He is now a University of Chicago professor.

BERRYMAN, JOHN (1914-   ), University of Minnesota Humanities Professor, was awarded the Pulitzer poetry prize in 1965 for *77 Dream Songs*. The collection of poems received enthusiastic reviews the year before. Berryman described the volume as part of a projected work, *The Dream Songs*. Fifteen "Dream Songs" appeared in *Ramparts* and won the magazine's highest award in 1963.

Over the past several years, Berryman has been a force in American poetry. He is truly original, sometimes difficult to follow, and has rare sensibility. His work is fascinating, moving, and often eloquent. Certain of his poems have been compared to Chinese paintings. Berryman is also a literary critic, has written short stories, and edited *Selected Poems of Ezra Pound*. *The Dispossessed* (1948) was his first book of poems. *Stephen Crane* (1950) is a critical biography of the author of *Red Badge of Courage*. *Homage to Mistress Bradstreet* (1956) is a long and powerful poem about Anne Dudley Bradstreet, America's first woman poet and wife of the Massachusetts Bay Colony governor.

John Berryman was born in McAlester, Okla., of Northern and Southern stock. He is a Columbia University graduate (1936), and has a degree from England's Cambridge University. He has received Rockefeller, Hodder, and Guggenheim fellowships, and taught at Harvard, Princeton, Cincinnati, Brown, and other universities.

See also PULITZER PRIZES.

BIOCHEMISTRY. For the first time, scientists worked out the exact structure of a *nucleic acid molecule*, one of the constituents of a cell that helps determine the development of its form and function. The accomplishment was hailed as a giant step in the struggle to understand the machinery of life. It was made possible through the work of Professor Robert W. Holley and his associates at Cornell University.

The nucleic acid they decoded is called "alanine transfer-RNA," and transfers an amino acid from one part of the cell to another. The team extracted and purified the nucleic acids for their study from cells of bakers' yeast. They used specific enzymes to rupture the RNA chains, which make up the nucleic acids, and then analyzed the fragments. After long and painstaking work, they found that it was possible to determine the specific sequence of nucleotide bases in this particular RNA. A similar approach had been employed 15 years ago by the Nobel laureate, Frederick Sanger, to determine the amino acid sequence in the protein insulin.

Synthesis of a Nucleic Acid. The first test tube synthesis of a substance that can replicate itself was accomplished by Professor Sol Spiegelman and his associates at the University of Illinois. The genetic molecule they synthesized was RNA, obtained originally from a virus called Q-beta.

A major obstacle to this development had been the inability to obtain a pure enzyme, free of other substances, particularly enzymes that carry out a series of related processes. Spiegelman and his co-workers succeeded in isolating such an enzyme, appropriately named *replicase*, which they obtained from cells infected with the Q-beta virus. The enzyme is not present in noninfected cells. The purified enzyme, with no additions other than the nucleotide building blocks of RNA, magnesium salts, and a bit of Q-beta replicase to act as a template, generated identical copies of Q-beta RNA.

The stage has now been set to examine details of the genetic copying process. It has been shown that the enzyme is quite specific and will not use fragmented or foreign RNA as templates.

Chemistry and Learning. It is well known that the ability of animals to learn can be altered by chemical means. One approach to understanding this process comes from the laboratory of Professor Bernard W. Agranoff at the University of Michigan. He trained goldfish to avoid an electric shock. When puromycin, an antibiotic substance which inhibits protein synthesis, was injected into the goldfish, the trained fish no longer avoided the electric shock.

Learning experiments in man indicate that there is short-term as well as long-term memory. In the studies with goldfish, puromycin interfered with the formation of long-term memory but did not affect their short-term memory.

Other laboratory observations involving rats and other animals agree that memory may be coded in the molecular structure of RNA (see PSYCHOLOGY). The experiments with puromycin, on the other hand, would suggest that the memory coding takes place by altering protein structure. It is possible that alterations in both RNA and in protein occur. Though much controversy exists in this area, it is conceivable that some of the memory and learning processes will soon be described on a chemical basis.

Growth Hormones. Little is known about the control of cell functions by large protein hormones, such as insulin or growth hormones, except that the cell is able to "recognize" the hormone. While insulin derived from cows is effective in the treatment of human diabetes, a growth hormone from the same animal is useless in the treatment of human dwarfism. The only source of growth hormone at present is human pituitary glands, and the amounts obtained from this source are inadequate relative to the needs.

The similarity of the structure of insulin from cows to that of insulin from human beings may explain its effectiveness in the treatment of human diseases. The bovine form of growth hormones, on the other hand, is a much larger molecule than the human form of growth hormones. Research at the Sloan-Kettering Institute in New York City had been directed toward the breaking of the bovine hormone into smaller fragments by using the enzyme *trypsin*. Fragments thus obtained have been used successfully to treat human dwarfism. It is plausible that one of these large fragments may have the same amino acid sequence as does the human hormone, which would explain why it has succeeded in therapy for human beings.

Origin of Life. Scientists believe that the earth's atmosphere before the advent of life consisted of hydrogen, water vapor, and ammonia. Energy from the sun, in the form of heat and ultraviolet light, and electrical energy in the form of lightning, acted on this atmosphere to produce organic chemicals which became building blocks for living matter. A number of years ago, amino acids were formed in the laboratory under conditions simulating this primordial environment. The formation of the much more complicated nucleic acid bases as well as the linking together of these molecules has been reported by Cyril Ponnamperuma, who directs the program in chemical evolution at the Exobiology Division of the National Aeronautics and Space Administration at the Ames Research Center in California. All five of the fundamental units of the nucleic acids have been produced from simpler subunits and these were demonstrated to arise from the simplest simulated primordial system.

Ponnamperuma has also shown that two subunits of nucleic acid will form and join under fairly simple conditions, and has suggested that the first nucleic acid chain originated in this manner. HAROLD FEINBERG

See also BIOLOGY; BOTANY; CHEMISTRY; MEDICINE; PSYCHOLOGY.

BIOLOGY. Clues to the origin and development of life on this planet have been found in ancient rocks that contain substances that were trapped during the early periods of the earth's history. Nobel prize winner Melvin Calvin reported in 1965 that he and a team of researchers from the University of California, Berkeley, had found phytane and pristane embedded in shale from the Soudan iron formation in Minnesota. Both substances are carbon-hydrogen compounds, and could only have been produced by living creatures.

The shale from this site is considered to be at least 2,500,000,000 years old, so that the finding pushes back previous estimates of the age of life on earth by a full 800,000,000 years. Calvin suggests that the two substances were synthesized by chlorophyll-containing plants. Since the green plant is a relatively high form of life, there must have been living things long before those that produced the phytane and pristane.

Life in Outer Space? Another source of information about life's origin, not only on earth but elsewhere in the universe, may be found through analysis of meteorites. At the Enrico Fermi Institute of the University of Chicago, Ryoichi Hayatsu and his co-workers extracted adenine and guanine from such objects. These amino acids are constituents of DNA, the genetic molecules basic to living things. Hayatsu is of the opinion, however, that such organic substances in meteorites—as well as those found in ancient rocks—reflect a random distribution of material throughout the solar system rather than the residue of living forms.

Nitrogen Fixation. Living organisms that take nitrogen from the atmosphere and use it in the production of protein, a process called nitrogen fixation, accomplish something that chemists are unable to duplicate under conditions of normal temperature and pressure. Two enzyme systems of the organisms are essential in this process. The first, hydrogenase, changes hydrogen ions into molecular hydrogen. This enzyme reaction could not take place without an electron carrier called ferrodoxin. The second enzyme system, nitrogenase, transfers molecular hydrogen to nitrogen, thus forming ammonia.

Many of these same microorganisms are also capable of photosynthesis, the process by which plants produce carbohydrates. Scientists seeking a link between photosynthesis and nitrogen fixation have noted that both make use of ferrodoxin. The findings are of important interest in that the same electron carrier participates in the two fundamental processes involving the incorporation of atmospheric gases into organic substances. They have now discovered that blue-green algae, capable of photosynthesis, also efficiently fix nitrogen. Thus it is possible that this abundant life-form may be an important source of protein.

Cell Division. The development of plants and animals from a single seed, or fertilized egg, is a subject of unceasing interest to biologists. Recently, scientists at the Rockefeller Institute studied this development in the eggs of certain snails, which are tri-lobed for a short period before they divide into two cells. The scientists found that they could remove a single lobe of these embryos without interfering with the cell nucleus. However, after the embryonic development was complete, the snails lacked certain tissues. The results were interpreted as evidence that various regions of the cell contribute genetic information to the developing organism.

Homing Salmon. The ability of spawning salmon to search out their home waters after years in the open sea has long aroused the curiosity of biologists. Experiments measuring the electrical activity of the salmon brain have provided evidence that salmon derive their homing capability from an extremely keen sense of smell.

Intense electrical activity in the olfactory lobe was recorded when adult salmon were exposed to water taken from their hatching sites. Thus it appears that salmon find their homeward migration path by their ability to sense the odor of highly diluted samples of home waters found downstream. Nonmigratory fish in the same locale were also tested, but did not respond to the odor of the waters with the same intensity.   HAROLD FEINBERG

See also BIOCHEMISTRY; BOTANY; INSECT.

BIRCH, JOHN, SOCIETY. See JOHN BIRCH SOCIETY.

BLINDNESS. The lack of accurate estimates of the world's blind population was stressed in the publications of the National Institute of Neurological Diseases and Blindness and of the American Association of Workers for the Blind during 1965. Estimates ranged from between 10,000,000 and 15,000,000, the wide variance being attributed to the fact that blindness is defined differently in various countries.

The concept of total rehabilitation of the blind adult, including independent travel, continued to gain wide acceptance. A greater number of vocations were opened to blind persons and emphasis in rehabilitation was placed on competition in open industry rather than in sheltered workshops.

Education. The process of integrated education, in which the blind child is taught in public schools alongside sighted children, continued to accelerate, especially in the underdeveloped areas of the world. It has been shown that the system can be introduced at much less cost than separate schooling programs, and it often has been shown to result in a much better social and psychological climate for the blind child.

According to the American Printing House for the Blind, 10,381 blind children in the United States attended ordinary local public schools, compared with 8,035 in special residential schools, in 1965.

International Programs. The World Health Organization (WHO), the World Council for the Welfare of the Blind, and the International Society for the Prevention of Blindness conducted cooperative programs to control the major blinding diseases and to greatly widen the availability of ophthalmic services.

The U.S. Vocational Rehabilitation Administration, in cooperation with the Indian government, conducted an experiment in industrial training in Bombay and in other cities for placement of blind persons in competitive employment. Similar work was carried on in Israel, where blind persons were trained to work in cotton mills and to operate data processing machines. Model rehabilitation centers designed to teach handicrafts and farming methods were also established by the U.S. Vocational Rehabilitation Administration in India and Syria. Similar facilities have been established in Ghana, Guatemala, Tanzania, Thailand, and Uganda by other global organizations, such as the American Foundation for Overseas Blind and the Royal Commonwealth Society for the Blind.

Braille. The availability of literature for blind people was greatly enlarged through the establishment of braille printing plants throughout the world and through the standardization by the World Braille Council of a system for adapting braille to all languages. Countries of Western Europe are now recording and duplicating books on tape, and the practice is gradually spreading to other sections of the world.   DOUGLAS C. MACFARLAND

BOATS AND BOATING enjoyed another growth year, both as an industry and as a sport. Retail sales rose an estimated 3 per cent, and sales at the New York City National Motor Boat Show hit a new record despite a decline in attendance.

By the year's end, the industry's trade associations estimated that 39,325,000 people had participated in recreational boating at least once in 1965. A total of 7,860,000 boats of all sizes and shapes were being used for recreation.

The great horsepower race in outboard motors continued. Kiekhaefer Corporation broke the 100-horsepower (hp) barrier with a new 110-hp model, the most powerful ever built. Although relatively new to the outboard field, Chrysler shortly thereafter announced a 105-hp motor, and Evinrude and Johnson each produced their most powerful engines yet, rated at 100 hp.

Kiekhaefer also took a lead in the growing inboard-outboard field by introducing a 60-hp stern drive unit, the smallest yet made.

Inventions. New ideas and products included:

A *hydrofoil kit*, suitable for installation on most conventional outboard hulls. For a cost of $450, including installation, the foils allow the boat's hull to cruise a foot out of the water, increasing speed 40 per cent while cutting fuel consumption by a similar amount.

A *one-man submarine*, made in Germany. Named the Porpoise, it is 10 feet 2 inches long; weighs

Pictorial Parade

TRIUMPH for sailor Bob Manry, who crossed the Atlantic Ocean in 79 days from Falmouth, Mass., to Falmouth, Cornwall, in his 13½-foot sailboat, the Tinkerbelle.

1,389 pounds; descends to 164 feet; and stays under water up to four hours. It costs about $3,900.

A communications system for skin divers, called the "Yack-Yack." This features a lightweight face mask with microphone and a special sound diffuser to eliminate bubble sounds. With its battery, amplifier, and speaker, the Yack-Yack amplifies the voice so that it can be heard by a diver 50 feet away.

Hydro-karting, a new form of boat racing using one-man sledlike boards propelled by tiny gasoline engines. The karts, averaging only eight feet long, reach speeds as high as 50 miles per hour. They provide the thrills of racing at a cost of $200 or less.

Legislation. The National Association of State Boating Law Administrators proposed two law revisions. They would have the effect of requiring state registration of all motorboats, including those under 10 hp, which are now exempted by the Federal Boating Act of 1958.

Sailing. William Snaith's *Figaro IV* won the Southern Ocean Racing Conference series, with victories in the Nassau Cup race and the 403-mile St. Petersburg-to-Fort Lauderdale race. The Northern Ocean Racing competition went for the second time to Sumner Long's *Ondine*, which also won the 1,300-mile Buenos Aires-to-Rio de Janeiro sail.

Ticonderoga, the 72-foot ketch skippered by Robert Johnson of Portland, Ore., beat *Ondine* by less than two hours in the 844-mile Miami-to-Montego Bay race and also finished first in the Transpacific Yacht Race, though the winner on corrected time was Don Salisbury's *Psyche*.

On the Great Lakes, Bill and Ted Schoendorf's 56-foot cutter *Blitzen* swept the Chicago-to-Mackinac race, and *Gypsy*, the 54-foot sloop skippered by Charles Kotovic of Milwaukee, won the 235-mile Port Huron-to-Mackinac race for the third time.

Donald Bever of Vermilion, Ohio, won the world star class title. The Mallory Cup for the men's national sailing championship was won by Cornelius Shields, Jr. The Adams Cup for women went to Mrs. Timothea (Schneider) Larr of Oyster Bay, N.Y. The Sears Cup for juniors was successfully defended by Robert Doyle of Marblehead, Mass., and Colin Park of Vancouver, B.C., took the O'Day Trophy for the North American single-handed title.

The University of Rhode Island beat out San Diego State for the North American collegiate championship.

Motor Racing. In unlimited hydroplane racing, the season featured nine races with prize money reaching $275,000, the highest ever. Ron Musson, driving *Miss Bardahl*, won the driving championship for the third straight year. Musson also won the prestigious Gold Cup race for the third year in a row. Then, for the first time, a "world championship" regatta was held for 180-mile-an-hour hydroplanes. The championship, and first-place money of $36,050, went to—who else?—Ron Musson in *Miss Bardahl*.—James O. Dunaway.

BOLIVIA found its government pitted against tin miners in a year-long battle to put the all-important mines on a paying basis. On May 17, the government declared a state of siege following an uprising by the miners over the banishment of Juan Lechin Oquendo, a major leftist union leader.

A state of siege was again declared on September 20 when the tin miners went on strike over a pay dispute. The government held fast. It exiled communist and leftist union bosses, reduced the wages of many miners, and abolished bonuses.

The government, determined to disarm the miners and end their role as a major political force, offered to increase wages in return for a pledge of normal operations. These efforts resulted in foreign loans for the rehabilitation of the mines.

General Alfred Obando Candia, commander in chief of the armed forces, was installed as co-president on May 26, assuming authority equal to that of junta chief René Barrientos Ortuño.

Population: 4,188,000. **Government:** Co-Presidents General René Barrientos Ortuño; General Alfred Obando Candia. **Monetary Unit:** peso (11.88 = U.S. $1). **Foreign Trade:** exports, $86,000,000; imports, $97,000,000. **Principal Exports:** lead, silver, tin.   MARY C. WEBSTER

See also LATIN AMERICA.

BOOKS. See CANADIAN LITERATURE; LITERATURE; LITERATURE FOR CHILDREN.

BOSTOCK, HUGH SAMUEL (1901-   ), a member of the Geological Survey of Canada for some 40 years, was awarded the Massey medal in 1965. The Royal Canadian Geographical Society cited him for contributions to the knowledge of the Western Cordillera and the Yukon Territory. Bostock's field work as head of the survey's Yukon section (1931-1949) has made him the greatest living authority on that vast, rugged country. He has been head of the Geological Survey Cordillera (British Columbia and Yukon) section since 1949. His fields of investigations include archaeology, geology, and historical geography.

During his early years with the Survey, Bostock made the first topographical maps of British Columbia's Chilcotin country. He did glaciological and physiographical studies along with geological mapping in the province. His "Physiography of the Northern Cordillera" added greatly to the geographical knowledge of the region and the headwaters of its rivers. His reports on the archaeological riches, mineral resources, and economic potential of the Yukon are invaluable. He is now preparing a glacial geology map of the Yukon.

Hugh Bostock trained as a mining engineer and geologist. He is a Royal Military College graduate (1922), and received B.Sc. (1924) and M.Sc. (1925) degrees at McGill University, and his Ph.D. in geology at the University of Wisconsin (1929). Bostock was born in Vancouver, British Columbia.

BOSTON will build an all-weather stadium as part of an $80,000,000 sports center in the city's South Station area. The stadium will have a retractable roof 720 feet in diameter that will protect 45,000 fans for baseball and 55,000 for football games. The center will also contain an 18,000-seat arena for hockey, basketball, and other entertainments.

Continuing a hectic pace in urban renewal, the city's Redevelopment Authority announced in July, 1965, a six-to-10-year plan for 31 acres adjacent to Prudential Center in the Back Bay area. Nearly half the site will become a church center for the sponsor of the $71,000,000 plan, the First Church of Christ, Scientist. The remaining 16 acres, will be leased by the church to private developers.

Government Center's first building, a 22-story state office tower, opened its doors to 3,500 employees in November. The first segment of One Center Plaza, a privately financed office building in Government Center, was to open in December.

Controversial new state legislation calling for an end to racial imbalance in public schools became a hot local issue. In November, Mrs. Louise Day Hicks won a smashing re-election as chairman of the Boston School Committee, the policy-making body. Opposed to busing students to attain racial balance, Mrs. Hicks became a strong contender for the 1967 mayoral campaign.   DONALD W. LIEF

See also Section Two, THE NEW NEW ENGLAND.

BOTANY. Scientists learned new facts about the complex process by which plants take nitrogen from the air and change it into valuable protein. In terms of man's food supply, the process is second in importance only to photosynthesis, whereby plants manufacture carbohydrates. Dr. Robert H. Burris of the University of Wisconsin reported that he and other researchers have isolated an enzyme, or chemical helper, which plays a key role in this process. The process is known as nitrogen fixation. See BIOCHEMISTRY.

Scientists believe that the enzyme binds nitrogen atoms to its surface while the nitrogen reacts to form ammonia—the first step in a long chain of reactions leading to the production of protein. Later steps in the cycle have been better understood than this first ammonia-forming step. Nearly 5,500,000 tons of nitrogen are converted each year by this nitrogen-fixation process of plants in the United States alone. The plants with this special ability are the legumes, the second largest group of flowering plants.

Fruit Ripening is known to be caused by a volatile hydrocarbon chemical called ethylene. Found in fruit tissue, the chemical acts as a hormone to stimulate ripening and make apples turn red and bananas turn yellow. Recent studies by Stanley P. Burg and Ellen A. Burg at the University of Miami (Fla.) School of Medicine have now shown that the ripening action of ethylene in fruit is greater after the fruit has been picked. According to the Burgs, this

255

BOUMEDIENNE, HOUARI

may be because a substance from the living plant inhibits ethylene's ripening action prior to harvest.

Barriers of fire-resistant plants are being seeded on the hills near Los Angeles, Calif., in an attempt to stop the brush fires that cause significant property damage each year. According to Dr. Robert Gonderman of the Los Angeles State and County Arboretum and head of the project, such fire-resistant plants do not carry a flame, but just blacken and curl up when exposed to fire.

Besides being flame-resistant, the plants must also be able to compete with natural vegetation, resist drought, and provide food for native wildlife. Included in the flameless group are Arabian scurf pea, coast saltbrush, creeping rosemary, ivy, sun rose, and yerba santa. Researchers also hope to find nonflammable plants for use in mountain areas.

Medicinal Greenhouse. A $285,000 climate-controlled greenhouse for investigating plants as potential sources of drugs was opened this year near Chicago. The new medicinal plant research station is operated by the departments of pharmacognosy and pharmacology of the University of Illinois. (Pharmacognosy is the study of the source of drugs.) Of approximately 350,000 plant species known, only about 20,000 have been screened as potential sources of drugs, according to Dr. Ralph F. Voigt, director of the station.   SERGEI LENORMAND

See also GARDEN AND LAWN.

BOUMEDIENNE, HOUARI (1925-   ), an army colonel, seized power as Algeria's chief of state on June 19, 1965. In command of about 1,000 troops, he took over government offices in Algiers and ousted Ahmed Ben Bella, who was president of Algeria since 1962.

Boumedienne had been a trusted follower of Ben Bella for 13 years. During the Algerian struggle for independence from France, Boumedienne trained troops in Tunisia and Morocco. He returned to Algeria in 1957 to command rebel forces. The following year, he was named the new nation's defense minister and first vice-president. By early 1965, however, Boumedienne had joined the steadily growing opposition to Ben Bella's rule.

Boumedienne was born to an impoverished peasant family at Guelma in northeastern Algeria. His original name was MOHAMMED BOUKHAROUBA; the name, "Boumedienne" was adopted as an alias during the war against France. Most of his education was at Islamic schools, including Al-Azhar University at Cairo, Egypt, where he first met Ben Bella.

A slim, sharp-featured man of seemingly inexhaustible energy, Boumedienne, unlike most of his compatriots, has reddish-brown hair and green eyes. His appearance brought him the nickname: "The Swede." Boumedienne is considered more of a doer than he is a speechmaker.   WALTER F. MORSE

See also ALGERIA.

256

BOWLING. Dick Weber of St. Louis won his third All-Star championship, beating Jim St. John of Santa Clara, Calif., in the final three-game series. The women's championship went to Ann Slattery of Salt Lake City, who defeated Sandy Hooper of Anaheim, Calif. It was her first major title.

The American Bowling Congress (ABC) tournament at St. Paul closed after 68 days of competition among more than 28,500 men, with Tom Hathaway of Los Angeles the all-events winner. Ken Roeth of Detroit won the singles title, and Dan Slak and Buz Bosler of Milwaukee won the doubles title.

Billy Welu of St. Louis successfully defended his ABC Masters title by beating Don Ellis of Houston in the final. The $25,000 first prize of the Firestone Tournament went to Billy Hardwick of San Mateo, Calif. In winning the tournament, Hardwick beat Weber and Joe Joseph of Lansing, Mich.

The Woman's International Bowling Congress (WIBC) tournament ended with Doris Rudell of Whittier, Calif., the singles winner. The event lasted 42 days and included more than 20,000 contestants. Donna Zimmerman of Norwalk, Conn., was the all-events titlist, and Betty Remmick and Mary Ann White, both of Denver, Colo., were the winners of the doubles championship.

Alfonso Martini of Milan, Italy, won the title in the first Round-the-World bowling tournament held in Flushing, N.Y., in July.   STANLEY ISAACS

BOXING. Controversy raged over heavyweight champion Muhammad Ali's behavior both in and out of the ring. Ali, who was born Cassius Marcellus Clay, successfully defended his title twice, even though he had been stripped of the title in 1964 by the World Boxing Association (WBA). Despite both victories, the 22-year-old champion remained unpopular with many boxing fans because of his tactics in the ring and his espousal of the Black Muslim sect. See Section One, RED SMITH ON SPORTS.

In May, at Lewiston, Me., Ali knocked out Sonny Liston in the first round with one punch. In November, at Las Vegas, Nev., a flamboyant and taunting Ali jabbed and hooked Floyd Patterson almost at will before the fight was stopped in the 12th round.

In the Patterson fight, Ali knocked his opponent down in the sixth round, but was unwilling or unable to floor him after that. Critics accused Ali of carrying the fight in order to punish Patterson. Ali, however, contended he was unable to deliver the knockout punch because he had hurt his hand late in the fight.

Ernie Terrell of Houston, Tex., defended his WBA version of the heavyweight title in February, in New York, by beating George Chuvalo of Toronto. Terrell looked forward to a bout with Ali, whom most people recognized as the champion even though the WBA did not.

New Champions. Five championships changed hands. Jose Torres of New York won the light-

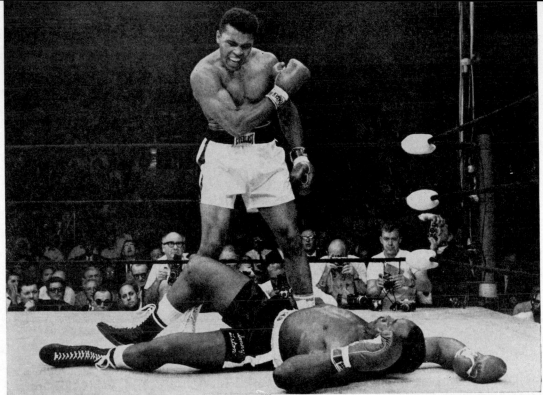

GET UP! *Heavyweight champion Cassius Clay stands over fallen challenger Sonny Liston shouting and gesturing after he knocked him down at Lewiston, Me.*

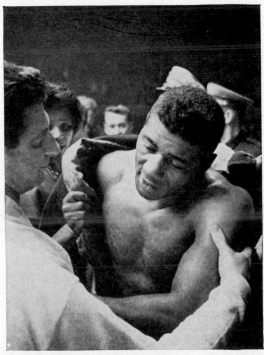

BIG BACKACHE. *Trainer Al Silvani assists Floyd Patterson, suffering from a back ailment, to corner after final round of Las Vegas fight.*

heavyweight title at New York in March by scoring a nine-round technical knockout over Willie Pastrano. Dick Tiger of Nigeria and New York regained the middleweight crown he had lost to Joey Giardello in 1963 with an easy 15-round decision over Giardello at New York in October. Eder Joffre's

WORLD CHAMPION BOXERS

Division	Champion	Where Fought	Year Won
Heavyweight	Muhammad Ali	Miami	1964
Light-Heavyweight	Jose Torres	New York	1965
Middleweight	Dick Tiger	New York	1965
Welterweight	Emile Griffith	New York	1962
Lightweight	Carlos Ortiz	San Juan	1965
Featherweight	Vincente Saldivar	Mexico City	1964
Bantamweight	Masahiko Harada	Japan	1965
Flyweight	Salvatore Burruni	Rome	1965

five-year reign as bantamweight champion came to an end with a 15-round loss to Masahiko (Fighting) Harada of Japan in a match at Nagoya, Japan, in May. Salvatore Burruni of Italy, who had a victory record of 56 straight bouts, won the flyweight title at Rome in April, with a 15-round decision over Pone Kingpetch of Thailand.

Carlos Ortiz at 29, lost and regained the lightweight title. He dropped a 15-round decision to 22-year-old Panamanian Ismael Laguna at Panamá in April, then won a 15-round decision over Laguna at San Juan, Puerto Rico, in November. STANLEY ISAACS

257

BOY SCOUTS OF AMERICA

BOY SCOUTS OF AMERICA began an expansion program in 1965 under the slogan "Breakthrough for Youth." Specially trained Scout leaders were sent to selected areas to work with local Scout councils in developing ways to attract more boys to Scouting. A highlight was a cooperative arrangement with the Public Housing Administration (PHA) to intensify Boy Scout programs in 3,700 public housing projects throughout the country. The expansion program also included efforts to interest corporations and labor unions in sponsoring troops.

The Farragut Wildlife Area, Idaho, was selected as the site for the 12th World Scout Jamboree to be held during the week of August 1, 1967. This will be the first of the quadrennial World Jamborees ever held in the United States. The Boy Scouts of America will be host to an expected 17,000 Scouts representing nearly 100 countries.

Silver Buffalo awards for distinguished service to boyhood were presented to Irving Ben Cooper; Austin T. Cushman; Harry J. Delaney; Royal Firman, Jr.; John H. Glenn, Jr.; Harry J. Johnson; Harry G. McGavran; David Sarnoff; Jo S. Strong; and Gustavo J. Vollmer.

Delegates to the annual meeting, held in May at Miami Beach, Fla., approved new merit badges for space exploration and communications. They also re-elected Thomas A. Watson, Jr., president of the National Council. — JOSEPH P. ANDERSON

BOYS' CLUBS OF AMERICA

BOYS' CLUBS OF AMERICA established the Herbert Hoover Memorial Award to honor the memory of the former President, who served as the organization's chairman of the board for 27 years. The award, a gold medallion, will be presented each year "to the man who has done the most for underprivileged youth." President Lyndon B. Johnson was the first to receive the award. The presentation was made at the White House on April 21 by Edwin Bassemier, 17, of Evansville, Ind., who had been named the 1965 "Boy of the Year."

Representatives of Boys' Clubs in Great Britain concluded plans with representatives of clubs in the United States for an exchange program to begin in the spring of 1966. Workers from England's National Association of Boys' Clubs will spend three months working with selected units of Boys' Clubs of America. An equal number of U.S. workers will spend three months in England. The program will enable the workers to share common concerns and program techniques.

Boys' Clubs in both countries were experimenting with programs designed to reach groups of boys designated as the hard-to-serve and the hard-to-reach. The first group is composed of boys who have joined a club but are then unable or unwilling to participate in program activities. The second group is made up of boys who cause concern and disturbance in the community but do not join any Boys' Club. — JOSEPH P. ANDERSON

BRAZIL

BRAZIL was widely praised abroad for the efforts it made in 1965 to improve its economy. It was successful, for the most part, in moderating an inflationary spiral. It was also able to set its economy on a solid foundation and thus form a basis for economic growth and social progress.

At home, however, criticism of the administration of President Humberto de Alencar Castelo Branco was at times bitter. This was due largely to the government's fiscal and monetary reforms and its austerity and stabilization programs. Credit was tightened, wages frozen, and price ceilings placed on many farm and manufactured products. Brazil was thus able to hold the cost-of-living increase to 39.2 per cent for the first nine months of 1965 versus 59.6 per cent in the same period for 1964.

Economic Action. A major effort was made to keep wage increases in private enterprises below the rise in living costs. Government officials also decreed that there would be no wage increases in 1965 for 500,000 civil servants and members of the armed forces. To spur the economy, the petrochemical fields and Brazil's vast petroleum-bearing shale deposits were opened to development by private investors.

Incentives, such as improved profit remittances and guaranteed convertibility of monies entering the republic were also introduced to encourage foreign investment. Brazil re-established its international credit standing by renegotiating its heavy short-term debt and improving its monetary reserve position to about $470,000,000 by the end of September, 1965.

Political Defeat. Although the administration scored important economic successes, they were achieved via admittedly unpopular measures. This was reflected in the gubernatorial elections held on October 3, which saw parties opposed to the government sweep 10 of the 11 races. The results were a clear indication that the government had failed to establish a broad popular base.

Two antigovernment groups—the Social Democratic party of former President Juscillino Kubitschek and the Brazilian Labor party of ousted President João Goulart—scored impressive victories at the polls. The military, fearing a return to left of center political thinking, forced the government to take action. On October 27, President Castelo Branco suspended constitutional guarantees, dissolved all political parties, and gave his administration broad powers to rule by decree. On November 21, however, the president issued a decree permitting a limited revival of political organizations.

Population: 82,696,000. **Government:** President Humberto de Alencar Castelo Branco. **Monetary Unit:** cruzeiro (2,200 = U.S. $1). **Gross National Product:** 455,000,000,000 cruzeiros. **Foreign Trade:** exports, $1,433,000,000; imports, $263,000,000. **Principal Exports:** coffee, cotton, ore. — MARY C. WEBSTER

See also LATIN AMERICA.

BRIDGE AND TUNNEL. Following completion of cable spinning for Portugal's great new bridge over the Tejo (Tagus) River at Lisbon, work began on the deck that will carry highway and, later, rail traffic between the northern and southern parts of the country. The bridge, when completed in 1966, will have the longest suspension span (3,323 feet) outside the United States.

Opening of Brazil's Friendship Bridge over the Paraná River, on March 27, provided the last link in a 736-mile highway between the Atlantic port of Paranaguá, Brazil, and landlocked Asunción, Paraguay's capital. The 1,812-foot cast-in-place concrete bridge includes a 952-foot clear span.

New U.S. Bridges. Work started early in the year on a new Mississippi River crossing at St. Louis. It will be the nation's first major highway bridge of orthotropic plate design when it is completed in 1967. In an orthotropic bridge, huge steel plates serve both as the roadway deck and the top flange of the main girders. A joint project of the states of Missouri and Illinois, the bridge will feature phenomenal span lengths—up to 600 feet between piers—for a bridge of this type.

Late in the year, the second Cooper River Bridge was completed at Charleston, S.C. It parallels an existing bridge built in 1929. The new $15,000,000 bridge consists of truss and steel girder spans.

New Tunnels. The long-awaited Mont Blanc Tunnel, connecting the Italian village of Entrèves and the French village of Les Pélerins, under the highest peak in the Alps, was officially opened to traffic on July 16. Its $7\frac{1}{4}$-mile length makes it the longest highway tunnel in the world. Earlier in the year, another Alpine highway tunnel was bored under southern Switzerland's San Bernardino pass. The tunnel was expected to open by 1968.

Construction started in July on the $133,000,000, six-mile underwater transit tunnel to connect San Francisco with Oakland, Calif. It will be the key link in the Bay Area Rapid Transit District's new 75-mile rail system. It will be built by a combination of sunken-tube assembly and tunnel boring.

Late in the year, first contracts were awarded for a nine-mile-long bridge-tunnel crossing the Northumberland Strait between New Brunswick and Prince Edward Island in eastern Canada. Designed for use by both rail and highway traffic, the double-deck toll crossing will include a precast trench-type tunnel and three causeways (see map, *below*).

Swiss-born Othmar H. Ammann, designer of two of the world's "longest" suspension spans, died in New York City at the age of 86. His famous bridges were the George Washington, across the Hudson River; and the Verrazano-Narrows, between Brooklyn, N.Y., and Staten Island.   M. E. JESSUP

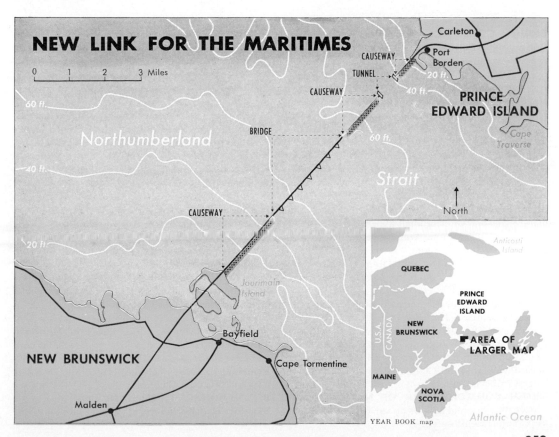

NEW LINK FOR THE MARITIMES

BRIDGE, CONTRACT

SCANDAL marred the world bridge match when members of the British team were accused of using finger signals. Two fingers held closely together, left, allegedly indicated two hearts; figure "V" signal, right, meant five hearts.

BRIDGE, CONTRACT. The international bridge world was rocked by charges of cheating leveled against two members of the British team at the world contract bridge championship at Buenos Aires, Argentina, in May. The two, Terrence Reese and Boris Schapiro, were among the world's leading players. They denied the charges, and the British Bridge League instigated an inquiry. An Italian team won the event.

In one of the most dramatic finishes in the history of the event, a team captained by Oswald Jacoby of Dallas won the Harold S. Vanderbilt Cup at the spring tournament of the American Contract Bridge League (ACBL) at Cleveland. The winning margin was four international match points. Other members of the winning team were Jacoby's son, James Jacoby, and Dr. John Fisher, both of Dallas; Ira Rubin of Fair Lawn, N.J.; Philip Feldesman of Queens Village, N.Y.; and Albert Weiss of Miami Beach, Fla.

At the ACBL summer tournament in Chicago, a team successfully defended its title in the Spingold trophy event for the first time in 30 years. The winners, all from Toronto, Canada, were Eric Murray, Sammy Kehela, Bruce Elliot, and Percy Sheardown. Entries—14,511 tables—made it the biggest in bridge history.   THEODORE M. O'LEARY

BRITISH COMMONWEALTH OF NATIONS. See GREAT BRITAIN; and articles on various countries of the Commonwealth.

BRITISH GUIANA was headed for independence after 162 years of British colonial rule. In mid-November, following 17 days of talks with Guianese leaders in London, British Colonial Secretary Anthony Greenwood announced that the colony would gain its independence on May 26, 1966.

The constitutional conference in London had succeeded largely through the efforts of the Guianese coalition government headed by Forbes Burnham, leader of the Negro-dominated People's National Congress party. Burnham had worked hard to end the internal strife that had erupted all too frequently in the past between Negroes and East Indians. Burnham, working with Peter D'Aguiar, leader of the United Force party, had introduced a budget that would devote $65,900,000 to current spending and development. A series of tax measures promulgated by former premier Cheddi B. Jagan, was swept aside. Meanwhile, Jagan continued to denounce the Burnham regime. His People's Progressive party had boycotted the constitutional conference.

Population: 683,000. **Government:** Governor Sir Richard Luyt; Premier Forbes Burnham. **Monetary Unit:** British Guiana dollar (1.75 = U.S. $1). **Foreign Trade:** exports, $95,000,000; imports, $87,000,000. **Principal Exports:** rice, rum, sugar.   ALASTAIR BURNET
See also GREAT BRITAIN.

BRITISH HONDURAS. See GREAT BRITAIN.
BRITISH WEST INDIES. See JAMAICA; TRINIDAD AND TOBAGO.